Every once in a while an interview comes along that is so outstanding, that makes such an emotional connection with me, I realize all over again why I do this job every day. One that stands out in my memory was with Steven McDonald, the New York City cop who was wounded in action and left paralyzed. It was the only time I ever recall crying on the air.

His wife, Patti Ann, was two months pregnant at the time he was shot, and since his son was born, Steven hasn't been able to hold him in his arms. McDonald still thinks of himself as a cop. He still thinks he'll walk one day.

He feels sympathy for the young black kid who shot him. He would like to meet the kid. Visit him and tell him he understands that those kids had different breaks than he had. "And while it's never an excuse to shoot anyone, let alone a police officer," Steven said, "I know, that as a white kid growing up, I had opportunities he didn't have."

I've never talked to someone like him. With all the racism rampant in our society, here's a guy confined to a wheelchair, possibly for the rest of his life, showing that kind of compassion.

So when people ask me who is the best interview I ever did, I could say Frank Sinatra, or Mario Cuomo, or Bette Davis; but I could also say Steven McDonald.

ALSO BY LARRY KING

Larry King
Tell It to the King
Mr. King, You're Having a Heart Attack

TELL ME MORE

LARRY KING

WITH PETER OCCHIOGROSSO

ST. MARTIN'S PAPERBACKS

*This book is dedicated to Mrs. Julie King,
who completed the circle*

The author gratefully acknowledges permission granted by the Estate of A. Bartlett Giamatti to quote from "The Green Fields of the Mind" copyright © 1977 by A. Bartlett Giamatti.

Published by arrangement with G.P. Putnam's Sons

TELL ME MORE

Library of Congress Catalog Card Number: 90-8458

ISBN: 0-312-92690-1

Printed in the United States of America

G.P. Putnam's edition/September 1990
St. Martin's Paperbacks edition/March 1992

10 9 8 7 6 5 4 3 2 1

CONTENTS

ACKNOWLEDGMENTS

I would like to acknowledge a few people in my life, without whom my life would be a lot more difficult:

Judy Thomas, my assistant, who keeps my schedule in order. Without her you would look up "calamity" in the dictionary and find a picture of me.

Tammy Haddad, the executive producer of my TV show and my personal shield against the forces of darkness.

Pat Piper, the nonpareil producer of my radio show, who always seems to be there when I need him without my having to ask for him.

Ellen and Herb Cohen, my best friends yesterday, today, and tomorrow.

My brother, Marty, and sister-in-law, Ellen, who are always there for me.

Neil Nyren, my editor, who wins all the disputes.

Peter Occhiogrosso, who captures the sound of me better than me.

And finally, Duke Zeibert, my Father-in-residence.

LARRY KING

Prologue:
Here's That Rainy Day

Since *Tell It to the King* came out, a lot has happened to me, as you probably know by now, most of it for the better. I've had heart bypass surgery, I've gone on a serious exercise regimen, and I feel like a million bucks. I've received new radio and television contracts, so now I'm *worth* a million dollars— me, Larry Zeiger! From Brooklyn. As the great hotelier Henri Lewin once said to me, "Money isn't everything. Health is two percent."

But as somebody else once said, nothing is more boring than good news and high figures. So as I sat down to compile my new collection of stories, reminiscences, and anecdotes about the great, near-great, and just plain weird whom I've gotten to know over the course of my career, I began to worry. How was I going to top the opening of *Tell It to the King?* If you read that book, you remember that it began with me lying on a hospital gurney in excruciating pain, asking the doctor if I was going to die. That incident gave me a reason to look back and examine my life, to think about what I'd remember and what I'd miss. But what could I say this time that might create the proper framework, that would set off the flood of new material I'd put together?

And then it happened. One rainy November day, I accepted an invitation to a party for Shimon Peres at the Israeli ambas-

sador's home in Washington, D.C. The Israeli ambassador lives
off Connecticut Avenue, in an attractive residential area, the
sort of place where guns and violence are furthest from your
mind. The invitation said six-thirty P.M., and when I arrived at
about twenty to seven, it was raining. I parked around the corner, opened my umbrella, and started walking toward the ambassador's house. As I walked along, I noticed that the street
was completely deserted. I saw someone in an overcoat behind
me, but I couldn't see anybody else or any other cars on the
block.

Just then a big black car pulled up, which I later learned was
a SWAT team car. Nobody got out of this car, and I just kept
walking. Another car came up and six or eight Israeli security
guys got out. I knew they had guns in their pockets because I
could see the bulges under their coats. The American Secret
Service guys were at the end of the block, and I was in the
middle of the block, still walking toward the house with my
umbrella up, when I recognized Peres starting to get out of the
second car.

All of a sudden, this one Israeli security guy looked up and
saw me, gave me a dirty look, and put his hand right into his
pocket. I got the feeling I was in terrible trouble. Something
told me he was going to shoot, because these guys take no prisoners and they don't ask questions first. I was so certain that I
was about to die that I did what anyone else would do in that
situation. I froze.

After the Israeli started for his gun, he glanced a little to his
right and saw the American Secret Service man, who nodded
at him that I was okay. So the Israeli put the gun back in his
pocket, and I walked into the house. I felt my heart do a triple
beat, and I knew that I had been within a second of dying. In
fact, the whole episode had taken only a few seconds.

At the party my anxiety receded and I began to feel foolish.
These guys weren't really going to shoot me—that kind of cow-
boy stuff was only in the movies. As I was leaving the party,
though, I ran into the American Secret Service man from the
street, and I had to ask: "Would they have shot me?"

"Probably," he said.

"But why?" I asked, gulping.

The problem, he said, was that the Israelis had a copy of the official itinerary, and they had been told that nobody was supposed to be on the block when Peres arrived. "What happened," the Secret Service man told me, "was that you parked your car and started to walk toward the residence. I saw you, and the other guy on our team saw you. We acknowledged to each other who you were. We figured it was going to be too much hassle to have you back your car all the way around, and it was all right just to let you go through. I thought that the guy ahead of me would signal the Israeli that this one guy on the street's okay. See, we do these things by hand or by head. We nod. But for some reason he forgot to do that, so the Israeli got no signal. The itinerary says, 'Nobody on the street,' and here's this fucking guy with an umbrella. It's raining and the Israeli can't see too clearly. He doesn't know if you have a gun under your coat, or a bomb, or what. So he's gonna gun you down before you get close enough for him to find out. Why take a chance? If he didn't look one degree to the right to see me nod, if he turned to the left instead of the right, you're gone."

"What excuse would they have given?" I asked.

He shrugged. "Who knows?"

I thought, These are my people! I could see the headlines: LARRY KING GUNNED DOWN BY THE JEWS. I can still see that Israeli agent, his blue coat dripping rain. I can still see his face. He had that look, that hard, cold stare that says, "You're gone, man."

But, as you can see, I'm still very much here. My latest brush with death was just the thing to put an edge on my appetite for storytelling. And maybe it sets the proper tone for the loony quality my life has taken on these days, despite all the good news I told you about. How could it be any other way for someone who spends his hours interviewing upwards of thirty different people a week, people from all walks of life and some that defy description? Talking to the likes of Frank Sinatra and Swami Satchidananda, Ronald Reagan and Grace Slick, keeps me ridiculously well informed, if nothing else. But it sometimes makes me feel as if my life is constantly bouncing along like one of those high-speed trains in Japan, passing the countryside so rapidly that a building or field is hardly in view before it's replaced by something else. In other words, lots of fun but a little dizzying at times.

I hope I've been able to capture some of that feeling here, but if you start getting dizzy or light-headed, just turn the page until it passes. And whatever you do, don't try reading this book while driving or operating heavy machinery.

1

Comedy Tonight: Mason, Wright, Leno, & Brooks

There's no question in my mind that the face of comedy has changed over the years, but describing that change is not so easy. On the minus side, there is nobody around today who can do what Lenny Bruce did, which was to make you fall down laughing and to think at the same time. Robin Williams is brilliant and I love him, but two minutes after you've split your sides laughing at his act you can't remember what he said to make you laugh so hard. George Carlin probably comes closest of anyone today, and he does a marvelous Lenny Bruce imitation, but he isn't Lenny either. Johnny Carson actually has more consistently biting political humor in his monologues than any other stand-up comedian I can think of. Dick Gregory has pretty much given up comedy. Even Mort Sahl isn't Mort Sahl anymore. He gave Al Haig the line that Haig was throwing his "helmet into the ring," which was pretty funny, but would Lenny Bruce have been writing lines for Nixon?

So we don't have a major political and social commentator in the country anymore, and that's a shame. But the legacy of Lenny and Mort Sahl can be felt everywhere nonetheless. Largely because of their impact, the newer comics have moved away from the tired shtick of the Borscht Belt comedians and the old routines of vaudeville and have begun to shape material based on their own lives and on current events. George Carlin

have made a fortune doing just that. And
e followed their lead have had to be even
ioning entire stage personalities as vehicles
absurd or surreal observations on modern
aren't exactly Lenny, they sure as hell aren't Buddy
Hackett.

I'm not putting the old Jewish comics down, because beyond the shtick and the old routines, some of them were just plain funny, and they could tell a joke. I remember seeing Jan Murray at the Copacabana for my high school prom, and one of the jokes he told still makes me laugh. A guy is leaving an insane asylum after visiting a friend, and as he's walking out he sees a man in front with a paintbrush and a can of paint, and he's painting the lawn green. As the guy walks by, the inmate with the paintbrush says, "Hey! Come 'ere." He's talking under his breath now. "I've got a hundred thousand dollars buried outside," he says. "I'll give you the location. If you go get it and bring me fifty, you can keep the other fifty."

He gives the guy a map and explains how to find the money. The guy has to go down the road two hundred yards, turn right for fifty feet, come to a tree, mark off six paces to the left, dig down a foot, two feet, ten feet, and he'll find a metal box with the money in it. So the guy takes the map and goes home, gets a shovel, and starts to follow the map. He gets to the tree and digs a foot, two feet, ten feet, and finds nothing. He digs another ten feet. Nothing. The next day he goes back to the asylum, and the same guy is out in front painting the lawn. The guy walks over to him and the inmate says, "So, did you do what I told you?"

He says, "Yeah."

"Did you walk two hundred yards, turn right, and see the tree?"

He says, "Yeah."

Inmate says, "Did you mark off the six paces to the left?"

"Yeah."

He says, "Did you dig a foot, two feet?"

The guy says, "Yeah."

He says, "Did you dig ten feet?"

The guy says, "Ten feet? I dug twenty feet."

Inmate says, "Pick up a brush."

* * *

Of all the New York Jewish comics who came up through the Borscht Belt, Jackie Mason may have been the best, as his recent resurgence bears out. I think Jay Leno is among the best of today's comics at working off what's in the papers on any given day. So is Albert Brooks, except that Albert combines that ability with a gift for impersonation and endless invention that puts him in a class by himself. And Steven Wright is a prime example of the young generation of comics who have created stage personas based on their own quirks and shortcomings and turned them into comic gold. Each of the four has something to tell us about where comedy is today and maybe where it's going tomorrow.

Those four comics may not all be household names yet, and none of them is as enormously popular as Jackie Gleason and Milton Berle were in their heyday, but no one ever will be. Part of the reason is that it's just not possible for a performer to dominate television now the way he could in the fifties. But more to the point, the best comics at any given time are not necessarily the best known. In Miami in the early sixties, I was familiar with a great group of stand-up comics, of whom only Don Rickles went on to become famous. Jackie Gayle, who moved out to Hollywood, Jackie Vernon, Paul Grey, and Dick Havilland were all as popular as Rickles was down there, and just as funny. They worked either the Playboy Club or Murray Franklin's, and they sparkled with a brilliantly individualistic kind of wit. You couldn't lump them with the Borscht Belt comics from the North because they were hipper. The crazy, offbeat style to their jokes and stories has more in common with some of the off-center young comedians of today than with anything the popular comics of their own day were doing.

As a small example, the joke I remember best from that time and place was originally told by Dick Havilland, who swore it was a true story. And he's dead now, so we'll have to take his word for it. Dick said it happened to him when he was working on a vaudeville bill in Boston in the forties. On the bill with him were Siamese twin singers attached at the hip. One of the twins took a fancy to him. Dick was in Boston for two weeks, and they all went around together, the three of them. He ended up having an affair with one of them that lasted until he left

Boston. The other twin didn't have much choice in the matter. As Dick said, "It was strange, but what the hell?"

Anyway, three years later, he's back in Boston on another vaudeville bill, and the Siamese twins are booked again on the same bill. Dick is standing in the wings waiting to go on when he feels a tap on the shoulder. He turns around, and the twins are there. And the one he had the affair with says, "You probably won't remember me. . . ."

Jackie Mason was not a member of that Miami circle of comics, although that was where I got to know him when he first came on my show. Jackie was a Borscht Belt boy all the way except that, like the Miami comics I just mentioned, he was hipper and more creative than the average Borscht Belt stand-up. One of the reasons Jackie was ahead of his time was that he didn't rely on the same old boring routines about shlubby husbands and castrating wives that had proved successful for so many Jewish comedians who worked the Catskill hotels beginning in the thirties. Jackie was a true maverick who wrote original material based on the weirdness of life in those hotels. As a "social director" in the Catskills, he built his routines on careful observation of and skewed insights into the basic craziness of civilized life. He continues to write the same kind of stuff today, although his subject matter has expanded. His idiom may be New York Jewish, but his approach is inventive beyond category. And unlike the safe, stodgy comics of the Catskills, who could be acceptably vulgar, Jackie always lived perilously close to the edge of unacceptability. Maybe it shouldn't have come as such a surprise that Ed Sullivan thought Mason was giving him the finger when he was just horsing around. Jackie emanates that kind of irreverent energy.

For instance, Jackie is able to do an act that bristles with borderline offensive humor and still leave his targets laughing. Just what a thin line he walks was demonstrated in the 1989 New York mayoral race when some of his statements off the stage got out of hand, and he was attacked by both blacks and Jews for his remarks about David Dinkins. But when Jackie is onstage, nobody is funnier at mining ethnic humor. "I love the Italian people," Jackie will say. "You bother an Italian on the street, you look at him the wrong way, he'll kill you. Put him in an army, he surrenders. Now a Jew on the other hand, look at him the wrong way, he runs across the street, he hides. Put him in an army, he invades countries ten times larger than his."

In some ways, Jackie is the embodiment of the modern comic's paradoxical stance: a scathing view of society undercut by an all-too-keen awareness of his own imperfections. For all Jackie's sarcasm and bravado, he's had an almost melancholy attitude for as long as I've known him. When I first met Mason and interviewed him in Miami more than twenty years ago, he told me his life story in a nutshell. And although the facts of his life have changed—he's much better known and infinitely more successful today than he was back then—the tone has remained pretty much the same. Besides everything else, his story is a classic tale of the comic as underdog, making it against all odds and despite his own gaping insecurities.

"I'm basically a tragic child," Jackie told me then. "I was a very tragic figure as a human being in my earliest days. I was a very miserable, unhappy, sad, lonely kid. I felt I was rejected in my own home because I had three older brothers who congregated together and enjoyed each other. They had a fantastic rapport playing ball together, jumping, running, flying, learning, everything they did together. But they were too tall for me. It came time to play ball, they threw the ball, they gave it to me, and I didn't know where to go with it. So they figured, this guy don't belong with us. And I had three younger sisters, but I didn't seem to fit with them either. I mean, how would I look walking around with them, especially with the same outfit? So I was too much of a man for the women and too much of a woman for the men. On top of that, I had an older brother who was so fantastically brilliant that I couldn't find any way to compete with him. He was graduating from high school when he was thirteen and a half. He was graduating from college when he was fifteen. I thought I was a genius, but every time I saw him I said, 'Wait a second, am I mentally retarded?' I couldn't even talk to him. I said hello, he knew the answer."

"How does this put you into comedy?" I asked.

"That's exactly what puts you into comedy," Jackie said. "People take different tacks to compensate for their misery. One

ompensate. One person fights back. One person
..self. And that's the tradition of the Jew. The his-
.. Jew is enacted in my own life. It's traditional that
the ... becomes either a comedian or a scholar."

Clearly, Jackie took the former route. "When I was sixteen
or seventeen," Jackie said, "I found myself with a group of kids
and I always aimed at the joke. That was the only way I could
attract attention to myself. One brother was smarter than me,
so I couldn't compete with him at that level. And they all played
ball better than me, so I couldn't compete with them at that
level. Now the only way I could become a hit was to be funnier
than them."

As we know, Jackie's father wanted him to be a rabbi, and
Jackie trained for the rabbinate for some time. When I asked
him if his affinity for joke telling helped him as a rabbi, he said
that every great speaker, if he has any ability at all, tries to take
advantage of his ability to tell a joke. "You can always develop
a point sharper with a joke," he told me. "You can always build
an analogy with jokes. Adlai Stevenson was a great humorist.
So was Abraham Lincoln. It doesn't negate the message if you
tell a joke. It sometimes adds to it and sometimes creates it."

But Jackie's interest in being a rabbi turned out to be secondary to his interest in telling jokes. So after he quit the rabbinate,
he started looking around for a way to support himself. "I knew
that I couldn't become a master builder," Jackie said. "It's all
Gentiles. I knew I couldn't go to Egypt—Arabs. Or Germany—
Hitler. There were very few places to go."

Jackie ultimately decided that since he was so successful at
comedy from the pulpit and since he was able to make so many
jokes out of truths he was trying to deliver, he would turn his
humor to more important things—philosophical and social
commentary. The hope that he could do this for money in front
of an audience led him to take a job as a social director at
Jewish hotels in the Catskills. This was a mixed blessing. I once
asked him if it was easy to get that kind of job, and his answer
sounded like one of his typical early bits.

"It was very easy," he said. "I found that it's no trick if you're
a liar. I lied that I had been a social director before. You see,
the mountains have four hundred hotels. Three hotels book regular social directors or regular stars. Most of the others each

hold three hundred people who require entertainment all week. And it's traditional that they have a social director who bothers them to enjoy themselves. Now, a guy don't want to be bothered, and he don't want to enjoy himself. His conception of enjoyment is to sit quiet. He's sixty-five, he can't get up from the chair. But they hire a guy to force him to play basketball. He thanks God he can walk, now he's playing basketball.

"On top of that, you have to wake the same old man up at eight o'clock in the morning to do calisthenics. He didn't know he was supposed to do this either. He gets up eight o'clock in the morning all year round, and he comes here to sleep. I'm chasing him: 'Go ahead, jump!' He didn't want to jump. I wanted to jump less than him. I came there to rest too, but they hired me for the job. I killed seven old men in one day. And at night you're supposed to tell jokes too. I always made sure I took the job at night. So I figured if I wasn't such a hit with the calisthenics, they saw me as a comedian. If I got laughs, at least I lasted another day. By the time they noticed I didn't get up for the calisthenics, I've got the job another day."

When I asked Jackie where he got his material in those days, he seemed insulted that I'd asked. "I didn't get it," he said. "I was writing it."

I was surprised by this, because back then it was common for successful performers to buy jokes and other material from writers. Remember, Woody Allen got his start by selling jokes to comedians. "You did all your own stuff?" I asked incredulously.

"I was sitting around all during the day," Jackie said, "and I used to think of jokes about the hotel, the owner, the boss, the waiter, the food, the cars, the bellhops, the this, the that. I used to try to see what I found funny about this hotel. And I would do homework all day long to write the jokes for the night. And I would do it every day, but every day in a different hotel. Because as soon as I didn't do the calisthenics, I was out another job."

It seems that every time Jackie showed up at a new hotel applying for a job as a social director, he would be looked on dubiously by the management, something that he found both frustrating and paradoxical. When I asked him why he had so much difficulty with Jewish managers, Jackie fumed.

"Because they could see I talked with an accent," he said,

"and they were ashamed of it. Jews were always more ashamed of my accent than Gentiles. Gentiles found me funny. Jews just thought I was a 'mockie.' I sounded so much like the manager that he figured, Why do I need him when I could do it myself? He wants me to entertain his guests. His guests are all old, broken-down Jews who can't talk a word of English. But for them he wants to prove that he's got a great hotel, so he wants a guy who sounds like Laurence Olivier to entertain them. They don't understand a guy like Laurence Olivier. But he wants to prove that he's got a high-class hotel."

Jackie finally managed to overcome the Jewish prejudice against him when he got booked into a hot nightclub on La Cienega Boulevard in Beverly Hills run by the Slate Brothers, retired vaudeville performers. It was the same club where Don Rickles became an instant success. Jackie was a big hit opening night, despite his jitters.

"I was panicky," he said, "but I was also hilarious. As I started to talk, before I even knew what I was talking about, they were laughing. They thought it was uproarious. The Jews who thought the Gentiles couldn't stand me were sitting in the back of the place hiding because they were ashamed. They figured, If the Gentiles hear this, we're all finished. Instead, the Gentiles were breaking up, they loved it. It was an immediate sensation."

Bill Dana, who was then the head writer for *The Steve Allen Show*, came in and heard Mason's act and got him booked on the show. "I went to Steve Allen's show panting in front of the camera," Jackie told me. "I didn't remember my jokes. I don't know if I got any out. But I was a sensation there, too, because my accent and my character were something they loved immediately. And I went from three hundred dollars a week to a thousand dollars a week from one *Steve Allen Show.*"

I wondered what his father's reaction was to all this. "My father didn't even know about it," Jackie said. "I didn't tell him."

"He didn't see you on television?"

"No, I didn't tell him that first time. I didn't think that he would be ready to accept it."

After Steve Allen, Jackie's next big hit was on Jack Paar's *Tonight Show*. To Jackie, Paar is the greatest salesman of our time. "If he liked you and he thought you were great," Mason said, "even if you stunk right in front of the whole country and everybody saw you stink the house out, they thought you were great because Paar said so. They figured, He knows something. And if he knows, who are they to say it stinks? So Jack Paar was the prime thing for me because he took an immediate liking to me. He was discovering a Jew every week."

"Was it a plan?" I asked. "A Jew-a-Week Plan?"

"It almost worked out that way," Jackie said. "I think he did more for the Jews than Moses."

Jackie also explained the origin of his stage attitude, his "I don't need it, I'm a star, I'm the biggest thing in the world," which he used in his recent hit Broadway show, *The World According to Me!* Once again, that classic comic's paradox comes into play.

"I honestly don't know how that evolved," he said. "I think it probably came from the fact that I had an intense inferiority complex. I unconsciously expected to be rejected. Even though I said to myself, I'm great, inside I probably wasn't that sure, and I was really more frightened than I cared to admit. So I used to go on the stage with some kind of defensive attitude. And my defensive attitude was, 'Here I am, the greatest comedian in the world.' I was trying to win over the audience's sympathy by making it very clear that I wasn't sure of myself, by howling 'I'm the greatest,' when I was obviously unknown. I've made it such a farce that it becomes ridiculous of itself."

"Are you over that now completely?"

"I don't think I'm over it. I think deep in my heart I'm still very insecure."

"Have you ever sought help for it?"

"Oh sure, I went to a psychiatrist for years."

"Did it help you?"

"Sure, he told me that I'm all right, but he told me *you're* not so great."

Jackie also went to the psychiatrist because of intense guilt feelings at having disappointed his father by not becoming a rabbi. Jackie used to say that the guilt feelings became so debilitating that he sometimes went onstage and totally forgot what he was talking about—his lines, his whole routines.

In thinking back on Jackie through all the years I've known

him, I'm amazed at how little he has changed, from his attitude and his accent to the kind of humor he creates. All that has happened in twenty years is that the rest of the country has caught up with him. The network may have canceled his television show, but the guy with the accent is a star.

Steven Wright is one of the youngest representatives of the new wave of comics who don't do shtick. He's not Jewish, and he's not from New York, so he may seem as far removed as can be from someone like Jackie Mason. Yet he has one very important trait in common with Jackie—he doesn't try to be something he's not. Jackie didn't try to hide his heavy ethnic accent and, despite the initial resistance to him, he proved that his uniqueness could be his drawing card. Steven Wright's surreal kind of humor is unique in a different way, like his delivery, which seems to be based on the persona of a hopelessly shy high school kid who stumbles and mumbles his way through life at an infuriatingly slow pace.

But the factor that links Wright not only to Jackie Mason but also to other new comics like Emo Phillips is that the weird persona he uses onstage is who he actually is. This distinguishes him from comics of the past such as Bill Dana, say, who created goofy stage personalities out of whole cloth. Then you'd meet them on the street and they wouldn't be anything like who they were onstage. But Steven onstage, it turns out—in large concert halls and on Carson and Letterman—is the same Steven offstage. I asked him if, like most professional comics, he had been the class clown in school. "They really didn't know I was there," he told me. "I would kid around with close friends, but I definitely didn't want any attention. So why did *this* happen?"

"That's the next question," I said.

"You're right," Steven said. "I'm outta here."

That's the way Steven talks. Interviewing him was like trying to drag information out of a very introverted kid who isn't quite sure he wants to answer you.

"I had a fantasy from about the time I was sixteen," Steven said, "about standing in front of an audience and making them laugh. But I was so shy that I would rather have stood in a closet by myself. So finally I *forced* myself to do it. I was twenty-three years old, and I decided I had to confront this fantasy so

I wouldn't be wondering about it all my life. I didn't want to be forty years old, selling insurance in Wyoming and wondering what might have happened. I put together two minutes' worth of material and forced myself to go down to a new comedy club that had opened in Boston. I came out onstage, shaking and feeling insane. I had no concept of waiting for the laughs. I just rattled off the material I had prepared, and when I forgot the next thing I just stood there. Then I remembered and I kept going. And then I forgot, and then I kept going."

"In a strange way," I asked, "do you think that caught on?"

"Yeah. After months of forgetting, I realized that even when I forgot, no one would talk. I kept their attention even though I wasn't speaking. So then I started to do that on purpose."

"That's true," I said. "The person you are is the person you take onstage—and the audience accepts it. You're still the shy kid in high school."

"Yeah. Now I'm the shy kid in front of fifteen million people."

But they laugh and they pay him. What an amazing country this is. When you work the way Steven does, you have certain advantages: you don't have to buy a tuxedo, you don't have to dress up, you don't have to comb your hair. Steven is balding, with unruly curly hair that looks like it hasn't seen a comb since high school, and he wears rumpled clothes onstage. He admitted that sometimes he would walk around with his back to the audience. "The main thing to me," he said, "was the material, and to make the audience laugh. I didn't think about how I looked."

Steven taped that first two-minute appearance, and he was a little depressed when he got home and played the tape and discovered that they hadn't laughed at half the stuff he'd done. Then he realized that this meant they *were* laughing at the other half, and that charged him up to go out and do it again. After three years of playing in small clubs like that first one, Steven got his big break. But finding out the details was like pulling teeth. Peter LaSalley, the coproducer of the *Tonight Show*, was in Boston with his sons, scouting out colleges. They stopped by the club where Steven was working and caught his act, but then he didn't hear anything and figured that was it.

"The back of this place where I was working was a Chinese restaurant, and the front was a comedy club," Steven said. "It was called Ding Ho's Comedy Club. The kitchen divided the comedy room from the restaurant."

"So did Peter come backstage and say, 'I want you on the *Tonight Show*'?" I asked.

"No, he just left. Two weeks later I'm sitting in my apartment in Boston with my roommate. We had no furniture. No kitchen table, nothing. The TV was on a tree stump."

"The phone rings," I prodded.

"The phone rings. But the rug was brown, and the phone was brown, too. So the phone rang, but I didn't know where it was."

Well, to make an excruciatingly long story short, it was the *Tonight Show* calling. They offered him a spot on the show, sent him some plane tickets, and he was on his way. I asked Steven if he was as nervous backstage waiting to go on the Carson show as he was in Boston the first two minutes he'd ever been onstage in front of people. "I was twice as nervous," he said. "I was nervous squared. The studio audience had five hundred people, and that alone was the largest audience I'd ever played before."

His first bit from that night was typical. "I had a dream that all the babies prevented by the pill showed up," he said. "They were mad." He got an immediate laugh, and that calmed him down.

"They had told me to look into the cameras, but I couldn't do that," he said. "I tried to block out that it was on television, and I tried to play the studio audience like I'd been doing in nightclubs for three years. I asked them if I could use a hand mike with a mike stand. Most people use the boom mike, but I needed that hand mike for security. I played the studio audience like it was a nightclub, and it worked. That first joke got a big laugh, and then they laughed at the next one, and the next one, and then I heard Johnny laugh. And I thought, Johnny Carson's laughing at what I'm saying! So then I calmed down and just kept doing it."

Johnny raved about him and they brought him back the following week, which was a little unusual. Everything else followed quickly from that. Apparently things haven't changed much on TV since the days of Jack Paar.

The first time I interviewed Steven on radio, I decided to close by holding the first ever Steven Wright Press Conference. I don't know why we called it a press conference, since we were just fielding questions from the live audience, but we did. One guy there had a great question, for which Steven had the perfect answer.

"Steven," the guy asked, "I was wondering if you still get amnesia and déjà vu at the same time?"

"Yes, I still do," Steven said. "Did I say that already?"

Then a woman in the audience said, "I have two questions for you—"

"Okay," Steven said, "ask me the second one first, please."

"Have you ever been in love?"

"Yeah, a few times."

"Are you more inspired when you're in love?"

"Yeah, but not for my career."

Then I asked him, "Do you have any brothers and sisters?"

"Yes," he said, "I have two brothers and one sister, and my sister has three brothers and no sisters. It's weird that we're all in the same family."

Someone asked what his favorite subject area was for material.

He said, "Time." I asked him why. "I don't know," he said. "It's so básic. I like twisting the concept of time. Like the police stopped me for speeding, and they said, 'Do you know the speed limit is fifty-five miles per hour?' And I said, 'Yeah, I know, but I wasn't gonna be out that long.' "

Like I said, surreal.

Next to doing a national weather report, the thing I would most like to do that I've never done is stand-up comedy. At least that's what I think every time I watch somebody like Jay Leno go to work. Jay is deceptively funny, which is a little like saying a pitcher is "sneaky fast." What do I mean? For one thing, a lot of Jay's material, like Jackie Mason's, is built around observations of daily life, although Jay's insights are somewhat less acerbic. But Jay is one of the best at tapping the other source of material that has marked the great modern-day comic since Sahl and Lenny—current events. When Leno works his way around from personal observation to the social and political stuff taken from the day's newspapers, he's in top form. You've probably gotten used to seeing Jay sit behind the desk as guest host on the *Tonight Show*, but check out his monologue some night. His jokes have a lot of the same political bite that Johnny's monologue is notable for. He may use Johnny's writers for that, but his own material is just as pointed.

I saw Jay's stand-up show when I was out in Vegas a few years ago, and when I had him on the radio later that same night, I asked him what kinds of jokes get the biggest laughs in his shows. He told me the hottest jokes are usually based on things that have been in the news that day or just previously. "For example," he said, "almost any joke you tell in the next two weeks about Jimmy Swaggart will get a laugh."

The story had recently broken that Swaggart had been involved with a prostitute in New Orleans, so I asked Jay exactly what jokes he was telling about Swaggart.

"Well, I think there are some good side effects to the Bakker thing and the Swaggart thing," he said. "Even people who are atheists are starting to say, 'Hey, maybe there *is* a God.' "

"What about Jimmy himself?" I asked.

"For years," Jay said, "what did he tell people? If you've ever watched him, what would he say? 'Stay out of porno bookstores, stay out of cheap motels, because you'll see something you shouldn't see.' And apparently it was *him*. But I saw one of those PTL guys on your show. What was his name, Dortch?"

"Reverend Richard Dortch," I said. He'd been second in command of Bakker's PTL organization.

"Yes, and this is exactly what he said. What he wants to do is establish a code of ethics for TV ministers. You know, I thought they *had* a code of ethics. It was called the Bible. Whatever happened to that? Do we really need an eleventh commandment? *Thou shalt not play the pirate and the slave girl in cheap motels.* Do you have to write that down now?"

When I asked Leno if he was doing any Jesse Jackson stuff, his answer gave me another insight into what works and what doesn't in the area of topical comedy.

"I don't do much on Jesse," he said. "You've got to give him a little more time. Other than trying to find a word to rhyme with 'orange,' Jesse hasn't made any promises yet that I can really hold against him. But you know what it is, too? People say comics are not making fun of him because he's black and the comics are afraid they'll be seen as racist. But Jesse *is* the candidate of the underdog, and from a comedy point of view you really can't make fun of the underdog. Because the comic sees himself as the underdog. When a politician says that his platform is to stop drugs and to help the farmers and working people—well, that's good. You can't say much against that. Comedy is always knocking down the pompous, so you want to go after the candidate who's the guy of the rich and powerful. So it's not really true that comics are laying off Jesse because he's black. You make fun of him the way you make fun of any other candidate. It's just that he doesn't have the big money interests behind him, so there's really nothing you can nail him on. At least not yet. But we'll find something."

Then I asked Jay if there was anything that ticks him off these days. Again, I saw a side of him I hadn't been aware of.

"You know how they ask, Is America falling behind and Japan getting ahead?" Jay said. "I saw something on TV the other night that is a perfect example of what's wrong with this country. I saw ads for two products. One was for a Japanese product and one was for an American product. And just the fact that they ran back to back was a perfect metaphor for what's wrong in this country.

"First there was the Japanese product. They showed the new Honda Prelude, and they said, 'State-of-the-art Japanese technology.' They showed the four-wheel steering, the antilock brakes, the sixteen-valve engine. Next was the ad for the American product: 'The hamburger that's cool on *this* side . . . and hot on *this* side. But *you* have to put it together.' So do you think we'll win the science fair this year?"

Besides being great at working with topical material, Jay Leno does another thing that puts him very much at the forefront of the current crop of comics. He makes virtually no distinction between the Leno you see onstage and off. For instance, he talks about motorcycles a lot in his act because he likes to ride them. I was amazed the night I did the *Tonight Show* to watch him put on a leather jacket after the show and ride off

on one. He also collects them. When I asked him about his love
for motorcycles, he acknowledged that he preferred American
motorcycles and "the old English stuff" because they hold their
market value better. "I'm not a big fan of Japanese motorcycles," Jay said. "When I do commercials, I don't do foreign
products. I only do American products."

"This is a rule of yours?" I asked.

"Yes," he said. "I don't do that much performing in Tokyo,
actually. I'm not at Ho Ho's a lot."

"But do you have a concept that you will not work for a
foreign product?"

"I just don't. I don't sell beer and wine either, because I don't
drink. You've got to keep things reasonably close to reality. See,
it's fun for me to go out because when I meet people, I'm the
same person onstage or offstage. Like, I don't drink beer. But
if I did a beer ad, and if I went to a place and went to the bar,
someone might say, 'Oh, let me buy you a beer.' Then I'd say,
'I don't drink beer.' And then people would get annoyed because I'm being a hypocrite. I go to a bar now and people say,
if they've seen me on the *Tonight Show*, 'I know you don't drink.
Can I buy you a soda or something?' And then we can talk. By
the same token, if you're on a sitcom and you play a tough guy,
or a lover, or whatever, there's always somebody who wants to
fight you—or make love to you, I guess. I never thought of it
quite that way, but. . . ."

"By the way, is that something you'd like?" I asked.

"To make love to someone? Yes."

"No, the *Jay Leno Show*. A Jay Leno sitcom?"

"No, no, not me."

"Jay Leno in *Happiness at Five?*"

"No, I don't want to be in *Who's Got the Butter?* or anything
like that. I like what I'm doing. I do TV to get people to come
to live shows. I don't really want to sit in a rehearsal hall with
a box of doughnuts because then I have the worst fear of all,
which is talking with actors. And you know just how frighten-
ing that can be. Not that comics are the brightest people in the
world, but at least with comics you talk about things. When
you sit with actors and talk about the election, they say stuff
like, 'Well, Shirley MacLaine feels. . . .' "

* * *

Of course, there's always something to be said for the good, old-fashioned joke teller. Few people alive today can tell a joke better than Milton Berle, for all his vaudeville-Catskills shtick. Berle has adapted to the times and can use material based on current events and concerns, as he did in the joke he told me about Alzheimer's disease. An old man is sitting on a park bench, moaning and crying out loud, "Woe is me! Woe is me!" Finally someone comes over to him and asks, "What's the matter?"

"I'm eighty-three years old," the man says, "and I've got a twenty-seven-year-old wife. She's crazy about me and I love her. Fortunately, I've got enormous stamina for a man of my age. We make love eleven times a day." Then he goes back to screaming and moaning.

The other guy says, "So why are you crying?"

The old man says, "I forgot where I live."

But when you talk about comics who can work off the events of the day, the guy I think is the best in the business is probably also this country's best-kept comedic secret. And that's regrettable, because Albert Brooks is a genius. His films—*Real Life, Modern Romance,* and *Lost in America*—have remained cult hits without ever becoming big box office favorites. He was nominated for an Oscar for his brilliant supporting role in *Broadcast News.* But Albert followed up his critical success by carefully avoiding acting roles for the next few years. Some people feel that he has a thing about success—he's terrified of it. But me, I think that's just Albert, always doing the unexpected. Like when I try to get him to come on my radio show and he says, "No chance," and then shows up at the last minute, unannounced.

I don't know how to explain Albert Brooks's fractured comic genius if you haven't already experienced it, other than to give you one thin slice of his bizarre brain in action. With his IQ, I'm sure he can spare a sliver. We were talking shortly after the Supreme Court had handed down its controversial ruling that the Texas law against flag burning was unconstitutional. If you recall, that same day the Court also released its decision that those 976 phone numbers, the ones people call for phone sex, were legal. Putting this all together, Albert said he had an idea for a new phone line: 976-FLAG. You call and hear the flag being burned.

"You would just hear a guy giving directions," Albert said. "You know: 'Okay, Bob, lay it out. Put kerosene on the stars and put Union oil on the stripes. All right, light up the torch! Wohhhhhh!!' And then they hang up like they do on the sex phones. You have to call back to hear it actually burning."

That was a throwaway that came up accidentally, but you get the idea. Albert told me that when he was starting out as a comic, the biggest deal in the world for him or any other comic was going on the *Tonight Show* with Johnny Carson. It was so traumatic and he worked on his material so hard and in such excruciating detail—and Albert is a perfectionist to begin with—that he just can't bring himself to go through that kind of torture anymore. It's not any easier for him today than it was ten or fifteen years ago. That he was brilliant at it and that it may have come across as being very off the cuff doesn't belie the fact that it was all sweat and blood.

In fact, Albert won't do *any* TV show now, including mine, even though he'll come on the radio just about anytime he feels like it. He claims that he made a promise to Johnny Carson that if he ever comes back on television, he has to do the *Tonight Show* first. I don't know if I buy that, but just in case it's true, I wish Johnny would call Albert and release him from his vow.

If Albert doesn't drop by on the radio, he may call up the show, although I never know when he's going to call. Once in 1985, on the eve of Reagan's much-criticized trip to Bitburg to lay a wreath at a cemetery that contained the graves of Nazi SS troops, Albert called in during the Open Phone America segment as President Reagan. Among other things, Albert does a marvelous impersonation of Reagan, and there he was in my ear saying he didn't understand what all the fuss was about a trip to Pittsburgh.

I think I'm now Albert's official sounding board for new material. He'll call me and say something like, "I want to do this George Bush thing. What do you think of it?" Or he may just call in *as* George Bush and go right into a bit. When Albert does an impression, he aims at the psyche of his target rather than just the voice and mannerisms. One night after I had finished interviewing Shirley MacLaine and had gone to open phones, I got a signal from the control room that Albert was on the line as President Bush. I guess he'd been working on Bush and wanted to try out his impression in a national forum.

"I understand that George Bush is with us," I said. "Hello?"

"I guess I'm talking to Larry now," Albert said in a hesitant semidrawl that made him immediately recognizable as George Bush.

"Mr. President?"

"Larry?"

"Yes."

"Up late here. Workin'. Heard ya. Heard that Shirley MacLaine there."

"What did you think?"

"Don't believe in it."

"But you like her, don't you?"

"Like her very much, Larry. *Irma La Douce*, favorite film. *Terms of Endearment*, liked that. Called up, Larry, to say hi and to have you ask me a few things."

"I'm honored to have you join us here."

"Y'know, the regular press doesn't ask me the good stuff."

"I'm glad you're up, glad you're listening, glad you're hard at work. Would you say that we're having a tough time getting a good read on your administration? In other words, there are jokes that you've hit the ground standing still, that nothing's really happening, there's no energy, no philosophy. How do you assess that?"

"Don't believe it. Don't think it's true. You know, I'm the education president. You're gettin' a good read. You know Larry, one hundred days aren't up yet. I heard Shirley say the Lord made the earth in seven days. I have twenty days left. We're gonna do it out there. We're doin' it now. Right now, we're doin' it in two of the rooms here. We're doin' it."

"Doing what?"

"Don't know."

"How's your wife, how's she doing?"

"Feelin' good. Larry, so glad to find out that's what it was. We thought she was in, like, a permanent menstrual thing there. Most irritable gal y'ever saw. Looked good, lost weight there, but irritable. Feelin' much better."

"How did you feel about your loss on the John Tower thing? Did it bug you?"

"Don't feel good about it. Good man. Sober, drunk, still good man. I've got to level with you now. Now I can say these things. You know, ya gotta drink a little, ya run the Defense Department. Ever walk a carrier? Four hundred yards. You want to have a drink just walkin' it. Buyin' one, ya *gotta* have a drink, gotta do it. Have to drink a little."

"What about the North trial?"

"No comment on it. Don't want to hear it."

"Wait a minute."

"Fella's bein' tried four hundred yards away. I'm not going to comment on it. I wouldn't have called you if I thought this was gonna be—"

Now I could hear him turn his mouth away from the phone and say, as if to an adviser, "He's askin' me the same crap."

"Okay, I'm sorry," I said.

"Go ahead, ask it," he said.

"Okay, the North defense wound up today, and they're going to have closing arguments, and you have been mentioned in this trial."

"So have a lot of people."

"They said, in effect, that you knew what you said you didn't know. You said you did not know about Iran-contra. Mr. North, called by the president prior to you 'an American hero,' said you did know. So one of you is lying."

"Larry, read some of the testimony of those fellas goin' to the electric chair. They'll say anything. What do you think the fella's gonna say? He did it? Larry—"

Again you could hear him talking to someone in the room with him. "I can't tell him. Can I do it? No? Sorry, Larry, can't comment on it."

"Do you still regard North as an American hero?"

"Never did. Heard today Franklin Mint's gonna have a plate for the fella, with his right arm up there, and his lawyer's gonna be on the plate. Big argument. His lawyer got on the plate. Do consider him an American hero, but Larry, you know, everyone's a hero. Isn't that what Shirley said earlier?"

"Yes, she did."

"We're all heroes in some lifetime. Maybe this isn't the one. Don't know."

In response to a question about how he saw his job, "George" replied, "My job, Larry, is to really ride right down the middle of the rail. Gotta take a little from the left, the right—"

"Don't you think a president should lead us?"

"Don't think so, no. I think the president is sort of like the conductor, comin' through the car, takin' the tickets, announc-in' the stops. If the conductor drives the train, you're gonna have a big crash, Larry. Don't think the president should. Don't like to do that. Sure, in an emergency we'll do it. Don't think that's m'job. You know I don't ride in the back of the limo? Don't like doin' it. Ride up front with Jerome there, the black fella."

Finally Albert came back to reality and we talked briefly about how he works on getting a character down.

"I love doin' him," he said of Bush. "Sometimes my voice goes in and out, but I have his psyche down. Oh, there's one thing I forgot, one thing I love. They asked him, 'What are you going to do with this piece of legislation, the budget?'

" 'We're gonna put it on the table. Look at it. Pick it up. Take it off the table. Look at it there. Put it back on the table. Look at it again. Take it off. Put it away for a year. See if anybody thinks about it.' "

I pointed out to Albert that he is not really a political hu-morist, and he agreed. "But George Bush is the most nonpolit-ical politician that ever lived," he said. "He's running the hardware store of the universe."

"That's right," I said. "It's really like a sitcom."

Albert said that, indeed, Bush reminded him a lot of those Hollywood husbands of the fifties, like Dagwood. "If Bush is not reelected," he said, "I see a solid summer stock career for him. Because he could be in any Neil Simon play. His team cheer is F-E-L-L-A, Fella. I'll tell you when I lost all faith in everything, though. When he came out with the gun issue and I thought, He's going to talk. But the guy managed to go right down the middle of the gun issue: 'Hunters there, don't wanna take it away from a hunter. By the way, more humane to kill a deer that way than a single bullet. Ya wanna put forty or fifty in it. By the same token, don't like to see children gettin' shot. Workin' on a compromise—maybe send deer to school.'

"I don't know how he did it. But somehow you thought, Oh my God, he's for the gun—no, he wants *no* guns. I was thinking, What kind of plan is he going to come up with so everyone can have a gun but no one gets shot? 'Gonna have a thing there. No barrel open. So we have a closed barrel. Shoot it. Heats up the metal. Bullet doesn't come out.'

"I don't know, but I get the feeling that there will be no big decisions made by Bush at a time when it would be great if there were. That's just my opinion."

Albert had one final insight about Bush that I found hilarious. "George Bush is a little like Al Kelly," he said. "Remember him, the great double-talking comedian? I think I understand Bush, and then eleven words in, I don't even know what he was talking about. He always stops in the middle of the sentence and begins again, like he just thought of something important. So he has fourteen sentences that have no ending: 'You know, Larry. You know I've got a funny story, Larry, which you'll appreciate. And by the way, a man came up to me yesterday— Oh, and Larry, this reminds me of a thing that happened—'

"But you know, a terrible thing did happen to Mrs. Bush," Albert concluded. "Willard Scott accidentally wished her a happy one-hundredth birthday on the *Today* show. He was severely reprimanded."

Another time, Albert called up with a bit about Ronald Reagan two years from now, when he and Nancy have become totally boring in retirement. He's got the maître d' at Chasen's answering the phone. " 'Hello? Ah yes, Mr. President, how are you? Oh, you're coming in again tonight? Party of four? Eight-thirty? Ah, Mr. President, we're packed tonight. I mean, we're really jammed tonight. I mean, you're here every night. What? Yes, I'll hold on. . . . Yes, Mrs. Reagan. Yes, Mrs. Reagan. Okay, Mrs. Reagan.' "

And then he's a Ford dealer taking Reagan's call: " 'You got the Lincoln all right, Ron? Yeah, Ron, what's the matter? The rear disk. You know, I can't spare a guy to come out. I just can't get a guy up there today. I mean, you've only had the car two weeks. You get a new car every six months. Yeah, I'll hold on. . . . Yes, Mrs. Reagan. *Yes*, Mrs. Reagan.' "

* * *

The show I remember best with Albert was the time he came on not long after the summer Olympics had concluded in a cloud of steroid-induced infamy for the Canadian sprinter Ben Johnson and other athletes. Once again, he had repeatedly told my radio producer, Pat Piper, that he would not come on, even though we were broadcasting live from Los Angeles, where he lives. Instead he just walked up to the microphone after I had finished interviewing the actor Robert Wohl.

"Larry, I have some very, *very* bad news," Albert said. "This is a sad, black day for Canada. I heard driving over here to-night that Gordon Lightfoot tested positive for steroids, and apparently all of his records have been removed. His new hit, 'Fly Me to the Moon or I'll Bring It Down Here,' has been recalled."

"Albert, you look sensational," I said. "What's going on, are you doing a film?"

"I'm on steroids," he said. "By the way, I brought a friend of mine named Willy Allen with me, an athlete who was sup-posed to be in the decathlon, and I wanted you to talk to him."

"Willy Allen?" I asked. I didn't see anyone else in the room with us. "Where is he?"

"Right here," Albert said. "Can I bring him in?"

"Yes."

"Willy, you want to come in here?"

I thought I was going nuts. "I don't see him," I said. Sud-denly I woke up to what Albert was doing. *He* was Willy Allen. "Oh, Willy," I said, recovering. "We have Willy Allen with us, who was supposed to compete in Seoul and apparently has de-clined to go. A friend of Albert Brooks. Why didn't you go, Willy?"

"Well, I mus' tell you somethin', Larry," Albert said, the black accent captured as faithfully as Albert does all his imper-sonations. "I was supposed to be in the decathlon. And I was up front about it, because I fully believe in steroids. I've been takin' 'em fourteen years, an' I don't see any physical damage it's done to me. They aksed me if it hurt my sex life. And the last time I had sex was 1971 and as far as I remember, it went very well."

"So you're here on behalf of steroids?"

"I'm here on behalf of steroids. Larry, let me tell you somethin'. I had entered the decathlon, I had broken every world record in the Olympic. I was given my choice. I was allowed to get into ever' single event in the Olympic. I didn't do well with the horses, because there's no pill that can really make you like a horse if you don' like it. You gotta like the horse naturally."

"In other words, you could take steroids and you could break swimming records?"

"I broke every single record, Larry. Let me tell you somethin'. I had dinner the night before with Ben Johnson. And personally, it's not his fault. We went out to a Korean restaurant, and he had what's called Steroid Duck. It's a very muscular duck and they douse it with steroid, and I think that must've been what happened. Because I know he don' take the steroid, because I offered it to him.

"But I had run the hundred meter, Larry, in the trials, in 4.1. I beat a Toyota flat out. That's the honest truth. I'm not kidding you. I threw the javelin, Larry, I hit a light plane. The shotput I put through a concession stand. And I'm very excited because Albert and I, we've just come from a meeting with Barry Diller, and we have just sold the Steroid Olympic to Fox. We're going to have the All-Steroid Olympic."

"So in other words," I said, "steroids are banned but you're going to have a Steroid Olympics. Where are you going to hold this?"

"Let me tell you," Willy said. "It don' matter, Larry. I think we're going to go back to Seoul, because Ben Johnson wants to light the torch and then burn the city down. And I don't blame him. I think it was unfair."

"You think he was robbed."

"Let me tell you somethin'. The people want to see athletes do as good as they can. Now you know, they did this study. Fifty percent of the athletes said they would die in five years if they could take the steroid and win the gold medal. Did you hear about that study? That's the honest truth. A few people said they would live seven and a half years if they could win the silver. And nine years, four months, if they could win the bronze. That was the whole shot. Now let me tell you, I ran the hurdles. The thing about steroids, you don't really have to clear the hurdle. You can go right through it. Do I look bad to you? I have my clothes on now, and you can see all my ligaments completely."

"You're an amazing physical specimen. How did you get to know Albert? Albert doesn't exercise at all."

"No, but Albert was one of the few comics who was doin' what was called blood dopin' when he was working onstage. Matter of fact, we used to call him the Blood Dope. That was his affectionate nickname."

"I've got to take a break," I said.

"All right, I've got to go now," Willy said, "because I'm coming down from the steroid and, you know, quite frankly, it's like havin' an extra ball. I don't know if I could say that on the radio."

"An extra—"

"Testicle. It's like a three-testicled person. And I get upset. I'm real angry atcha now, and I don't quite know why. Lemme run around the buildin', Larry. You don't need your car lifted, do you?"

Later in the show, Albert told one of his classic stories about the terrors of everyday life. Just as his humor based on current events goes beyond mere jokes into the psyche of a Bush or a Reagan, Albert also goes beyond the simple observations of most new comics. He's more like a jazz musician, improvising on a single riff and building it into a small masterpiece.

"I usually go to a 7-Eleven near where I live," Albert began. "Now, the Iranian people, I think, are very nice people. I have no problems with them, but there *is* something interesting about them. They have no period of development from when they are calm to when they are extremely angry. Like if you bother another person, if you go to a guy and say, 'Hey, can you fix my car?' he says, 'We don't fix cars here, this is a bakery.'

" 'I see, but I need my car fixed.'

" *'Buddy, I don't fix cars! It's a bakery!'*

" 'What time can I get my car back?'

" 'I DON'T WORK ON CARS!!'

"With other people there's a buildup. The Iranian doesn't do that at all. Like if you ask the guy at the 7-Eleven, 'What time are you open till?'

" 'Twenty-four hours.'

" 'That means you're open all night?'

" 'OPEN ALL NIGHT! I KILL YOU! GET OUT OF HERE, I KILL YOU!!'

"Sort of like from zero to one hundred in two seconds. Anyway, they have a self-serve machine at the 7-Eleven for Coca-Cola Slurpees. I know it's bad, and you'd probably kill me for eating this stuff, but I got hooked this summer. They come out of the machine, they're ice, and you're supposed to get it yourself. But they don't tell you about the Slurpee machine. You've got to have a lot of knowledge. You have to stop it about a quarter of the way before the top because it continues to grow. It's like the Slurpee that ate Cincinnati. It just moves up and up the cup before you know it.

"So the first time I came in was early in the summer. It was very hot, about a hundred here. I got that ninety-one-ounce deal they have. It's like the diabetic special. It's one in the morning. The guy is *way* down at the other end of the store waiting on people. I open up the faucet. I mean, Slurpee comes out like a fire hose. Industrial Slurpee. It came all the way to the top, Larry. It came over on the floor. It was like Yosemite. Tourists were camping out watching me do this. It went all over the place. Well, the Iranian guy went crazy.

" 'WHAT ARE YOU DOING? I KILL YOU!! DON'T USE MY MACHINE!! I DO THAT FOR YOU!!'

" 'But it's self-service,' I said.

" 'I DON'T WANT YOU IN MY STORE!! GET OUT OF MY STORE!!'

"Same thing with the newspaper. You pick up the paper. If you don't buy it within a second, he's on top of you. 'DON'T YOU READ MY PAPER HERE! BUY IT AND READ IT AT HOME!!'

"So the Slurpee went all over the floor. He went nuts. Then I wanted to get on his nerves. I looked at every sloppy thing he was selling and tried to buy it. Hot dogs with melted cheese— also self-serve. I said, 'I'm going to take that melted cheese.'

" 'I DO THAT FOR YOU! I FIX THIS! STAY AWAY FROM

THE CHEESE! DON'T USE ANYTHING THAT'S SOFT!
NOTHING YOU MAY TOUCH! NOTHING! ONLY HARD
THINGS IN PACKAGES! NO SOFT ITEMS! GET AWAY! I
KILL YOU! I KILL YOU!!!'

"Basically, they put in self-serve so it would be easy for the
guy. And now he's got to do the hardest job in the world. He's
got to wait on people *and* look out of the corner of his eye. I
made him paranoid about the Slurpee machine. So now for the
rest of the summer, he's there: 'Yes, sir, that's forty-nine cen—
Just a minute! NO NO NO NO WAIT!! STOP THAT MA-
CHINE!!' Or 'Just a minute, sir, that's not on special—STOP
THAT!! DON'T DO THIS TO ME!!' "

Then we came back to another theme of the evening.

"Do a lot of people in Hollywood use steroids?" I asked. "Why
would actors use steroids?"

"I know personally a lot of people at Disney do."

"Disney?"

"Yes."

"For what reason?"

"Well, you've got to be a real man to work with all those
people with those costumes all the time. You get annoyed, you
want to say, 'Get out of here, mouse.' I don't know, but now
that I'm really into steroids I can see what they do. There are
a lot of people in Hollywood who are extraordinarily built up.
You know, these producers who have a lot of muscles. And I
don't know if they come so naturally. And by the way, now
that I know about steroids, I'm reading scripts that I've gotten
and I'm a little suspicious. Like the sequel to *Gone With the
Wind—Come Back, Damn Wind!* I think this may have been
steroid-written. Or the *Ordinary People* sequel: *Those Horrible
People, I Want to Strangle Them.* I think that might have been
a steroid script."

The calls were coming in from Albert's army of radio fans.
"I'd like to know," one caller asked, "if Roger Maris gets an
asterisk next to his name in the record book, does that mean
Ben Johnson gets an asteroid?"

"You know I really have feelings about this," said Albert. "I
don't think they should wipe off these athletes completely. I
think they should put an asterisk. They should put the name

Ben Johnson and then put 'Artificially Fueled'—the initials AF.
And still put his time. Because, you know, guys can do amazing
things on steroids, Larry. I was at the UCLA track. The guys
were doing steroids, and they were high-jumping fourteen-
eight."

"Artificially fueled, huh?"

"AF, a little symbol, so you have your natural athletes and
your artificial. Because may I tell you something? Why should
we be so cocky? If we're ever visited by UFOs, do you think
people from another planet are going to get here on the natch?
Not on steroids? You don't fly seventy-one light-years on the
natch. You take uppers and steroids and get in your craft and
go. They're gonna *want* to see other people on steroids. The
Mr. Universe Contest? What if there really *is* one? This is going
to be a guy on a lot of steroids. 'All right, the man from Venus
is into his final pose-down. He was going to take a urine test,
but from Venus, as you know, they have no urine. They just
yawn and they feel better.'

"Here's the thing about the Olympics that I think is tragic.
There were those girls from Rumania. I saw the mini-doc on
Rumania. It made Rumania sound like a bad place. They said
they have electricity only two hours a day. Well, I just had a
big meeting with the Southern California Edison Company, and
there are brand-new generators that can be run by humans flip-
ping around over and over. So why not put these talented
women to work?"

"The gymnasts?" I asked.

"Yes," said Albert. "They could run power. There are brand-
new generators that if you do extra flips and degrees of difficulty— Put all those girls inside a glass thing and let them run
that country so they can get electricity more than two hours a
day."

"That's a great idea, Albert."

"That was a steroid idea, Larry."

There was one sequel to that night's insanity. The following
week, I was told that a group had been formed in Chicago
called Iranians for Albert. I have yet to see any proof of this
group's existence, but I'm willing to buy it since that's the kind

of fanatical following Albert seems to attract. Naturally, when I asked him about it the next time he was on the show, he took exception to the idea that he might have insulted Iranians with his routine. I said, "But you said that all 7-Elevens are run by Iranians."

"That's not a joke," Albert said. "I was reading out of *USA Today*. There was a graph of what Iranians do in this country and where the Iranian's head went up to one hundred it said '7-Elevens.' Now, Larry, you go into 7-Elevens occasionally, right? Close your eyes and tell me if this sounds like a 7-Eleven. 'Howdy. Whatcha goana have? Goana have a Sluhrpee?' "

"Okay, that doesn't sound right," I admitted. "How does a 7-Eleven sound?"

"HEY, DON'T READ THAT HERE PLEASE! DON'T USE THE PHONE HERE!! NO, SORRY, CAN'T CHANGE A TWENTY!!"

2

Caught in the Act

As kids growing up in Brooklyn, my friends and I were theater freaks.

That may sound a little strange to anybody who grew up outside of New York or who came of age after the advent of television. It may even seem unbelievable coming from a guy who grew up in a working-class neighborhood in Brooklyn where our biggest heroes were Sandy Koufax and Jackie Robinson. But beginning as young as age twelve or thirteen, back in the late forties, we usually managed to come up with a couple of bucks for balcony seats to a Broadway matinee, after which we'd have a bowl of spaghetti somewhere and then go see the Knicks. My mother had gotten me started by taking me to Yiddish theater, where I saw the likes of Menasha Skulnik and Muni Weisenfreund, who later became famous as Paul Muni. I didn't understand Yiddish, but I laughed at the actors' delivery and extravagant mannerisms. When my friends and I were old enough to go to Broadway shows on our own, we would read the opening night reviews and then one of us would wait on line to buy matinee tickets. I saw *South Pacific* from the second balcony at a Saturday matinee for $2.80, although most musicals were $2.40 then. I think *Death of a Salesman* was $1.80 for a matinee. Top ticket prices then were about $6 or $7, which sounded outrageous to us. After all, a first-run double feature was ninety cents with a stage show—Sinatra at the Paramount or Gleason at Loew's State—so even $2.40 was high. But like I said, we were theater freaks.

We weren't interested in Shakespeare or the classics—although I later enjoyed Lee J. Cobb's *King Lear* and Michael Moriarty's *Richard III*—but we loved mainstream dramas and musicals with big stars: Paul Muni and Ed Begley in *Inherit the Wind*, Fredric March in *Long Day's Journey*, *Top Banana* with Phil Silvers, and *A Funny Thing Happened on the Way to the Forum* starring Zero Mostel. I didn't see Brando do *Streetcar*, but I saw Jack Palance do it. We caught Irving Berlin's *Miss Liberty*, which didn't make it, and *Annie Get Your Gun*, which did. I saw Anthony Quinn do *Tchin-Tchin* with Margaret Leighton and a very young Charles Grodin, and I watched John Garfield's last play, *Golden Boy*, with Lee J. Cobb at the ANTA Playhouse. Garfield died three days later. I even got to see Menasha Skulnik again when he made it to Broadway in *The Fifth Season* and *Uncle Willie*. *The Fifth Season* was set in the Garment District and it had a funny premise: the four seasons are spring, summer, fall, and winter, and the fifth season is pants. Richard Whorf played Skulnik's son and he would say something like, "But Dad, it's the fall season." And Skulnik would say, "Fall, vinter, spring, summer! There's only *von* season—pents!"

We weren't the brightest kids, but we didn't have television and we loved the excitement of going into Manhattan and seeing a live show—a show where anything could happen, where the actors might even make a mistake. After the show, on our way to get a hot dog and maybe take in a ballgame, my friends and I would discuss the merits of what we had seen, not only the plays but the actors. Wasn't Muni great? Was Cobb better than Karl Malden? The arguments were as exciting as the dramas we had been watching. We'd go back to see the same play with a different star in the lead, and it was always a kick to watch an actor we'd seen develop onstage suddenly starring in a big Hollywood movie. It was almost as if we had a personal stake in his or her career. The excitement and vitality of live theater carry over to this day for me, and even now when I watch a movie, it's the acting that holds me more than anything

else. Maybe that explains why I still get such a charge out of
seeing popular actors in the flesh. Having the chance to talk to
them and ask them about how they do the things they do is a
bonus.

Over the years, I've developed certain theories about actors
from interviewing them and watching them work, both onstage
and on the screen. It's probably not original to say, and it may
even sound oversimplified, but it seems to me that most actors
fall into either of two basic categories, with a little overlap here
and there. On one side of the aisle are the Method actors—the
ones who spend weeks preparing and researching and use all
sorts of psychological and physical devices to give their char-
acterizations the ring of realism. Here I'd include Marlon
Brando, Paul Newman, Anthony Quinn, Robert De Niro, Meryl
Streep, Michael Moriarty, and Tony Randall. On the other side
are the naturals, the kinds of actors who say, "Just give me my
lines and tell me where to stand." This bunch includes Robert
Mitchum, Jackie Gleason, and Spencer Tracy. It should be clear
from this brief sampling that it doesn't really matter which style
an actor favors because there are plenty of greats in both camps,
but it can make their performances all the more interesting to
understand the tension between these two approaches to acting.

I know Jackie Gleason isn't usually mentioned in lists of great
modern actors, but I think he was vastly underrated, partly
because of all the television work he did. His performances in
The Hustler and *Requiem for a Heavyweight* were so naturally
understated that it's possible to forget how well crafted they
were. But then that was Jackie's style. He hated to make a big
deal out of acting, and he loved to kid the Method actors who
sweated and strained over every line to get it just so. When they
worked on their "off-shots," in which the camera films one actor
while the other actor stands off-camera and just says his lines,
Jackie would try to crack up the other guy. He'd say his lines
in some kind of goofy voice, and if the guy didn't laugh, Jackie
would say, "Come on, loosen up. It's just a part."

That's not to say these different acting styles didn't mesh perfectly at times. Paul Newman is a classic Method actor, and he
got along brilliantly with Gleason in *The Hustler,* just as Quinn
and Gleason worked well in *Requiem for a Heavyweight. The*

Hustler was filmed at Vassar, and that's where Willie Mosconi taught Newman how to shoot pool. Although the close-ups of the trick shots were of Mosconi, Newman and Gleason had to do their own long shots, and Paul worked like crazy to make his Fast Eddie character look authentic. But Gleason didn't have to do a lick of preparation to make his own shots—not because he didn't believe in it, but because he was already a great pool player himself. That's one reason he looked so comfortable in the role.

Jackie also happened to have been a pool hustler in his early days; when he couldn't get work he used to go around New York hustling games for food money. In fact, he told me a funny story about Leo Durocher, who was also a pool hustler when he was young. I think Durocher was managing the Giants by the time he met Gleason, and one day they were sitting around talking about how they both used to hustle pool for eating money. So they decided to play each other, starting with a small wager, two hundred bucks or something. "I'm playing Leo," Gleason told me, "and here we are, two pros and we're both trying to lose. And we both know we're trying to lose. I'm missing easy shots and setting him up, and then Leo's missing even easier shots. Finally one of us says, 'Fuck this. Who's kidding who here? Ten grand! We're playin' this next game for ten grand!' "

So then they played for real, and according to Gleason, Durocher was a monster. Jackie won, but it went right down to the last shot.

As Method actors go, Jackie said that Paul Newman was not as infuriating as someone like Tony Quinn, who was always saying, "Uh, I think maybe the scene ought to go *this* way" or "I think we should change this line" or "I think I ought to be out of breath when I do this scene so I'm gonna run around the block." Jackie referred to this as "having the I-thinks." He would say, "*I think* we oughta finish this picture." Newman spent hours getting into character in his trailer or dressing room before the scene, but at least he didn't have the "I-thinks."

But Gleason had a good reason for his attitude. Burt Reynolds told me that Jackie's first take was always better than his second, and his second was better than his third. That's why Jackie

liked doing live television more than tape or film. And maybe
that's why I always felt such an affinity for him. Frank Sinatra
is the same way. John Frankenheimer, who directed Sinatra in
The Manchurian Candidate, said he was amazed at Sinatra's
performance in that film. He had heard all the stories about
Frank being difficult, a prima donna, but the only request Sinatra made was that they try to get everything on the first take.
"I'm a one-take actor," he told Frankenheimer. "I'm much better on the first take than on the second." Frankenheimer would
have loved to oblige him, but as he said, "We've got to do some
tricky things in this movie."

In that regard, Sinatra and Gleason were similar, but in other
ways as actors they were dead opposites. In one of the final
scenes in *Manchurian Candidate*, Sinatra had to run up a dozen
flights of stairs to get to the upper room from which Laurence
Harvey had just shot his parents with a rifle. Usually in that
situation the actor can just run up a couple of flights and then
they'll edit the film to make it look like he's running up a dozen
flights, but Frank insisted on running up all the steps for real.
Sinatra ran the dozen flights and wanted to keep going. Gleason
never would have considered that. But Frankenheimer did say
that Frank sat around smoking and telling jokes right up to the
minute before he went in front of the camera. Laurence Harvey, by contrast, would become his character an hour before he
started shooting, and you couldn't talk to him.

That's the same thing Roseanne Barr told me about Meryl
Streep when they were filming *She-Devil*. "It was a riot," Roseanne said. "Meryl and I are friendly, and we're really getting
along. Then we go to do a scene, and in the scene Meryl hates
me. We get on the set and they're blocking us. We haven't begun to shoot and I start to say something to Meryl, and she
gives me this fuck-you look. I said, 'What are you doing? Talk
to me.' Meryl just glared and gave me another fuck-you. I
thought, Fuck you? We're gonna have lunch together in a few
minutes!"

Harvey could do that, but not Sinatra or Gleason. George C.
Scott uses elements of both approaches to acting, and Gleason
admired him when they worked on *The Hustler* because Scott
had done much more stage work then either Gleason or New-

man. Jackie was bored by stage work. I once asked him when he got tired of doing *Take Me Along,* in which he starred with Walter Pidgeon and Robert Morse. And Gleason said, "Fifteen minutes after the opening night curtain." As soon as he realized he'd have to do the same thing tomorrow, he lost interest. Sinatra will never do a Broadway show for the same reason. Some actors, like James Garner and Robert Taylor, stay away from Broadway because they're uncomfortable with it. They feel much better in front of the camera, which is no put-down since it takes a whole other set of skills to be a film actor. Gleason and Sinatra weren't uncomfortable because they were both used to stage work; in fact, Sinatra was offered a fortune to do a Broadway show. He just had no interest in doing the same thing every night. But for Method actors, that's never boring because they find something new each night.

Laurence Olivier, some people may be surprised to hear, was much closer in style to Gleason and Mitchum than to Streep and De Niro. Like Gleason, Olivier loved to mock the whole business. After Olivier died, Peter Ustinov told me a funny story about him. Sir Laurence, who insisted on being called Larry, had been awarded the O.M., which is the highest award in England. It's the Order of Merit, and only a handful of people ever get it. "Somebody asked him, just before he died," Ustinov said, "what O.M. stood for, and Olivier screamed, 'Old Man!' "

Ustinov also said that as great as Olivier was, Ustinov had trouble with his Hamlet, which was considered one of Olivier's most brilliant roles. "I liked Olivier when he was offbeat," Ustinov said. "But I couldn't believe him in *Hamlet* because I couldn't see someone with that jaw as the kind of man who is indecisive."

That was the only instance I'd ever heard of Olivier's face getting in the way of his performance. Certain actors have a style somewhere between the two basic types I've mentioned, and part of the reason is their looks. Karl Malden comes to mind here because although he is a classic Method actor, that schnozz makes it hard for him to disappear entirely into a character. You're always aware that it's Malden up there, in much the same way you're always aware it's Mitchum or Orson Welles. And Charlton Heston's face keeps him from playing certain kinds of roles. One way of evaluating an actor's performance is by asking yourself whether you willingly suspended your disbelief. Was Brando really a waterfront hood? Was Garfield a boxer in *Body and Soul*? Was Gleason a deaf-mute in *Gigot*? Tony Quinn has done a remarkable job of letting his face disappear in roles, which isn't easy when you have that kind of face. Paul Muni was probably the best at that in his day, as Robert De Niro is today. They always look different.

Recently I had a chance to interview two actors who exemplify as well as anyone can the two schools of acting, although neither has received the full measure of stardom he deserves. When the TV movie about the founding of Alcoholics Anonymous, *My Name Is Bill W.*, was made as a Hallmark Hall of Fame special, both James Garner, who produced and had a bit part in the film, and James Woods, who played the lead, came on my TV show to talk about the art of acting. I can hardly think of two actors more diametrically opposed in attitude, acting technique, and personal style than Woods and Garner. About all they have in common is great natural ability and their first names.

Garner and Woods not only get along well, they seem to have enormous respect for each other and in a very genuine way to love each other. Woods, who belongs to the studied category of actors, is more at home with intellectual dissection and analysis of roles, whereas Garner is enrolled in the Bob Mitchum school of explanation: "Hey, I learn my lines, I show up, the camera starts rolling, and I do it. No big deal."

So it was fun to watch Woods trying to explain how brilliant Garner is while Garner just sat there shaking his head. James Garner is the kind of guy who would read Pauline Kael and probably laugh. Don't forget that the role that made Garner famous was on *Maverick*, the first TV western with a sense of humor. Garner's sardonic and naturally unheroic character made that series a huge success in the late fifties, at a time when everyone else was playing it macho straight. A lot of what Garner said to me rang so true that I learned more about acting from him, and from James Woods, than I have in interviewing many of the classical actors I've known over the yeas. To begin with, Garner admitted that the reason he enjoys acting is that

he likes being someone else. When I asked him why he likes
being someone else, he laughed and said, "I'm not too happy
with me."

He may have laughed, but he wasn't joking. As Woods was
quick to point out, "Behind every joke there is a truth."

"That's why so many actors put on putty noses," Garner said.
"You take all that off, and they're not too interesting. I know
when I go out as myself on Sunday afternoon, I'm pretty nervous. But when I go onstage, I'm doing someone else's dialogue,
so I'm not that nervous."

To illustrate how far into a character a good actor can get,
Woods described a scene in the TV movie in which, as Bill W.,
the alcoholic who founded AA (a role for which he won his
second Emmy), he was having a conversation with another alcoholic. Bill has no booze left in his glass and is getting kind of
desperate, when he notices that the other guy has a little left in
his glass. The way the scene was scripted, they get up to walk
out of the room, and Woods drinks the booze in the other guy's
glass. When they finished rehearsing the scene, Garner, who
had been observing, said, "Why don't you pour the booze from
his glass into your glass and then drink it?" It was a small detail,
but Woods loved it. "It was a great idea," he said, "because
that's what an alcoholic would do to maintain his dignity somehow—drink it out of his own glass rather than the other guy's.
But it told me something about how Jim thinks, and it eluci-
dated something in my mind about acting, which is that actors
are like sociologists. I mean real actors—I'm not talking about
movie stars and that stuff. We love to see somebody and dissect
him."

Woods feels that the problem for actors who make it look as
effortless as Garner does is that people think it's just him being
natural. "But he does a lot of very well disguised, effortless-
seeming work that, in fact, takes a lot of detail and technique
and patience," Woods said. "A lot of people think Jim Garner's
this great easygoing personality, but in my mind he's very much
like Redford, who is one of the most underrated actors in the
world. People say Redford's good-looking and a great matinee
idol and so on. But look at him in *Downhill Racer* and *Butch
Cassidy and the Sundance Kid*. They're two totally different

characters, and he portrays them in a very fine, pointillistic kind of acting."

In *Promise*, another TV movie that Woods made with James Garner, Woods won his first Emmy as Garner's schizophrenic brother. But he seemed angry that Garner didn't win one too, comparing Garner and his understated style of acting to a cop who keeps the street safe without a lot of fanfare. "If a cop has a great arrest record," Woods said, "everybody thinks he's a great cop. But how about a cop who gets to know everybody on his beat and prevents crime and doesn't have one collar on his sheet? He ends up staying a private the rest of his life. And somebody says, 'This guy never did anything.' Yeah, because nobody ever committed a crime in his neighborhood."

Part of the reason Garner doesn't draw raves is that his personality is so indelibly imprinted in the American public's mind that sometimes we have trouble separating him from his characters. But that doesn't seem to bother him. "I don't know that I ever want anybody to separate them," he told me. "Spencer Tracy always said that he never wanted anybody to catch him acting, and I'm the same way. I don't want anybody to know I'm acting, ever. I want them to think that's me, doing what I'm doing. Because the minute the audience says, 'Boy, he's acting his heart out,' then they're out of the scene, they're out of the movie. Their minds are somewhere else. But if they're watching the character and continue to watch him and believe that's him, then they're with it."

When Garner said that, it looked like a light went on behind Woods's eyes. "You just gave me the answer to a question I have been asked by journalists for the past five years," he said. "People say to me, 'Why are you always so intense when you work?' And what I like to do is the same thing you like to do: make it look effortless. But it's even more fun to look effortless when you're doing a character who's really on the edge. The ultimate challenge is to make it look like that's really happening, when in fact it's just technique."

One of the questions that has always intrigued me is, What happens between actors during a production? Whether it's on-stage or in front of the cameras, what goes on if, for instance, one actor is markedly better than the other actor or actors in the same scene? Does he bring them up or do they take him down a notch? Woods told me, for openers, that it's more difficult to work with Hollywood personalities than with genuinely skilled actors because he puts so much energy into helping them out that he has less left for his own work. So in his estimation, it both lifts up the bad actor and exhausts the good one.

Another thing I've always wondered about actors is what's going on inside in that moment before the director calls "Action." When I asked James Garner, he laughed and said, "I'm wondering, 'What's my first line?'" That fits in perfectly with his natural style and is probably about the same answer you'd get from Mitchum or John Wayne. Woods, by contrast, saw it in almost existential terms. "It's probably kind of what a bronc rider feels when he's sitting in the gate," he said, "and before that monster underneath you starts heading for home. When they open the gate, you're finally so grateful just to be out there getting banged around. It's like, Let the artillery start falling so we can get into this battle and get on with it, because I'm getting tired of waiting."

It's not hard for me to think of Woods as a bronc rider because his acting is usually charged with that kind of manic energy. But James Garner, who has played plenty of western characters, strikes me as just the opposite. I asked him, "Are you Jim Garner five seconds before you go on?"

"Oh yeah," he said. "Five seconds before, yes I am."

"You could say, 'See you for lunch,' and then do it?" I asked.

"Yeah."

Then I asked Woods the same question. "Yes," he said, "but if you're still Jim Garner or Jim Woods five seconds *after* they say 'Action,' you've got a real problem."

It's clear to me that Garner's attitude toward acting comes from his take on life in general. Like me, Garner has been through bypass surgery. But I asked him if, like me, he had felt a little anger before going into the surgery, anger that it had happened to him. "Nope," Garner said. "I felt I deserved it. I had done everything in the world to myself, and I felt, Well, it's about time something went wrong."

Since I know that actors are sometimes taught to draw on their previous experiences when they need to react emotionally,

I asked Woods if he ever used anger from his own life in a scene that required him to be angry. He thought about it a moment and then turned the question around a little. "Let's take a scene where you have to cry, for instance," he said. And he proceeded to give me the best answer I've ever heard to the question of how actors get themselves to cry on cue.

"People say, 'How do you cry?'" Woods said. "And I say, 'Well, if the scene makes me cry, I cry.' And they say, 'What if it doesn't?' Then I say, 'It's bad writing and they've got to change it.' Because I presume that I'm a fairly sensitive person, and I might have some response to a situation. People say *Promise* must have been difficult, but it was the easiest job of my life. It had brilliant writing, brilliant directing, a brilliant co-star. I sat in my little chair. Jim said great stuff to me. I just said back what was written in the script, and halfway through the scene I'd be in tears because it was so moving to me."

As intelligent as that statement is, I know that Jackie Gleason would have laughed at it. Gleason would say, "Don't matter if the script is bad or good. If ya gotta cry, cry." That kind of intellectualizing about acting drove him up the wall. "If the scene says cry," Jackie once said to me, "and they're paying you money to act the part, then cry." Anthony Quinn would take it even further. Quinn is one of the great living Method actors, and he would never limit himself merely to what is written in the script. As Tony once told me, "I've always been accused of playing slightly bigger than life, and rightly so." But when I told him Gleason's complaint that "Quinn don't act, he marinates," Tony rolled his eyes. "Poor Jackie, he never understood. I marinated, but I marinated for twenty years."

While Quinn was getting ready to film a new TV movie of *The Old Man and the Sea* and he came down with a painful flu bug in his stomach, he refused to postpone filming. "Please don't change the dates," he told the producers, "because I want to play it with a bug in my stomach. I think the Old Man had a bug in his stomach." Tony insisted to me that it really helped the part. "The whole time we were filming I was saying to the bug, 'Please don't disappear while I'm doing this part. Let me keep my virus."

I think I'd have to agree with Jackie: that's sicko. Nor is Quinn satisfied by drawing on anger or sadness from his own life the way some actors do. He likes to imagine the entire inner life of the character he's playing and to build his onstage emotions from the ground up. For example, in 1962 Quinn starred in a Broadway play called *Tchin-Tchin*, about an aging Italian businessman and an American socialite who meet and have a brief affair in Italy. Margaret Leighton played the woman, and Charles Grodin, in his first Broadway role, played the woman's son. Quinn told me that during rehearsals he decided that his character's father must have died when the character was still quite young, and that affected Tony's interpretation of the role. Mind you, there was nothing about the man's father in the script. As a matter of fact, Tony asked the playwright about this, and the playwright told him he hadn't given it a thought. Quinn obviously gave it plenty of thought.

Another time, Quinn told me he held up shooting on *Lawrence of Arabia* for an entire day because he felt one of his scenes was not quite right. The scene called for Peter O'Toole as Lawrence to walk up to Quinn and say, "Tomorrow we attack Aqaba. Will you join me?" Quinn was supposed to look at O'Toole and say, "Yes." That was it. They ran through the scene at 9:30 in the morning, and David Lean, the director, could see that Quinn was unhappy about something. "What's the matter, Tony?" Lean asked.

"You know, Mr. Lean," Quinn said, "he asks me to attack Aqaba, and I know that my whole army can be killed. I can lose five thousand men in this fight because we don't know what we're facing against the Turks there. My saying 'Yes' to him is a tremendous decision. I have to go away and think about it."

"Do you?"

"Don't you think you'd think about it if you were in my place?" Quinn said.

"You're right," said Lean. "What do you want to do, Tony?"

"I'd like to walk over there and take a long look back at my army," Quinn said, "and then come back and say, 'Yes.' "

"Well," said Lean, "that means moving five thousand horses and two thousand elephants to begin with."

At that point Tony told Lean to forget his idea, that he'd be happy to do it the way Lean originally wanted. But the director wouldn't hear of it. It took them until five-thirty in the afternoon to move everyone into place while Tony sat with his head in his hands, muttering, "Oh my God, what have I done?"

Finally, they shot the scene. O'Toole said, "Tomorrow we attack Aqaba. Will you join us?"

Quinn looked at him, walked over and looked at his army, came back and said, "Yes."

Just then, the director called "Cut!" and the sun disappeared behind the horizon. And David Lean said to Anthony Quinn, "Damn nice, Tony, because we only had time for one take."

Afterward, Quinn kept trying to apologize for putting him through so much trouble, but Lean insisted that the scene worked great that way. Tony promised never to do it again, and Lean replied, "Tony, please don't. I'm not that insecure." Gleason would have called that a major case of the "I-thinks."

How far can you take that kind of thing? Unless you've worked with or hung around professional actors, you probably have no idea. I was backstage with Michael Moriarty and John Rubinstein when they were appearing in *The Caine Mutiny*. They'd been doing it for three months, and that's when they started switching roles. For the last few months they played each other's parts to keep from getting bored, and even then they were constantly making adjustments to keep things interesting. They had done a matinee the day I was backstage chatting with them. Moriarty was playing Captain Queeg, and he said to Rubinstein, "You know in the challenge scene, John, where I lean forward and you come at me?"

"Yeah?" Rubinstein said.

"Come at me harder, and I'm going to jump out of the chair and then sit back down, instead of holding on to the chair."

"Why are you going to do that?" Rubinstein asked.

"I think Queeg's losing his grip," Moriarty said, "so he's going to let go of the chair."

"But this is the guy who's spent all those years in the navy," Rubinstein said. "Do you think he's going to leave himself open enough to let go of that chair?"

"Just once," Moriarty said. "Just once in his life I think he'd do it."

It fascinated me to watch two veteran actors expend that much energy discussing one little maneuver. But it all made sense to them because they had become someone else. It's like what Tony Randall said when I asked him why he enjoys being an actor. "I can be anyone I want," he said. "I can be a kid. I can be crazy. I can be happy. I can be poor. I can be rich. I can have a sunny disposition or a gloomy one. I can be a killer or the nicest guy in the world. I can be anything—tonight! Why would I want to do anything else?"

Maybe that's what keeps drawing actors back to the theater, even after they've done films. It's not only the chance to be someone else but also to create that new persona, to shape it day by day in the theater and to reenter it each night on the stage. Randall said that the happiest moments of his life are when he's onstage. "I like an audience," he said. "Some actors don't. Some very fine actors are uncomfortable in front of an audience, and you can feel it. John Gielgud is one of the greatest actors living, but I always felt he was uncomfortable in front of an audience. I always thought his acting lacked charm and I knew that he was probably much better in rehearsal, until recently. In the last few years, suddenly he loves the audience, and his acting is just dripping with charm."

Getting back to James Garner for a minute, he's another of those actors Randall was talking about. I knew Garner had done some theater, so I asked him if he found it valuable to return to the stage every so often. "No, I don't go back to it," he said, "because I never really felt that that was where I should be. When I started acting I was an extreme introvert. I thought, I have to get over that. But in the process of getting over it, I couldn't project from here to the curtain. And so I said, If people are going to see what I'm doing, they're going to have to see it in the camera and in my eyes and with much more subtle movement."

"So you're an extreme introvert who liked the camera," I said.

"Yeah, I made friends with the camera. I understood the camera and now I use the camera. The proscenium stage is not necessarily my thing."

But James Woods keeps going back to the stage because he enjoys the immediacy of the response: "I like my gratification instantly." Robert Taylor told me that he was afraid to be a stage actor. He was a film actor and would have been nervous in front of a live audience. In films, you can always do a scene over if you blow it. What would he do if he forgot his lines onstage? He didn't want to find out. Someone told me that while Ronald Reagan was working in films he had the same fear about stage work, and judging from how he performed in press conferences and debates, I'd have to believe that. Yet even a performer who loves working live can find audiences unpredictable. Tony Bennett said once that he doesn't think the performer always creates the show; some nights the audience does. Or, as Tony Randall put it, "Audiences have their own personalities. There are nights in a comedy when you get no laughs. Every laugh disappears, and you don't know why. The next night they're back."

Tony told me a story about playing *The Odd Couple* in Chicago with an actor whose name was also Tony. "I looked out," he said, "and the audience was one hundred percent nuns. It was a benefit. The big joke in that play is the 'Fuck you' joke, and I whispered to Tony, who is an ardent Catholic, 'We better cut the 'Fuck you' joke.' He just shook his head. It was his joke, so he said it. It got the same huge laugh it always gets. I was embarrassed, but seven hundred nuns were screaming with laughter."

Unlike Taylor and Reagan, Randall feels he has nothing to be afraid of onstage. He firmly believes that as long as you bring yourself to the performance, bring everything that has ever happened to you in your life and call on it unashamed, you'll be all right. "What could they do?" he told me. "Throw stones at me? They're not going to do that. As Ethel Merman said, 'If they could sing as good as me, they'd be up here onstage.' "

I've been in a few movies myself, in very small parts. When I did a little part in *Ghostbusters*, playing myself, it was the first day of shooting. I was the first scene shot, which is considered good luck. When we started, Ivan Reitman, the director, asked me, "See the script?"

"I haven't read the script," I said. "I just read my page."

He said, "Jesus Christ, this thing is going to cost us thirty-five million dollars." It ended up costing about $37 million. "The script was written for John Belushi," Reitman said. "We have Bill Murray playing it, but we haven't changed the writing. Murray told me, 'Don't change a line,' and we didn't. On top of that, I don't know a fucking thing about special effects. I've got ghosts coming out of my head. I don't know how they're going to look. I've got cameras shooting blank walls. I've got the Teamsters running all these cars. They've got their own fleet and they're in charge. Anything moves, they move it. I mean, if this film makes it, God, it'll be a miracle."

Then he talked about the last scene. "The Pillsbury Dough-boy," he said. "How do you think that's going to work? Do you think this is going to get them? I have no idea how we're going to do this scene. They tell me they're going to do it with little cardboard slides. But I'm a director. I don't know from special effects. Aykroyd tells me that the Pillsbury Doughboy is the guaranteed laugh of the year. How am I going to direct this?"

Reitman was almost comical, he was so worried. But I had very little to worry about myself. They paid me $2,500 to do my one scene, and I had a deal on residuals because it was a speaking part. If the movie was sold, I would get four times my salary for each sale, plus another $2,500 for each re-showing. With foreign sales, cable and broadcast rights, and home video, I've made thousands of dollars from that one day of shooting. And I never thought I'd make it into the finished film. You still get paid the flat fee if they cut out your scene, but you don't get the residuals. They changed the scene a lot, but they left in the first twenty-five seconds, where I say, "This is the *Larry King Show*. Tonight's topic is ghosts and ghostbus-ters. We'll be getting your opinions." But they cut out the next part, where I said, "Are you kidding me with this? Why are we doing this? Ghosts? Are you putting me on?" I took calls from people who said things like, "I know a ghost, Larry." And I kept hanging up on them.

So you can see it wasn't a really hard part for me. James Woods told me I would be a good actor. He said, "Come on, you're acting already. You're acting on the air. You know what you're doing." Similarly, J. T. Walsh was doing a scene with me in the movie *Crazy People*, and he said, "Boy, you're very good."

But in the scene, I was playing Larry King. "What do you mean?" I said. "I'm just playing me."

"That's hard," he said. "This is not your set. It's not familiar circumstances. But you're really doing it well."

But I don't know. Compared with real actors liked Woods and Walsh, I think I'm just lucky to be up there. And as James Garner said, most actors like what they do because they're just more comfortable being somebody *else*. This common thread unites not only Garner and Woods but also, I'm sure, Al Pacino and Christine Lahti and John Wayne and Katharine Hepburn, and all the rest. Whether it's insecurity or shyness, I don't know, but many actors have explained to me how they merge with, or "become," the person they're playing. They have all told me, in essence, "It's much easier being that guy than being me." George Hamilton might be the exception, but he's really a businessman. He acts only because he's a good-looking guy and they give him a role to play.

Sylvester Stallone told me that he likes acting because, he said, "It's a kind of self-imposed schizophrenia that you can visit from time to time. It gives you a license to be outrageous, obnoxious, overbearing, comedic. And you're doing it under the guise of someone else. 'Ey, it's not *me*. I'm not really sayin' those things.' You are perpetuating and extending your childhood fantasies. All acting is, is pretending."

What's really interesting to watch is the *way* actors become someone else when they work. Take that actor I worked with in *Crazy People*, J. T. Walsh. I was sitting there memorizing my lines, which were easy lines. He, meanwhile, had to portray a slick advertising executive. The director said to him, "We see this character as a Donald Trump kind of guy."

The makeup people were doing his hair like Donald Trump. And as they were doing his hair, he started to change. His voice changed, his mannerisms changed. It was like a scene out of *Dr. Jekyll and Mr. Hyde*. He slowly became a Donald Trump kind of guy. They had six different jackets there, so he took off the one he was wearing and switched to a blue blazer. He was getting more like Trump all the time. We did eleven takes and he never left that character. On the break, when I'd start kidding around, he'd be hard to talk to. As soon as we were done, they said "Wrap," and he came out of it.

Then there are actors who always seem to be playing themselves. Like Bogart, for instance. On the screen, Bogey is always Bogey. And among living actors, I would have to give the all-time award for this style of acting to Robert Mitchum. It doesn't matter whether you look at his classic film noir roles from the forties in, say, *Out of the Past* and *The Big Steal*, or his recent work in *The Winds of War:* Mitchum is always Mitchum.

The irony is that, when I have Bob Mitchum sitting in front of me, most of the time I can't tell if he's putting me on or not. Every time I interview him and I ask him how he goes about his craft, he says things like, "Acting's acting, Larry. There ain't no skill to it. Just learn your part and stand there and do it. Don't matter if it wins an award."

The last time I saw him he was giving me the same bit, so I tried a different tack. "Okay, let's discuss some other actors," I said. "What do you think of Al Pacino?"

"Never seen him work," Mitchum said.

"Robert De Niro?" I asked.

"Can't say as I've seen him."

"Dustin Hoffman?"

"Nope, haven't seen any Dustin Hoffman movies."

"Do you *go* to movies?"

"Maybe twice in the eighties."

"Twice in the eighties?"

"Yeah."

"Why?"

"Well, one, it's hard to find parking. Two, I don't have any interest in movies."

"Do you watch movies on television?"

"Can't say as I do."

"Do you watch your own?"

"Nah."

"Ever had a problem with a director?"

"Once," he replied after some thought. "One time, John Huston said to me, 'In that second part there, Bob, give it a little more anger.' And I said 'Okay.' "

"That's your total memory of directors?" I asked.

"Yeah, total."

"You don't care who's directing you?"

"Nope," he said. "You tell me where to stand. I learn my lines. The other people know their lines. I act. It ain't no big thing. So why should I have trouble with the director?"

Again the question is, Was this whole interview a put-on? And the great thing about Robert Mitchum is, I don't know. Yet David Dukes told me Mitchum is great to work with. Dukes said that he's understated and he brings you right in to him— sort of what James Woods said about James Garner. So you can't really say that Mitchum has no style. Michael Moriarty said that when you're doing a scene with Mitchum, he'll be talking in that laid-back tone of voice, and pretty soon you've brought your voice level down to meet his. You start giving it a little of Mitchum's style. "Which is good," Moriarty said, "because he sure isn't going to change to *your* style."

I don't often ask stock questions, but one of the few I sometimes ask actors is whether they ever regretted turning down a role they were offered. One of the reasons I like asking it is that I never know what kind of answer I'm going to get. For instance, James Garner said there was no role that he regretted turning down, but there were a couple he was very sorry he couldn't do. One was the lead in *Lonesome Dove,* the TV movie based on Larry McMurtry's novel. Jim was offered the lead, but he had to turn it down because of his heart problem, and that hurt him. Robert Duvall played the part instead, and Garner said, "Robert Duvall did it beautifully, but God, I'd have played that role. It was about the only part that I ever read that I didn't get and that I really, really wanted."

Garner was also sorry that he missed out on *King Rat,* the 1965 film based on James Clavell's novel about a World War II Japanese POW camp. But the real shocker for me was when he told me that he turned down *Terms of Endearment* because he felt he couldn't communicate with James Brooks, the director. He was being considered for the role Jack Nicholson ended up playing, and he had a talk with Brooks. But during the meeting he began to lose interest, and by the time he walked out of the meeting he didn't want to do it. "Everybody always said I was a bright kid," Garner said with a laugh.

James Woods told me that he originally had been chosen for the Jim Belushi role in Oliver Stone's *Salvador*, which, along with *Once Upon a Time in America*, is his favorite of all his films. One day Stone said to him, "You know, I really don't see you as a B personality. You're more of a lead character. I don't see you as the henchman." And Woods said, "Well, there's one simple solution to that. Cast me in the lead." The actor who had been chosen for the lead role of the cynical journalist had complained to Stone about the violence and the vulgar language in the script. Woods wouldn't name him, but he said that this actor, because of his religious beliefs, wanted Stone to tone that stuff down. Stone talked to the actor about his objections but finally decided that it would be best if someone else took the role. That's how Woods got the lead in *Salvador*.

Jack Lemmon told me a great story about a role he had turned down. He was doing a play in New York when Robert Rossen sent him a script. Lemmon read the script and called up Rossen. "Are you kidding me?" he said to Rossen. "You're going to make a movie about shooting pool? Hey, man, listen. I appreciate it, Robert. When you get something good, send it to me. And good luck with this."

Lemmon told me, "It was all I could do not to laugh. Now I'm in London, a year later, doing a play. My wife says, 'Let's go to this new movie opening.' We walk into *The Hustler*. I couldn't believe it. They made this movie? And they got Gleason, who's a television star, not a movie actor? And who the hell is George C. Scott? I was congratulating myself for my good sense, but as I sat there, about ten minutes into the movie my heart started to sink. 'Oh, Jesus Christ!' I said to my wife. 'I turned this down.' "

Lemmon also turned down *Butch Cassidy and the Sundance Kid*. It was going to be Lemmon and Newman. He told me he had talked to Newman about it: "Paul, two guys running away on horses in the eighteen-eighties? It's a western, but it's not *really* a western. It's one of those borderline comedies that has to be done just right. I don't think we can do this."

Charles Grodin is an accomplished actor who has only re-

62   LARRY KING

cently begun to get the acclaim he deserves, but recognition might have been his much sooner if he hadn't turned down the lead role in *The Graduate* more than twenty years ago. He was the first choice for the part, and he was offered $500 a week to star. "I had to do a screen test," Grodin told me, "but they had no second choice. Still, five hundred dollars a week was about half of what I could make on a television show. It wasn't about the money, but it seemed odd that they were offering me so little for a studio film, and I kept making a point of this. So after two weeks of negotiation, Dustin Hoffman was the Graduate. The producers were convinced by then that I was going to be very difficult to work with, and I was convinced that they were very strange. They said, 'Look, everybody gets exploited in their first starring role.' But I couldn't willingly agree to be exploited."

My question about the role not taken isn't limited to film and theater. Angie Dickinson told me she turned down *Dynasty*, in which she was offered the part Linda Evans eventually took. Angie's very philosophical about it, and it's clear that the part wouldn't have meant as much for her already flourishing career as it meant for Linda Evans's.

Sammy Davis, Jr., not only turned down the song "Candy Man" the first time around, he hated it when he did make a record of it in 1972. He recorded it tongue-in-cheek and laughed when it was finished. "I said to myself, What's my career come to?" he told me. "I'm an artist. I'm a dancer. I think I'm a jazz singer. And I'm doing 'Candy Man'! 'Candy Man'!! Six months later, I'm driving in the car, and the disk jockey's on. He says, 'Number thirty-two in town and bursting onto the list. This one will grab you and you won't stop listening. "Candy Man" by Sammy Davis!' " It went to number one and became the biggest individual hit in Sammy's career, and he *still* hated it.

Kirk Douglas at first refused to answer my question about what roles he'd turned down that he shouldn't have. He said he was offered the role of a Nazi who was treated as a sympathetic character, and he didn't feel he could play such a part. But he wouldn't name the film because he didn't want to offend the actor who had taken the role. When I explained that I was asking if there were any roles he wished he *had* taken, he lit up and started laughing. "Oh, God, yes," he said. "I turned down *Stalag 17* and Bill Holden won an Oscar for it. I turned down *Cat Ballou* and Lee Marvin won an Oscar. Oh, I passed up some beauts."

I couldn't believe *Stalag 17*. Not only did it seem like a part that was made for Kirk Douglas, but it had been a hit play on Broadway. Why on earth would he have turned that down?

"I had seen the play," he said, "and even though it was a hit, I thought the play had a lot of weaknesses. But what I was stupid about was in not realizing that Billy Wilder was a great director and he could overcome the problems."

A year earlier, though, in 1952, Kirk had been the recipient of another actor's regrettable decision. "Clark Gable turned down *The Bad and the Beautiful* and I said, 'I'll take it!' " That movie ended up winning five Oscars.

I don't know if Barbra Streisand ever regretted turning down a role, but I do know a few people who have rued the day they took roles opposite her. I'd always heard that Streisand is impossible to work with, but I had never spoken to someone who'd made a film with her until I interviewed an actor who appeared with her in *Nuts*. They had just finished filming, and he told me, "The happiest day of my life was the last day of shooting *Nuts*. We all gathered around. Streisand left the room, and as she left we hugged and kissed. Richard Dreyfuss, Eli Wallach, and me. You could feel the relief in the air. She's gone!"

All of this was said off the air, during a break. I asked the actor if he would like to talk about working with Streisand when we went back on. He politely but emphatically declined. "I don't have bad words for most people," he said, "and she's got a lot of talent. God knows she's got a lot of talent. But Christ, were we glad when it was over!"

Not long after that interview, I was with Angie Dickinson at the racetrack. Martin Ritt, who directed *Nuts*, was also there. I went over to him and said, "We haven't met, but I'd like to introduce myself." Ritt knew my show and we chatted for a few minutes. Then I said, "I was just on the air talking about *Nuts*—"

At that point I stopped myself because Ritt made a face like an aardvark going into labor. "Never mention that word to me again," he said slowly. "Never again. I don't want to be in the same room, I don't want to be in the same universe or have anything to do with that movie. Never again will I undergo that."

"What was it like?" I asked.

"Larry, it's not describable."

I hadn't mentioned Streisand's name, mind you, only the name of the movie. On the other hand, Omar Sharif told me he never had a problem with Barbra. He played Nicki Arnstein in *Funny Girl*, and she didn't give him any trouble. Of course, Sharif had such an air about him that it probably didn't matter what she said or what she did. He was always ready. He was a professional. She was screaming at people all around them, he said, but she never screamed at him. He had an attitude, and I guess it was the right one.

More and more actors these days are moving to the other side of the camera or the footlights, prompted partly by the premise that nobody knows more about getting actors to perform than another actor. This change in roles can lead to some unanticipated problems, as Charles Grodin once explained to me. When I asked him what was the most difficult aspect of directing, he said, "Having to fire people." On the first Broadway show he directed, *Lovers and Other Strangers*, in 1968, the writers and the producer decided that an actress ought to be replaced.

"I really didn't agree with them," Grodin said, "but everybody else felt that the understudy should play the part. So I had to go to this young actress and give her the bad news. It took me so long to get around to telling her what I was talking about that she thought we were just having a little chat. And as I got closer to the subject, I actually started to get chest pains and I had to lie down. She got me a wet cloth and a glass of water, and as she was patting my forehead, I said, 'You're fired.' "

Grodin, by the way, had the best advice that I've ever heard, not only for aspiring actors but for anybody trying to make it in the entertainment business. I asked him why he stuck with acting for all those years before he became established. "I wanted to master a craft," he said, "the same way you did. But in this business they say to your face that you aren't any good. They said to me, 'Why are you here? Go away, we don't like you.' They *tell* you. They're not shy. It's a very insensitive, cold profession. I became successful, but I can't forget all the other people, the other actors, who were so wonderful and who are gone now. They didn't know that it was happening to everybody else. That's the whole point—you are not alone. This is happening to everybody, only they don't know that. This is my experience right now. I'm not rejected so much anymore as an actor, but I'm also a writer, and if I write a movie or a play and want to get it made, I'm in for it again. That's what happens. If you reach out for something, people are going to say no. And what I'm saying is, It's not just you. This is the way it is, so hang in."

My final story has nothing to do with acting, but it involves one of my favorite actors and reads like a Stephen King screenplay, so maybe it isn't totally out of place here. I interviewed Telly Savalas on TV a few years ago and, as usual, we had a great time. Telly loves horses, he loves Vegas, he loves action in general. He's also a no-nonsense guy who's fairly skeptical and doesn't suffer fools gladly. In short, he's my kind of guy. Near the end of the show, a caller asked if Telly would relate a story about something that happened to him after he had left the army years ago, something supernatural. Telly said he'd be happy to tell me the story, but we were out of time. I was working by remote—Telly wasn't in the studio with me—so I couldn't ask him about it after the show, but the next time I interviewed him it was the first thing I wanted to know about.

"You really want to hear it?" Telly asked.

"Yeah," I said.

"Tell it to you now?"

"Go."

"All right. True story. And it shouldn't happen to a guy like me. Many years ago when I was working with the State Department, years after I was out of the army, I was traveling home to Long Island. It was the summer of fifty-five and I was driving from Manhattan to Garden City, and I ran out of gas, which wasn't an unusual thing for me. There's a White Fortress

on a corner of Hillside Avenue in Queens and I go in there for
help. They tell me there's a gas station open where the Cross
Island Parkway meets Grand Central Parkway. They tell me I
can hitchhike there with no problem. I say, 'Great.'

"That's exactly what I did. But while I'm walking through
the woods, I hear a voice say, 'I'll give you a lift.' I turn around,
and I see this guy sitting there in his black Cadillac. Now, I
didn't hear the car pulling up, I didn't hear anything. I figured
maybe it's somebody makin' a move, but I'll take my chances.
I get in and let him take me to the gas station. When we get to
the gas station, I realize that I don't have any money. I was
intending to leave my watch there for security, but without my
telling him a thing he says, 'I'll lend you a dollar.' Are you still
interested, Larry?"

"I'm right with you."

"All right, babe. I go in, I get a gallon of gas, and he offers
to drive me back to my car. As he's driving me back, out of a
clear blue sky he says, in one of the strangest high-pitched voices
I've ever heard, 'I know Harry Agganis.' We hadn't been talking about anything. I ask, 'Who is he?'

"He says, 'He's a utility infielder for the Boston Red Sox.' I
say, 'Oh.' I thought it was kind of strange that he should come
out with information like that. Anyway, he takes me to my car.
I wanted to say I wasn't destitute and to send him the dollar
and a thank-you note. So I ask him to write his name down.

"So he does and, unsolicited, he also writes his phone number. He gives my car a push to get it started. I thanked him
very much. All in all, a very pleasant experience. I come out of
my office the next day and the *Journal-American* has a big story
announcing that Harry Agganis up in Boston, twenty-some-odd
years old, has died under mysterious circumstances at the exact
time that this guy in the black Cadillac said to me, 'I know
Harry Agganis.' I thought that was kind of . . . strange. I wish
it stopped there."

"Did you call the guy?" I asked.

"I go home that night," Telly said, "and I tell my mother,
who's a witch anyway. I say, 'Ma, look what happened to me.'
She says, 'Telly, life is full of strange things like that.' And then
I remember the piece of paper. I go to my jacket from the night

before and take out the piece of paper, and, sure enough, there's a name and a telephone number in Boston. I call and someone answers, 'Hello, Harry's Bar.'

"I say, 'Can I speak to Mr. Cullen, please?'

"The guy says, 'Who? Hey, just a minute.' A woman gets on the phone and I say, 'Can I speak with Mr. Cullen?'

"She says, 'He's not here. Who's calling?' I give her my name, and I tell her I was with him last night.

"She says, 'What did he look like?'

"I begin to describe him, and she breaks out into hysterical tears. She says, 'Look, you bastard, I don't know what you're trying to pull, but you're talking about my husband. He's been dead for two years.'

"Which in turn just shook me up. I apologized profusely. But I couldn't let it go. I finally went up to Boston and met her a couple of weeks later. The clothes I described to her that he was wearing that night were the clothes he was buried in. I told you he had a high voice, and I thought maybe he was a little fruity. His wife said that he committed suicide by shooting himself in the mouth. This is what happened, and I ain't gonna continue to tell you the rest of the story until I meet you next time. It's kinda scary, because I don't believe in nonsense like that. But I've become a believer since then. It's spooky, so let's talk about pleasant things."

I was doubly baffled because I knew about Harry Agganis, who was quite a fine athlete and who, like Telly, was of Greek ancestry. In fact, his nickname had been the Golden Greek. Agganis played a lot of sports, including football, and was in only his second season in the majors when he died at the age of twenty-five. What makes that story spooky to me is that if anyone else but Telly was telling it, you'd just say, Sure. If Shirley MacLaine told you, you wouldn't even blink. But Kojak? I don't usually believe "nonsense like that" either, but I can't wait for the next time I meet him so I can hear the rest of that story.

3

The Summer Game

Certain phrases refer only to baseball in the American consciousness. "Are you going to the game today?" means only baseball. The All-Star Game means only baseball. If you're talking about the NBA All-Star game, then it's the NBA All-Star game. Opening day means baseball. Who talks about opening day of the National Hockey League?

Maybe because baseball is a nonviolent, noncontact sport, baseball players seem to have a longer life span than other athletes; a good player can last twenty years in the majors. For that reason, we're more aware of the changing generations of baseball players—we see the aging catcher gradually give up his duties behind the plate to the young kids coming up, or the crafty veteran pitcher of forty-one or forty-five lose a little off his fastball but still get out the young hitters on guile. Every so often in football you might get one player, a George Blanda, who sticks around into his forties, but it's rare. In baseball, it's part of the game since the transitions take place over a longer period of time.

I thought Kevin Costner might have some insight about this since he'd just done two baseball movies—*Bull Durham* and *Field of Dreams*. I mentioned that we seem to be having a national love affair with baseball, including a slew of movies and a best-seller by David Halberstam, *Summer of '49*. Costner said the reason baseball is so popular is that it's ingrained in us. It's the one sport everyone grows up playing from childhood. And besides watching the majors, there's softball for the older guys, Little League for the kids. There are pickup games all over the place, and you can always go see a minor league or semi-pro game. You can walk into Central Park on any summer afternoon and watch a couple of dozen ballgames going on at once. And the same is true in small towns around the country. As Bart Giamatti told me not long before he died, "In a country that's not very old, baseball has been around a long time. It's one of the few free-standing institutions from before the Civil War that has survived intact. And it reminds America of rural origins that may never have existed, because baseball's origins aren't really that rural. But it reminds us of a kind of America that we like to think about."

Black, white, Latin, urban, rural—baseball is the one sport everybody plays and everybody watches. It's the same game here as in Nicaragua and Santo Domingo and Puerto Rico and Japan. You get a quintessential ethnic mixture, a pan-American rainbow coalition, of ballplayers. Sure, the NBA has a lot of black players. How many Hispanic players do they have? How many players from Latin American countries play in the NFL? And we won't even discuss hockey. But for all that diversity, baseball remains completely, reassuringly familiar. Giamatti told me that he was always intrigued by the term *home plate*. "I don't know why they didn't call it fourth base," he said. "In baseball, you start out at home and you try to get home again."

Someone once told me that he had never met a baseball fan who would not have gladly changed his career to be a good major league baseball player. If I were a major league ballplayer, I'd like to play for Tommy Lasorda, the manager of the Los Angeles Dodgers, because I like to be hugged. I like to be comforted. Not many managers do that, certainly not many good managers, and I think Lasorda is a great manager. It's like some of the old Dodgers used to say about Leo Durocher: "We felt like we had another man playing for us." If you got in a beef, Leo would be right there. And you feel that way with Tommy. If the pitcher throws at you while you're at the plate, Tommy is definitely going to have his pitcher stick it in the other guy's ear.

Recently, a San Francisco Giants pitching coach named Don

McMahon died of a heart attack right before a game. He had pitched for many years in the majors before ending his playing career with the Giants. Tommy Lasorda was there when McMahon had the heart attack, and while they were waiting for the ambulance and guys were working on McMahon, Tommy was crying and holding his hand, screaming, "Don't die, Don, don't die!"

Tommy has a great intensity to go with the caring and nurturing attitude he takes toward his players. After my bypass surgery, while I was recuperating in Miami, Lasorda invited me to a Dodgers spring training game. It was the first baseball game ever played in Robbie Stadium, which is a football arena that can be converted to baseball. Miami would love to get a baseball franchise, so they're doing whatever they can to attract attention. Anyway, Tommy was in classic form that afternoon. First he introduced me to Kirk Gibson, who gave me a sort of hasty, nonchalant handshake. Lasorda glared at him and said, "Hey, Kirk, shake his hand. Someday you're going to need him. Someday you're going to write a book and you're going to need this guy."

Then we started walking around the field together. It was a beautiful March day: there wasn't a cloud in the sky, and it was nice and warm. Eddie Murray was at first base, throwing the ball around the infield. Tommy ambled by and said "Hey, Eddie, how you doing?"

All Eddie said was, "Okay." Lasorda went wild.

"OK?" he said. "O fucking K? Two fucking million dollars a fucking year. It's March. There ain't a cloud in the sky. You're standing there wearing a major league uniform. You're thirty-three fucking years old, you're going to go to the fucking Hall of Fame, and you're saying O fucking K? You say, 'Great, Tommy!' " Murray looked at him like he was a maniac. "You say it: 'I feel great!' "

So Eddie started saying it: "I feel great!"

One of the enjoyable sidelights of my job is that every so often I get to hang out with and maybe, if I'm lucky, to become friends with someone I'd otherwise know about in only the most cursory way. It might even be someone I'd never dream of wanting to get to know until chance throws us together. When that happens, I often come away with a vitally different understanding of who the person is. A perfect example is Tony Kubek, the former infielder for the New York Yankees who has gone on to become one of the finest announcers in baseball.

As a player, Tony Kubek was a model of consistency. He was also everything I always hated about the Yankees. Kubek was a lifetime .266 hitter, which wasn't tremendous in the fifties and sixties—except that he always seemed to get the key hit. To Dodger fans like me and my friends from Brooklyn, God was always with the Yankees. We used to feel that God put pebbles in the infield; Yankee baseballs would hit them and then jump over the infielders' futilely extended gloves, because God, in his aristocracy, was a Yankee fan. And all the Yankees were Tony Kubeks and Mickey Mantles. They did not tire or age. Kubek is Polish, but he's the least ethnic-looking Pole I've ever seen. He could've been in those Arrow shirt ads. We had nobody on the Dodgers like that. And everything the Yankees did, they did correctly and with a minimum of strain. Those rare occasions when we would defeat them are etched as sharply in my memory as my first kiss or my first Carvel. Like 1955, when the Dodgers won the World Series from the Yankees in seven games. When Elston Howard grounded to Pee Wee Reese, who threw to Gil Hodges for the final out, that moment was among the five best moments of my life. It ranks with the Peabody Award, with the birth of my daughter. As I said many years later to Johnny Podres, the man who pitched the deciding game, "We knew we were going to lose three to two."

"I didn't think so," he said. "In fact, I told the guys, 'Get me one today. Just get me one run today.'"

Some of my suspicions in this regard, by the way, were confirmed in David Halberstam's book *Summer of '49*, wherein Halberstam recounts how Boston's Bobby Doerr watched "in utter disbelief" as the very elements of nature seemed to conspire to cheat the Red Sox out of a game at Yankee Stadium. Bobby Doerr was the power-hitting second baseman for the Boston Red Sox throughout the 1940s, and a Hall of Famer. Trailing 3-2 going into the ninth inning, the Red Sox managed to load the bases with one out. Al Zarilla, the right fielder, came to the plate, and as Doerr watched from the on-deck circle, he knew that just a fly ball to the outfield would tie it. But then a weird thing happened. "A sudden, violent storm blew into the Stadium," Halberstam writes. "Scorecards and debris swirled out of the stands." Play was halted momentarily, and when it resumed, the sky remained dark. So when Zarilla hit a sharp line drive to right field, the runner on third, Johnny Pesky, lost sight of it in the eerie darkness. Instead of racing for home, he ran back to third to tag, not knowing whether the ball would be caught. When the right fielder's throw sailed over the head of the cutoff man and reached Yogi Berra at home plate on one bounce, Pesky was forced out at home by inches. A certain run had been turned into the second out.

But Doerr had a chance to even things with the bases still loaded. "At least the wind was with him," Halberstam relates, "for it was blowing out to right. Raschi threw him a ball out over the plate, and when Doerr swung, he was sure that he had gotten all of it, that it was a certain home run. He had hit it toward right, where the grandstand rises in three tiers. He watched Mapes go back to the fence. Then in one terrible glance he watched Mapes, his back almost touching the wall, start to come in one step and then another. Then he caught the ball. Doerr had been cheated by a rare combination of the wind and the contours of the ball park: the wind had swept into the right-field wall and then bounced off, reversing its direction to come back toward the field, carrying the ball back with it." Even Bobby Doerr must have wondered if he wasn't seeing the hand of God working little miracles for the Yankees.

So when the ground ball hit Tony Kubek in the neck in the 1960 World Series, we all figured God must have been out to lunch that day. The Yankees lost the World Series to Pittsburgh, in part because of a bad-hop ground ball that crushed Kubek's Adam's apple. God never did things like that to Tony Kubek, or to any of the Yankees. He never did it before, he's never done it since. But that day, God went out to lunch, and the Yankees lost. Maybe now you'll understand why, when I later met Kubek through my friend Bob Costas, the announcer, I definitely had mixed feelings. For one thing, although I always felt a mixture of disdain, fear, and awe toward Yankees like Kubek, I also figured he got a bad deal. I *wanted* the Yankees to lose that World Series to Pittsburgh, but I certainly didn't want them to lose it on a career-shortening injury to Tony Kubek. I have come to like and respect Tony enormously since getting to know him. He is as likable as he is gifted as a broadcaster. But every time I see him again, all those memories of past games and years of hating and fearing the Yankees go through my mind as I talk with him.

The first day we met, Tony and I got into a discussion of the designated hitter in the American League. Kubek hates it as much as I do, but it was the detail and subtlety of his reasoning as much as his passion about it that made me feel an immediate connection. He began by talking about the "DH burnout" that is affecting American League pitchers. "Since you don't have to worry about taking the pitcher out for a pinch hitter in the fifth or sixth inning if you're down by two or three runs," he said, "a manager will leave his best pitchers in. Suddenly the American League has a lot more complete games, but I think a lot more arms are burned out because of it. It isn't only the increased number of innings but the quality of pitches you have to throw with nine hitters in the lineup. When you get to the eighth or ninth inning and you have to snap off a hard slider, that's going to lead to burnout."

But Tony was also upset, as I was, over a more fundamental imbalance the DH created. "Because of the DH, especially in smaller ballparks," he said, "you have more big innings, and so you see less of the hit and run and less base stealing. And not as much of a premium is placed on defense because of the DH. The emphasis is on getting more hitters to score more runs. The end result is that, on average, a National League game is a more stimulating game without the DH, mainly because of the greater emphasis on strategy and base running."

Discussions like that helped me feel a lot more comfortable around this dread Yankee of yore. I said before that we used to look at the Mantles and Kubeks as people who would never get old. The fact is that Tony Kubek is now somewhere in his midfifties and he looks about forty-one. You wouldn't think it at all odd to see him in uniform, playing shortstop again, and I don't mean in an Old-Timers game either.

In the summer of 1989, I went out to Memorial Stadium in Baltimore to watch the young Orioles in the midst of their remarkable comeback season, in which they had gone from laughable cellar dwellers the year before—owners of the dubious record of opening a season with twenty-one straight losses—to front-runners in the American League East. Even though they would wind up losing out to Toronto, the division race would come down to the last two days of the season, and for such a young team that was quite an astonishing turnaround. That afternoon they would play Tony LaRussa's Oakland A's, who went on to win the American League West and the World Series. I was also planning to meet up again with Kubek and Bob Costas, who would be announcing the game together for NBC. It was a beautiful sunny day in June, and I was down on the field watching the timeless daily ritual of batting practice. Maybe *timeless* is an overused word these days. People are always applying it to things that change every few years, but batting practice is unchanged in essence from the way it was done in the days of Ty Cobb and Honus Wagner, almost a hundred years ago.

Here's what you would see if you were standing on the field with me. Someone is pitching to the batter, who is standing in the cage, a large wire-mesh affair that resembles the chain-link backstops you might find behind amateur diamonds in any small town in the country. But this one is on wheels so it can be rolled on and off the field. On either side of the cage, coaches are standing in the fungo circles a few yards down the first and third base lines, hitting grounders to the infielders. This is all going on at once—pitch, left-side grounder, right-side grounder—and requires total awareness on the part of everyone involved so that nobody gets hit by a ball he didn't see coming. I've watched this ritual hundreds of times, but it never fails to mesmerize me. Meanwhile, the outfielders and pitchers are standing around in the outfield, shagging fly balls. The guy who's pitching batting practice grabs a few baseballs with each hand, pitches till they're gone, and the next batter steps into the cage. Meanwhile, I get to talk with whoever's waiting for his turn to bat.

While I'm standing near the batting cage watching the Oak-

land Athletics take their swings, this multileveled tableau is on
display, moving and shifting. Two Latin American ballplayers
are laughing and joking in Spanish, to the hilarity of a bunch
of their black teammates. Then Dave Parker walks over to the
cage to wait his turn. Parker looks huge in his dark green wind-
breaker, a small jeweled stud glinting in one earlobe. It occurs
to me that Parker is one of the few players who can sport an
adornment like that with impunity. But as he moves near the
batting cage, cries of "Dave! Autograph!" come from the row
of youngsters leaning along the short fence in front of the field
boxes. The kids yell and wave their programs but Parker stays
where he is, idly swinging a bat as he cocks an eye at them.
Talking in my direction but not *to* me—I've never met Dave,
and he's not the kind of guy you just strike up a conversation
with, uninvited—he says, "Sounds like an order to me!"

The idea of someone ordering the Cobra to do anything seems
fairly humorous, but Parker sounds serious about it. Or maybe
he feels the slightest need to explain his refusal to sign autographs. "Those same kids," he says, addressing the air again,
"come the seventh inning, they'll be calling me Bum!"

It's easy to imagine myself as a young kid at the ballpark with
my friends, watching a scene like this one. "Who's that guy
Dave Parker's talking to?" I'd want to know. "And what's Parker saying?" I feel enormously grateful that I've finally been
admitted to what, as a kid, seemed to me the inner sanctum of
life. And I never get over it.

Before driving out to Memorial Stadium, I'd had breakfast with
Kubek and Costas. Over cornflakes and strawberries, Kubek
was telling me about the bad-hop grounder off the bat of Bill
Virdon that bounced up and caught him in the Adam's apple
that fall afternoon in 1960. He flicked his head back to show
me that if he hadn't reacted quickly, the ball would have got
him in the face and done even more damage; but by reacting,
he'd exposed his neck, with devastating results. To me, the interesting detail in his story was his remembrance of listening to
the rest of the game on his way to the hospital, a game the
Yankees lost to the Pirates, along with the Series.

"We were still three runs up when I had to leave, and they

had two men on," Tony recalled. "Moose Skowron's playing first base, and with two outs Clemente chops a ball to Moose. Moose plays it and goes to underhand it to first, but Jimmy Coates, the pitcher who had come in to replace Bobby Shantz, forgot to cover. That's the third out. Coates froze and didn't cover. Then Smith comes up and hits a three-run home run— Hal Smith, who hit a total of fifty-eight home runs in his entire career. Everybody remembers Mazeroski's homer that won the game, but people forget Hal Smith's. Mazeroski's was the only home run ever to end a World Series, but you don't get Mazeroski's home run without Smith's three-run homer earlier. Who knows what might have happened? It's like everybody remembers Fisk's big homer in the 1975 Series—but how about Bernie Carbo? Carbo had the three-run home run that tied the game and allowed Fisk to hit his."

It was a wonderful fine point, the sort of thing I've learned to expect from Kubek. At the beginning of NBC Sports telecasts you could see the footage of Carlton Fisk applying body English to his long drive that sent the 1975 Series between Boston and Cincinnati to a seventh game. But without Carbo's homer in the eighth inning, Fisk might never have had his chance to win the game so dramatically.

Getting back to that 1960 Series, Tony had another point. "Dan Topping and the rest of the owners were looking for a reason to fire Casey Stengel because he was getting old and because he was growing impatient with younger ballplayers," Kubek said. "The key to utilizing the great Yankee farm system and preventing the Yankee teams from ever getting old was to keep at least one rookie in the starting lineup if you could, and Casey had begun to play all veterans. The owners were grooming Ralph Houk, the war hero, but they were afraid they were going to lose Houk to Detroit if they didn't give him the job soon enough. And when Casey didn't start Whitey Ford in game one of the Series, they had a pretty good excuse. Whitey was in the midst of breaking Babe Ruth's World Series consecutive inning shutout streak, which he broke the next year in Cincinnati. Whitey shut out the Pirates twice, but he got only two starts in the Series. Casey never explained why he didn't start Whitey, except to say that he wanted to start him in Yankee Stadium.

Whitey gets three starts otherwise. And maybe it wouldn't have gone to seven, you don't know, but. . . ."

My head was reeling from the wealth of detail in Tony's reminiscence. The thing that most amazes me about baseball players is their precise memory. In Halberstam's *Summer of '49*, Ted Williams recalled the last game of the 1949 season. The Red Sox and Yankees were tied for first place with one game to play: the winner of the game would go to the Series. It was the bottom of the eighth and the Yankees were ahead 2–0 with the bases loaded and two outs. Jerry Coleman hit a little pop fly to right center field.

"I can still see it with my eyes closed," Williams remembered. "Bobby is going back and Zeke is coming in. Zeke is diving for it, and then I see it squirting to the foul line." Three runs scored. Everything went out of him. "It's funny how you can remember something so painful so clearly," Williams said forty years later. "It was the worst thing that had ever happened." But he took you through every agonizing moment of it.

That day in Baltimore, I retold the story to Kubek, and then he told me *his* Ted Williams memory story. It took place at an All-Star Game in which Ted was playing and Tony was riding the bench with a pulled muscle. "Ted is the biggest cheerleader in the whole world," he said, imitating Williams's aggressive chatter. "He's yelling, 'Come on, guys, we gotta score some runs! We're the American League! We gotta beat these guys!' He was running up and down the bench, yelling, 'What was that pitch? What's this guy throwing? Who've they got in the bullpen?' Now, about the seventh inning, Turk Farrell comes in for the National League. Turk threw hard, had a great slider. Casey says, 'Ted, get ready. You're gonna pinch hit for the pitcher.'

"So Ted starts asking guys what Turk Farrell throws, and they tell him hard sliders. Ted claps his hands and says, 'Boy, he's gonna throw me a slider. I'm lookin' for a slider.' Ted must have been forty or forty-one years old, near the end of his career, and he was getting all keyed up for his one at bat in the All-Star Game. He gets up there and gets three sliders and strikes out swinging. Then, ten years ago, I saw Ted at a clinic and I said, 'Hey, Ted, you remember the time I was on the bench at the All-Star Game?' He says, 'Yeah, that son of a bitch Farrell, he threw me just what I was looking for. He threw me the slider.' Ted holds his hand half a foot from his chest and grimaces. 'The son of a bitch was *that* far inside and I swung at it!' Williams not only remembered the game situation, the pitcher, and the pitch, but he remembered exactly how far inside it was."

At breakfast, I asked Tony about his days as a Yankee rookie, when Mickey and Whitey and those guys would take him anywhere and tell him anything, and Kubek would go, "Realllly?" I'd heard the stories about how they would take Tony to dinner at Duke Zeibert's in Washington and say, "That's Senator So-and-so." Tony would just stare and say, "Realllly?"

"Yeah," Tony agreed affably. "I was a very quiet, naive young Polack from the south side of Milwaukee. What do you want?"

But the thing Tony didn't know was that Mickey would be faking it himself. Mantle didn't know who the hell was who in Washington. When I told Tony that, it got him going on some stories I hadn't heard before, little tales that give you an idea of life in the majors twenty-five or thirty years ago.

"You talk about Whitey and Mickey putting *me* on," Tony said. "Let me tell you what they did to Moose Skowron. Moose would hit .400 for the first two months of the season. He didn't have to take batting practice, he didn't need spring training. Mickey and Whitey would go up to him—'Watch this,' they'd tell the guys—they'd go to Moose and say, 'Moose, you know, you're not swinging the bat as well as you used to. Maybe if you put your hands down here, do this, turn your hands a little. . . .' And in a couple of weeks Moose would go down to about .300 or so. Then Mickey and Whitey would laugh and say to Moose, 'You dumb son of a bitch, you listened to us.' "

"You guys knew you were going to win the pennant anyway, so you didn't care," Costas interjected, and then he added some Moose Skowron stories of his own. "We were doing an Old-Timers Day game at Yankee Stadium last year, and Skowron came up in the booth. We're talking to him between pitches, and Tony says, 'Moose, we just saw Joe Pepitone before the game.' Joe was on a work release program after he'd done time on that drug rap. And Moose says, 'Yeah, Tony, I saw Pepi down there before the game, and I looked at him and I said, "Joe, just don't do anything wrong." ' "

According to Tony, who played with Skowron for quite a few years, Moose is the most gullible, sincere guy in the world. He is also one of the most conservative; even today he sports that old Marine flattop he wore in his playing days. Costas went on to recall talking to Moose recently about all the baseball movies that had come out. Skowron liked *Field of Dreams* all right, but *Bull Durham* was baffling to him. "I never saw that kind of thing going on in the locker room, and before a game," he told Costas, referring to the scene in which one of the players has sex with a woman in the locker room. "And that language!" Moose complained to Costas. "I walked out. But you know what movie I really like, Bob? I love that *Fatal Attraction*. I saw that three times. I'll tell you, Bob. If you're a man, *that*'ll make you think before you do anything, won't it?"

Later that day at the ballpark, as Tony and I strolled around the field, we started talking about managers, since two of the best—Frank Robinson and Tony LaRussa—happened to be in the dugouts that day. Kubek was commenting on a particularly astute managerial move Robinson had made in the previous night's game when I asked him, just out of curiosity, "Did Stengel manage that smart when you were with the Yankees?"

Kubek was off and running with a story about the kind of manager Casey was. "He took every coach and every scout and all the best prospects down to Huggins Field in St. Petersburg before we went to spring training," Kubek said. "Spring training started March 1, but we were down there February 1—guys like Bob Grim, who was rookie of the year a few years before me, and Bobby Richardson, who was at Petersburg with me. Even Marvelous Marv Throneberry was there two or three years in a row when he was a great prospect. He was hitting forty home runs and then he got burned out in the minor leagues—that was before free agency, of course. And Norm Siebern and Jerry Lumpe and Deron Johnson and a lot of other guys who went on to be good players for other teams in some cases. Now they call it the instructional period. Casey called it his acceleration camp, with the fifty or seventy-five best Yankee prospects, every manager from every Yankee farm club, fifteen or twenty back then, and the scouts who'd signed all these kids. He'd have you under his wing for a full month, and then you'd go off to spring training."

I wanted to know if there was a Yankee way of doing everything. "Here's what Casey did," Tony said. "I'll give you one example. Casey called it his offensive routine. He took us all into the clubhouse. 'Okay,' he would say, 'now you start thinking about the game in the clubhouse. Who's pitching today? What's he gonna throw you? Who are the relief pitchers who might come in? What kind of arms do they have in the outfield? What infielders can you bunt on? Do you know our signs? If you don't, you'd better learn them because they might change today.' And he'd always throw in stories to illustrate his points.

"Then he'd walk you into the dugout. 'Now you're in the game,' he'd say. He'd explain what you should be thinking about if you're in the lineup or if you're on the bench. Then he'd take you to the on-deck circle. 'Okay, now you're one hitter away from being in the ballgame. You've gotta go over the signs in your head.' Then he'd take you to home plate. 'Now you've gotta get the signs first. If you've got a sign for the runner, whatever it is, you'd better get it straight.'

"Next he'd tell you, if you get on base, how to cut the bags a certain way, how to round the bases. 'You get to first base, see? You put yer fuckin' foot on the bag, see? We don't want any hidden ball tricks on us. Happens every once in a while—most embarrassing thing in baseball. I know, I've been caught. You put yer foot on the first base bag and you don't talk to the first baseman. You look at the right fielder. Where's he playin'? Is he lefty or righty? What kind of arm's he got? Now you look at the center fielder—where's he playin'? You don't want to be lookin' around when the ball's hit, thinkin', Where's that guy, what's he doin'?'

"Then he took you to second base: same thing. He'd show you how to take your lead, how to take a walking lead in case the squeeze was on, or first and third if the double steal was on. And so on all around the bases. Actually, Casey took a lot longer; this is just the basic idea of how he did it. He'd do the whole thing himself, and sometimes it took a couple of hours. He would do that almost every day for a month. He'd always work in different stories and emphasize different things, but it was essentially the same drill.

"And then he had a defensive routine, which he also did himself. If you're on defense, how do you play different batters? If the ball is hit to the outfield and there are men on first and second, where should you go if you're an infielder—what cutoff position, what relay position? We're talking about half a century of knowledge that Casey had garnered playing against Cobb and Ruth and pitchers like Walter Johnson, and he would impart as much as he could to us. And he would insist that after we went back to our farm teams, the managers who were there with us would reinforce those skills all year long. They would have to do all that same stuff every day in the minor leagues during batting practice."

I was astounded. "I never thought of Casey in that vein," I said. "I thought of him as a strategist, but I never thought of him as a teacher."

"One of Casey's great expressions was 'There's no perfect player,' " Tony said. "Of course, Mantle was probably as close to perfect as Casey ever had, I think. But he'd say, 'Everybody's got weaknesses. You've gotta eliminate your weaknesses, but if you can't eliminate 'em, you gotta learn to protect 'em.' In other words, if you're a shortstop and you don't go to your right as well as you go to your left, you've got to play one step the other way. If you can't hit the low pitch, you've got to learn to lay off it and wait for the high pitch. He could talk for hours on that idea. And even when you made the team, you had to keep working on these things. After you took hitting, you didn't stand around the batting cage. You went out and ran the bases. You took your lead off first on the batting practice pitcher, then off second, off third, to learn how to get a walking lead, how to tag up. And you did that every day."

That was news to me. In all the years I've been going to games and watching batting practice, I can't remember ever seeing that happening. "Do any major league teams still go through that kind of instructional drill today?" I asked.

"I doubt if many other teams were doing it *then*," Kubek said. "That was just Casey's way of doing things. If you didn't take a certain amount of infield before every game, you couldn't play. That was a standard rule we had. They made exceptions for Mantle when his knees were bad and he had to spend time stretching, but otherwise you had to take eight rounds of infield. Now some guys do and some don't. Cal Ripken won't miss infield because he figures it's part of getting ready for the game, but he's an exception. Most guys just want to swing the bat.

"But talk to Whitey Herzog about the instructional training. Every spring, Whitey still brings in a fellow named Dick Tettelbach, who is a Yale graduate, now a retired businessman, and has him do Casey Stengel's routine. Tettelbach was a minor league player who just made it to the majors for a cup of coffee, but he impersonates Casey very well. Whitey does that for his *Cardinals*—for Willie McGee and those guys, not just the rookies. That's one of the reasons the Cardinals have such a fundamentally sound club and run the bases so well. And a lot of what Billy Martin did with Oakland and the Yankees, with Ricky Henderson, for instance, was taken from Casey's offensive routine, which included base running and base stealing."

"Then why was Casey's image one of a strategist but not a teacher?" I asked him.

"Casey was portrayed as a showman-entertainer, but he was really a baseball fundamentalist," Tony said. "And you talk about platooning now? Casey pioneered it. The reason wasn't strictly to play percentages, all that lefty-righty business. The reason was to keep his bench players involved, so they wouldn't sit there for two weeks and then, when someone got hurt, you'd have to throw a guy out there who hadn't played in all that time."

Stengel's platooning was legendary. Phil Rizzuto once told me that the players used to get mad at Stengel because of it. One time Stengel pinch hit for Rizzuto in the *second inning*. With the bases loaded, two out, the Yankees ahead 2–0, he batted Johnny Mize for Rizzuto. The other team had nobody warming up in the bullpen, they had a right-handed pitcher on the mound, and Johnny Mize, a left-hander, hit a grand slam. Rizzuto never came to bat in that game, but they were ahead 6–0. Phil complained, and Casey said, "How do I know if I'll have the bases loaded in the eighth inning?"

Kubek remembered that, on occasion, when Don Larsen or Tommy Byrne was pitching, they might bat seventh in the order instead of ninth. Casey might have Billy Martin and Jerry Coleman bat eighth and ninth because Larsen and Byrne were better hitters. "I'll tell you another thing," he said. "Casey hired the first advance scout in my first year, 1957, here in Baltimore. His name was Rudy York, and Casey admired him because Rudy could steal signs better than anybody. Not long after Casey hired him, we were in Baltimore for a Friday night game, and Connie Johnson, the big, tall right-hander, was going to pitch for them. He had a great screwball and really threw hard, and that year he was off to a terrific start. Rudy met with us at one o'clock Friday afternoon at the Lord Baltimore Hotel.

"Rudy told us that whenever Connie Johnson throws a screwball to left-handed hitters—and Casey's lineup was stacked with left-handed hitters—during his windup he moves from the center of the rubber a little bit toward the first base side of the rubber because it gives him a better angle on the outside corner against left-handed hitters. And when he gets above his head in the windup and you see a lot of white in the palm of his hands, it's a fastball. When you don't see much white, it's the breaking ball or curveball.

"Nobody I've spoken to can pinpoint a scout who advanced in that way before Rudy York for Casey. People talk about Huey Alexander being the first advance scout for the Phillies and other teams, but that was the early sixties already. Rudy wasn't on a permanent basis and didn't travel all year long, but whenever possible Casey would send him ahead to scout the big teams. There were occasions when the Yankee front office didn't want to spend the money on a guy like Rudy, of course, because the Yankees were a little tightfisted. Just look at their salary structure back then. They figured you were going to get your payoff when you won the World Series. That was your bonus, and that was what they told you every time you negotiated a contract. 'Why should we pay you more? You're gonna get a World Series check at the end.' That was George Weiss's philosophy, and he was usually right."

Tony also mentioned that advance scouting was hindered by train travel, which was how teams got from one city to another back then. I asked Kubek if traveling by train led to a closer team.

"No question," he said. "We used to spend thirty-six hours on

the train from New York to Kansas City. What can you do?
You play some cards, you have a beer, you eat together, you
sleep, and you listen to Casey talk baseball. I learned so much
from Jerry Coleman and Gil McDougald because I was on the
train with them for twelve or fourteen hours at a time."

I've often said that every time I go to a baseball game I learn
something I never knew. I always knew Casey was a great strategist and showman; I never knew he was a teacher. I would
never imagine Stengel taking fifty rookie prospects from the
clubhouse to the dugout to the batter's box and then around the
bases the way Kubek described it. I've never seen that written
anywhere, never heard anyone else talk about it.

But then that's one of the reasons I think Kubek is underap-
preciated as an announcer. He has a graphic memory and a
tremendous knowledge of the game. Maybe part of the problem
is that Kubek only got to do color on those NBC broadcasts.
Tim McCarver is awfully good at color, but McCarver does
play-by-play for the Mets, so he has more air time. And the
guys McCarver works with on the Mets broadcasts are not in
his league, so by comparison he seems even better than he is.
At NBC, Kubek was teamed with Bob Costas, who I think is
second to none in the business. Some bright network like ESPN
is going to hire Kubek and make him their lead announcer one
of these days. He's smart and analytical, but as long as he's been
in baseball, and as fine a player as he was, he's also intensely
curious. Most announcers who were outstanding ballplayers are
not all that curious because they already know the answers. I
saw Tony that afternoon with Elrod Hendricks, the Orioles'
bullpen catcher, having Hendricks show him how a catcher
cheats on pitches, pulling the glove back over the plate to try
to mislead the umpire. There was Kubek standing behind Ellie
in the umpire's position, seeing what it would look like. You
have to be very curious to go through that kind of effort.

Another way Kubek is better than most is that he is absolutely
fearless. He's one of those risk-takers I like to talk about. He's
not afraid to say anything on the air; he discusses racial problems in baseball and occasionally attacks the owners when he
thinks they're in the wrong. Rumor was that Steinbrenner tried
to get him fired a few years ago because he openly questioned

Steinbrenner's tactics and abilities. If you ask Tony about Steinbrenner, he'll acknowledge that they didn't get along, but then
he'll tell you that some people who are afraid to come to New
York use Steinbrenner as an excuse for not trying their luck in
the Big Town. "A lot of people won't go to New York—whether
as a ballplayer, manager, or broadcaster—not because of Steinbrenner but because of their fear of the intense media pressure
and the intense scrutiny of the fans and the fact that boy, you'd
better be good when you go there or you're in trouble. A lot of
people who don't have enough of a competitive nature fear that
kind of situation. But they'd rather take the easy way out, so
they say, 'Hey, I wouldn't go work for George.' " Tony obviously meant what he said because not long after he told me
this, he took the job as Yankee broadcaster.

While I'm on the subject of baseball announcers, I'd better say
a few more words about my good friend Bob Costas. Still in his
mid-thirties, Bob has already made a successful career as one of
the two or three best sportscasters on national television—and
if he seems too young to be making as much money as he does,
it just puts him in the same class as most of the gifted athletes
he talks about. In my heavily biased opinion, Costas is a great
baseball announcer. A great television sports announcer can relate what's in front of you in such a way that even though you're
watching the game yourself, your perception and appreciation
of it are enhanced by his commentary, and that's Bob.
  One of the things that makes Bob Costas a great announcer
is that he doesn't really change from the way he is off-mike to
the way he is when he's announcing a game for eight million
people. The key, as I've said before, is to be yourself. If you can
be yourself when the mike goes on, then you're in. The secret
is that there really is no secret. I've known Costas for seven or
eight years, and when I first met him he was making maybe
$60,000 to $70,000 a year. He's now well into seven figures,
and I haven't seen any change in him either personally or pro-
fessionally. The same is true of Tony Kubek, whom I met with
Costas, oddly enough, at Memorial Stadium about ten years
ago. Both of them are as enthusiastic, as turned on by the game,
when they're telling you about it in a hotel lobby as when

they're announcing for network television. If Costas were sitting next to you in your living room describing the game to you, he'd be exactly as he is on TV.

The difference between either of them and any ordinary announcer is easy to see. The ordinary announcer is different on and off the air. He could be standing talking to you one way, but when he goes on the air his entire character and personality suddenly change, and you hear *that voice*. There was a sportscaster for Yankee games named John Gordon, who is now in Minnesota. He can be very animated and friendly talking to you, but the minute the mike goes on, he puts on *that voice*. All of a sudden it's, "Well, hel-*lo* there, baseball fans across America."

Boring announcers think, "Gee, people are listening, I'd better put on a good show." They're afraid to be themselves. Good announcers trust their instincts. I'll give you one small example that I witnessed not long ago. Jon Miller was doing the NBC *Game of the Week* on national TV, announcing the game between Minnesota and Milwaukee. Jim Kaat, the former pitcher who was doing color on the broadcast, said, "Carmen Castillo is batting. Castillo's from the Dominican Republic. There are quite a few players from the Dominican Republic in baseball these days."

Suddenly Miller started doing the broadcast in Spanish. He just did a few moments of it, but it sounded wild coming out of nowhere. Of course, he had a pretty good reason for doing that. Teddy Higuera was pitching and NBC was broadcasting the game in Mexico, where he has a big following, much like Fernando Valenzuela does. They carry the game there and dub it into Spanish. Jon just thought he'd make everybody a little crazy by speaking Spanish: Hispanic Americans would love it, and the rest of the country would think they'd lost their minds for a minute, but so what? I can see one of the ordinary announcers saying, "Hey, gee, what if somebody turned on the game just then? He'd think he was getting a Spanish-language broadcast, and he might switch the channel." The minute you start doing the what-ifs, you're in trouble. Ninety-eight percent of broadcasters in America do the what-ifs. Miller, like Costas and Kubek, doesn't have a what-if.

Of course, you do have to draw the line somewhere. Frankie Frisch was one of my favorite baseball announcers, but not because he was good. On the contrary, his calls were so erratic they were hilarious. He used to say things like "It's a long fly ball out toward center field, curving foul." Another one went, "I can't see his number because his back is to me."

Another sign of a top announcer, I've always felt, is the ability to tell a story well. After all, that's what he's doing for you, whether you're listening to the game on the radio or watching on TV. You're counting on him to tell you the story of the game. And Bob can tell a story with the best of them, always keeping the rhythm going with style to spare.

One of his funniest stories has to do with a subject very close to my heart—gambling. Gamblers are a breed apart, strange denizens of a murky underworld both baffling and brightly exotic to those who have never plumbed its inner depths. It is forever cloaked in deep folds of cigar smoke, ringing with the strident voices of a million sports announcers all babbling at once, lost behind a curtain of impenetrable ritual. My father died when I was only ten, too young to have appreciated what I later learned of his passion for the well-placed bet, and so I have no childhood stories of my own to pass along on this subject. But it doesn't matter, because I don't know if I could have topped my all-time favorite gambling story as told to me by Bob Costas.

Bob grew up in the suburban blandness of Long Island, Connecticut, and California. His father died of a heart attack at the age of forty-two while walking through Kennedy Airport. Bob was eighteen at the time.

"My father," Bob told me, "was one of the most colorful characters I've ever known. Any kid views his father as larger than life, but the effect was even stronger in my case because I grew up in a suburban neighborhood, which made my father look more colorful by comparison. I'm talking about a white-picket-fence existence, and yet he knew people named Fury the Horse and Three-Finger Brown. I actually watched my father one day, on our way to Yankee Stadium, walk into a doughnut shop in Brooklyn, where a guy who looked like he was sent from a B-movie—shiny suit, pinkie ring, a nose you could annex and make into a state—slipped my father an envelope. The guy looked at me and said, 'That your boy?' My father said, 'Yeah,' and this guy just said, 'Nice boy.'

"My father took the envelope and we both went out to the car. I sat there in the front seat and watched him count out seventeen thousand dollars in hundred-dollar bills. This was in 1965—our *house* cost $19,990 on the GI bill. He had gone on a winning streak that started late in spring training and continued through the early part of the season. With those winnings he bought, in cash, a sixty-five Ford Mustang and an in-ground swimming pool. We had a nineteen-thousand-dollar house with a six-thousand-dollar swimming pool in the backyard. You have to understand, this guy was probably making twenty-five to thirty thousand dollars a year at the time.

"He bet baseball, football, basketball, hockey, and he was always very, very funny when he was gambling on these games. He would rock his head from side to side. People would have to remain sitting in the same positions they were in when things were going well. If you got up to go to the bathroom and Chamberlain made eight straight baskets for the Warriors and he had bet the Celtics, then you weren't allowed to go to the bathroom anymore.

"Anyway, one Sunday morning around that same time, my father looked in the papers to check the probable starting pitchers. Remember, this was before cable TV and Sports Phone and complete live access to everything that was going on, and it was not uncommon for him to send me out to the car to scan the dial to see if I could find, through the static, radio broadcasts of out-of-town games, which could include picking up hockey games in French. It would then be my responsibility to bring him back the reports.

"On this fateful Sunday, he looks in the papers and sees: Boston (Monbouquette and Morehead) at Detroit (Lolich and Sparma). He picks up the phone, he calls his bookie. He bets a thousand dollars on the Tigers, *'if* Lolich goes.' He's got Lolich in whatever game Lolich pitches—he assumes it's the first game. So we're watching the Yankees play on Channel Eleven in New York, and there's a fly ball to right field. As Maris settles under the fly ball, I can see, in the background, the auxiliary scoreboard. And I see: Boston 8, Detroit 0, in the second inning. I say, somewhat tremulously, 'Dad, I think the Red Sox are beating the Tigers eight to nothing.'

" 'No! *Impossible!*' he screams. 'Son of a *bitch*, I can't believe it! My life is shit!'

"By now, our only hope is that Lolich didn't pitch, that somehow he'll pitch the second game. So we wait. And we wait. And then Phil Rizzuto says, 'Ohh, Mickey Lolich didn't have it today. . . .' Before that sentence is even finished, my father has become apoplectic. 'Goddamn Mickey Lolich! Goddamn lard-assed, doughnut-eating son of a bitch! You call this guy a fucking pitcher? He oughta be working in a hardware store!' There was not an epithet that he would not apply to Lolich, in whatever creative combination he could come up with in his wrath. 'I shouldn't put fifty cents on this fucking hook-nosed, beer-swilling, pot-bellied motherfucker!'

"Okay. He's also got a smaller bet on the Yankee game and we keep watching. Periodic reports update the Detroit score. It's 8 to 2. It's 8 to 4. Then we hear Rizzuto: 'Oh, Joe. Al Kaline connected. It's 8 to 7!' Now I start whooping it up. My father raises his hand and stills the tumult. No one is to make a sound. So I settle back in my seat, hoping not to break whatever aura has been transmitted through the airwaves from Detroit to New York. We sit. The Tigers tie the game, and it goes to extra innings. In the thirteenth inning, Don Wert hits a home run to win the game, 9 to 8. Rizzuto says, 'Oh those Tigers! Down eight to nothing, they came back, McAuliffe and Kaline homered, and now Don Wert, in the bottom of the thirteenth. The Tigers win that first game over the Red Sox, 9 to 8!'

"I jump up, I thrust a fist into the air. My emotions rode on this, too, because I wanted my father to be in a good mood. How enjoyable dinner was depended on how these bets went. So I thrust my fist in the air and I look at my father, expecting him to be jubilant.

"He settles back in his chair, reaches into a drawer, and pulls out a giant Cuban cigar. He unwraps the cigar, taking great care, lights it, places it in his mouth, draws a long, luxuriant puff, blows out a smoke ring, looks at me, and says, 'Lemme tell you something, Robert. . . . This Lolich is *some fuckin' left-hander!*' "

* * *

Compared to baseball, with its leisurely sense of pace and nuance, football has always seemed a little crass and militaristic to me. Football is, at heart, a military sport. It's all about holding ground and gaining ground, penetrating your opponent's territory by breaking through his defenses. On every play in football, heavily armored men in strategic formations do their best to level each other. Violence is a major part of the game. Baseball is clearly a more civilized game that rarely involves intentional contact. Although it can be as dangerous as any sport, and people have died or been seriously injured by being hit with a baseball, that's not the object of the game. And in football, injuries occur more frequently and with more severity than in baseball. George Carlin put it a lot more succinctly when he said that in football you blitz, bomb, spear, march, and score, but in baseball you wait out a walk, go into a stretch, tap your spikes, play ball, and run home.

Football's militaristic attitude carries over into every aspect surrounding the game. For instance, media people, reporters, and announcers are not allowed on the field before a football game to talk to the players. It's as if those are gladiators down there. Before a baseball game, any announcer or writer with a field pass can go sit in the dugout, talk to the manager, walk around the field, get information that he can use during the broadcast or in his column. And baseball players themselves are fairly relaxed. They're joking, taking batting practice, having fun. Football players, in contrast, are pumped up mentally and physically and, in some cases, medicinally. An article in *Sports Illustrated* pointed out that one of Bo Jackson's problems—if he does have problems—is that he approaches baseball with a football mentality. He'll walk into the clubhouse and start cheering and yelling, "Come on, let's go get 'em, guys!" Meanwhile it's the second game of a three-day series, in the middle of a 12-game road trip, in a 162-game schedule. You want to say, "Hey, Bo, slow down." But Bo's going, "Come on, guys, this is a big one!" George Steinbrenner has a football mentality, too. And if it was ever clear that the two sports don't mix well, it's clear in him.

Earl Weaver explained the theory to me this way: "Would you want a baseball player talking like this: 'I'm going up there now, gimme that bat!' And he jumps into the batter's box and says, 'Come on, you mother! Throw the fuckin' ball, 'cause I'm gonna kill ya!' He's out on three pitches."

In fact, the whole secret of the successful at bat in baseball is to be as relaxed as you can. But the whole secret in football is not to relax for one instant. It's also generally accepted among journalists who follow the game that the NFL has a much worse record of race relations than major league baseball. There are far fewer blacks, in terms of percentage, in management or front-office positions in the NFL than in baseball. There are plenty of black pitchers in the major leagues; how many black quarterbacks are there? That fits in with my theory about football being a militaristic sport; what I'm really saying is that it's a more fascistic sport than baseball. Baseball, as many people have pointed out, is the game of failure. If you make an out seven times for every ten at bats, you're doing great—you're batting .300 and you're probably among the top ten hitters in your division. But imagine a quarterback completing only thirty percent of his passes, or a place kicker making only thirty percent of his kicks.

Weaver also had a theory about momentum in baseball. "It may have a place in other sports," he told me. "It has no place in baseball, because the pitcher changes everything. I remember once when we were in a pennant race. We're twelve games behind the Yankees, but then we start to make our move. We keep coming and coming and we get within one game. We're gonna catch them. The Yankees are in Oakland and we're in Seattle for a weekend series. The Yankees gotta play Oakland. All we gotta do is beat Seattle, who has one pitcher but other than that they stink. We're on a bus out to the Kingdome for the first game, and we're all chirpy. Batting practice moves along and we feel great. We're gonna be ahead of the Yankees by Sunday night. First batter steps up to the plate. Strike one, inside corner. He swings and misses, strike two. We got all this momentum going for us, right? Well, that one Seattle pitcher just stuffed the ball in our face. The Yankees beat Oakland and we got two hits. The moral of the story? Fuck momentum! The guy put the ball on the black, and we're gone."

John Bramlett is emblematic of the world of football. Bramlett was a Miami Dolphin, a pretty good linebacker on an expansion team. He grew up in Memphis and played at Memphis State. John was just wild. He would dye his hair pink and orange. On his first day in training camp, Larry Csonka asked him if he knew how to eat spaghetti. John said yeah and proceeded to show him by putting his face into the bowl of spaghetti and gobbling it up. He once saved my adopted son Andy's life in an elevator in New York when some people tried to stab him. Of course, Andy wouldn't have been in trouble in the first place if he hadn't been with John. It was always an adventure to go out with John.

John was also a close friend of Elvis Presley. The night Elvis died, I called Bramlett on the air and we talked. In fact, John was the one who told me what Elvis would have to do to play a pickup game of softball. Apparently Presley loved to play softball and could never figure out a way to play it without being bothered by fans. He couldn't just go to a public park or softball diamond and play without getting mobbed. So whenever Elvis and his friends wanted to play softball, they would pay the city of Memphis to keep the stadium open at night. City workers would open it up at two in the morning, turn on the lights, post a security guard around the stadium, and Elvis would play softball. Bramlett knew this because he was one of the guys who played with him in Memphis.

Bramlett was a charming guy, but he's indicative of the crazy atmosphere that pervades football. You get very few maniacal superstars in any sport. Kirk Gibson, the Dodger outfielder, comes to mind. I once saw him pop out in a game, and when the camera followed him back to the dugout you could see him smash his bat against the wall, then throw his helmet and bounce it off the floor of the dugout. He was berserk because he had popped out. He brings a football player's mentality to baseball. In fact, Gibson was a great college football player, an All-American wide receiver at Michigan State. Pete Rose wasn't as maniacal as Gibson, but he had a kind of arrogance that at times seemed out of place in baseball. I know a lot of people worshiped him, and he was Charlie Hustle and all that, but I can't forget that he ended the career of the great Oakland catcher Ray Fosse when he lowered his shoulder and plowed into Fosse at the plate *in an All-Star Game*. It didn't count in the standings, it was being played for fun and for the glory of the game, and Rose laid a football block on a guy who, under the circumstances, probably wasn't expecting it.

Dick Butkus had that same mentality and the same maniacal energy in professional football. Larry Csonka told me about the time he was in a pile-up on the field with Butkus, and Butkus bit him. Csonka looked him in the eye as they were lying there on the ground and said, "You're a college graduate, University of Illinois. This is an exhibition game, and you're biting me?"

Butkus said, "You're damn right I am."

Whereupon Larry Csonka—an A student with a 3.8 grade point average at the University of Syracuse—promptly bit Dick Butkus back. Csonka told me that at the time he didn't know if that was what you were supposed to do. He thought that maybe as one attained manhood in the world of professional football, one bit one's opponents. For most of his career, though, Csonka maintained his cool, as did most of the superstars of football. Few of the great quarterbacks were bombastic or crazy, and the same goes for the great wide receivers and running backs, the Fred Biletnikofs, the Herschel Walkers. They're confident and cocky; only Butkus was insane *and* great. His coach, Charlie Hallas, told me that no player he ever saw had the sense of the ball that Dick Butkus had. Wherever the ball was, there was Butkus. Wayne Gretzky has that same sense about the hockey puck. It's a sense that can't be taught.

Of course, that doesn't mean everyone who ever played football is automatically an animal who thrives on the smell of blood and the sound of tendons popping. The great wide receiver Paul Warfield, for instance, had a thorough understanding of the subtleties of the game and of what made a great player different from an ordinary one. Warfield once told me that there are seven hundred guys who can run twenty yards in four seconds, cut on a dime, and catch a pass. But a great athlete does that when the ball is *not* going to be thrown to him. He does it for the six times when the ball is not coming to him so that on the seventh time, when it is, the defender won't know the difference. The second-rate athlete, when he knows the ball isn't going to come to him, will take five or six steps and make a halfhearted cut. The difference is a matter of concentration and effort. But then again, that applies to all sports. I asked Bill Hartack once what makes a jockey good and he said, "Horses run for him."

And yet something has happened to our perception of these sports heroes over the years, whether you're talking about Butkus, Warfield, or Gretzky, and I think television has had a lot to do with it. Television has made sports figures so accessible to us that the magic and mystery with which childhood imbued them have begun to drain out of those all-too-familiar faces. I know Isiah Thomas so well from all those close-ups that there's nothing left to wonder about him. His face is embedded in my mind and needs no fantasizing. When Hearns and Leonard were talking after their last fight, I had the impression that these were two guys I'd known most of my adult life. It was like a walk in the park. I knew what Leonard was going to say. I knew what Hearns was going to say. Television has destroyed my innocence about sports stars.

So why don't fans get fed up with all this familiarity? That's a good question, and the answer is not so surprising. The one thing that keeps me going as a sports fan is that when I get up today, I know that fourteen games are going to be played tonight, and I have no idea who's going to win any of them. I am going to open tomorrow morning's paper and be surprised. And there's a finality to those results that is lacking in most of the other news reported in the paper, with the possible exception of the obituary pages. There is a winner and a loser, and there ain't many gray areas. I once heard a reporter who'd been covering the Washington political scene announce that he was leaving to take a job as a sports columnist at a midwestern newspaper. He said his colleagues couldn't understand why anybody who'd been in the thick of the Beltway fray could settle for writing about something as relatively insignificant as sports. His answer was simple and went something like this: "I have never yet watched a game at night in which the St. Louis Cardinals were defeated by the Chicago Cubs and opened the paper the next morning to read a statement by Whitey Herzog that although his team may have appeared to lose, they had exceeded expectations."

When it comes to sports, it's impossible to have certain expectations anyway. Every time I think I've seen it all, I see something I've never seen before. Just a few days before I went out to watch the Orioles and A's play that day in Memorial Stadium, I was watching an Orioles game on television. I saw a Yankee batter hit a fly ball that the center fielder *lost in the fog*, and as a result the Yankees beat the Orioles. In the forty-five or so years I've been going to games and watching baseball on TV, I never saw a guy lose a fly ball in the fog. Who would have guessed that? Of course, now that I've become an Orioles fan since moving to Washington, it figures that the Yankees would be up to their old tricks, finding new ways to beat my team. Can it be that after all these years, God is still a Yankee fan?

4

"Who do you like?"

You might be surprised to know the names of some of the prominent people who have been great horse handicappers throughout the years, men from public life who like to bet the ponies. Let's begin with General Omar Bradley, John Edgar Hoover—the handicap at Pimlico is named after him—and Winston Churchill, who was a major horse handicapper. And the sheet goes on.

There is something enthralling about the *Daily Racing Form*, as I once discussed with Jack Klugman at an OTB parlor in New York. It is the most mind-boggling daily paper in America. Here are all these animals, and the *Form* lays out in front of you their prior records: who rode them and what races they were in, how they finished and under what circumstances. He went from the 7 but it was sloppy that day. But now he's coming down in class. See, he ran for $8,000, now he's claiming for $6,000. He won last time out, so why are his owners dropping him in class? Was there an injury? Do they know something we don't? This other horse ran fourth last time, but that was on the grass, and today he's on a dirt track. What does that mean? Nowadays you can punch a button at the track and they'll show you your horse's last race on videotape. It can help you decide whether that last win was meaningful or if he came on strong at the end.

Racing is a world unto itself; the track is another life. Klugman and I spent hours just talking about the *Daily Racing Form*, the racetrack Bible. Let's take a quick look at today's issue of the Bible. Here's the second race at Laurel. They're going five furlongs; that's five-eighths of a mile—a furlong is an eighth of a mile—a short race. This is a maiden claiming race, with a $10,000 purse to the winner, and it's for two-year-old fillies— young females. "Maiden" means the horses have never won, "claiming" means you can buy any horse in the race. For this race, the claiming price is $16,000. And if a horse runs for less than $16,000—you can enter for $14,000—it's allowed one pound off. So you can buy, let's say, Revenge for $16,000. Revenge is a gray filly, two years old. Then they give you the name of the father, the mother, and the father of the mother. They list the breeder and where the horse was born. You get as much information as the stock market gives a potential buyer of stock: its highs and lows over the past few races and its positions at the quarter poles through those races.

Handicapping is an art, and people do it as a mental exercise or discipline as much as for any other reason, like doing crossword puzzles or double crostics. J. Edgar Hoover used to spend an hour every morning with the *Form*, doping the races even if he wasn't going to the track that day. It's a great intellectual exercise. It always tests your ability, and it's a great ego reward to win. But it's also a great humbler of the intellect. You can think you've got it all perfectly doped out and then lose by a nose. So it's the ultimate exercise in woulda, coulda, shoulda.

Handicappers love to go back over the *Racing Form* for a race they lost. Let's say the long shot was at 70 to 1, no chance of winning, and it comes in first. The handicapper will say, "Oh sure, of course, it was all right here. Look. Back last May at Hialeah, the horse ran here, against this kind of competition, wet track. Of course, I should have known! It was right in front of me."

For all that it's an art, handicapping is an extremely inexact science, since you're dealing with so many variables. And the greatest variable of all is the horse. As Bill Hartack, one of my favorite jockeys, once said, "We have never interviewed a horse." Therefore, the main player in this sport is a question

mark. We know certain elements of the horse's life—its gene-
alogy, breeder, trainer, past record—and we can extrapolate
from there. But you never really know for sure. We know that
human heart problems are inherited, but not every heart attack
means that the victim's father had heart problems. Likewise,
we know that if a horse has run only on the grass and then runs
on the dirt, his first race on the dirt is generally a pretty good
race. But no one knows why. Nor does it mean that will happen
today. But historically, a horse coming off the grass is going to
run a little better on a dirt track.

And, as in baseball, you learn something new all the time.
Down through history, horses have done thoroughly unpredictable things. Why did Easy Goer win the Belmont after losing
in the Derby and the Preakness to Sunday Silence? It's possible,
if we had interviewed Sunday Silence before the Belmont, as
Hartack suggested, that he might have said, "Man, I had some
headache this morning! Jesus Christ! I woke up and it was
throbbing. No way I felt like running."

Thoroughbred racing is called the sport of kings for the simple reason that kings used to race their horses against each other.
A crowd would come to watch and bet on the horses. And at
some point, one of the kings must have said, Why not let the
public participate in owning and breeding the horses? So they
started with claiming horses. The king would take some of his
cheaper horses and put them on sale, and people started to buy
horses. The public now could not only bet but also own horses
and collect the purse if they won.

How obsessive are people about going to the track? I'm not
talking about compulsive gamblers here. I just mean people who
get caught up in the sport, in the handicapping, in the *feeling*
of being at a racetrack. Tim Conway says, "I'll get in my car.
I don't want to go to the track. The car goes to the track. I go
to the track on off days, when nobody's running, just to sit
around."

I knew Count Basie, a major racetrack fanatic, pretty well.
Sinatra told me a story about how cool he thought Basie was.
He sang with Basie's band many times, and one time Frank
comes onstage opening night at the Fontainebleau and starts
singing "Come Fly with Me." The band is swinging, Basie's

cooking. He looks down and sees that Basie has some paper in front of him at the piano. He's reading. Frank does a double take because he's never seen Basie read a score during a show. Basie never needs the music, but Basie's reading from this paper. Frank strolls over with the mike in his hand, still singing, to get a closer look. You guessed it—the *Racing Form*. It's opening night and Basie is doping the horses for the next day's race at Hialeah, doing it all without missing a note at the piano, and leading the band at the same time. Sinatra was impressed. In fact, Basie was such a horse freak that near the end of his life, when he had to use a motorized wheelchair to get around, he would go to the track in his wheelchair whenever he could.

Bettors aren't the only obsessives around the track. Jockeys are a breed apart. Riding a racehorse is a very tough job, when you think about it—it takes not only tremendous skill and coordination but more courage than many contact sports. For that reason, I think that Willie Shoemaker, pound for pound, may have been the best athlete in America in his time. One of the biggest dangers jockeys face, believe it or not, is visibility. Jockeys now wear five or six pairs of goggles on a muddy track and just flick off each pair as it gets coated with mud; it's easy to be blinded out there. Bill Hartack told me that the first time he rode in a race, he was so nervous when the gate opened that he forgot to put his goggles down. Dirt splattered in his face all the way around the track. The second time he rode, he did the same thing. He was lucky to finish. Make one bad move at those speeds and you can find yourself under the horse instead of on it.

Bill Hartack, now a racing steward in Chicago, was one of the great jockeys. He won five Kentucky Derbys, and he's the only man to win the jockey title three years in a row. That means riding the most winners, period. One of my favorite Hartack stories out of hundreds he's told me over the years is testimony to jockeys' superb athleticism, and this one has a bit of the Hartack slapstick about it as well. One day Bill was racing in a rainstorm, and as they were going into the turn, the horse next to him leaned too close. A black jockey was riding the other horse, and at that moment the black jockey started to slide from his mount in the rain. Hartack reached out to hold him up and they got tangled up with each other. Somehow in the confusion, they ended up switching mounts just to avoid falling off, which would mean instant injury, if not death. So they finished the race on each other's horse.

When the trainer of Bill's horse came out to meet them, he saw the black jock riding in on Bill's horse. All the jockey said to the trainer was, "Hey, great horse. I'd like to ride him again."

Hartack was the Ted Williams of riding in his dealings with the press. He was unusually honest, possibly too honest for his own good, and one of the first of the rebel athletes. Trainers love to hear bullshit about their horses when they don't win— he stepped in a hole, he's really getting better, that kind of thing. Hartack would just come out and tell them, "Look, your horse is no good." He hated the name Willie, and if reporters referred to him as Willie Hartack, he thought they did it for spite. But he wanted to win so badly that he used to say, "I ride in anger." Bill Hartack told me he bit a horse once. He wasn't angry at the horse, though. He'd lost his whip, and coming down the stretch he bit the horse on the mane because he had no other way to goad it.

Betting takes place on most professional sports, but only horse racing, dog racing, and jai alai exist solely for the purpose of gambling on the results. The bizarre behavior of racetrack bettors is legendary, and over the years a whole body of folklore and humor has grown up around it. For instance, the story goes, the richest bettor in the world could walk by a bum, and the bum could say, "I love the 5 horse," and the rich guy would go bet the 5 and lose. Now if the bum knows what's going on, why is he a bum? Why would you take a tip from a bum? But you would.

There's another joke about how anything can change a bettor's mind at a racetrack. This guy goes to the track and he's convinced the 3 horse is going to win the first race. He gets on line at the window, and the guy in front of him turns around and says, "I like the 4." So he bets the 4, and sure enough the 3 wins.

Later his friend says, "What happened? I thought you liked the 3."

He says, "I met this guy. . . ." In the next race he likes the 5 and meets a guy who likes the 6. He changes his mind, the 5 wins. The guy's going crazy. So now it's the sixth race, and he's lost every race because somebody keeps changing his mind. Finally he tells his friend, "I've had enough, I need a rest. I'm going to get a hot dog. I'll be right back." He leaves and comes back with a hamburger.

The friend says, "What are you doing with a hamburger?"

He says, "I met this guy. . . ."

Maybe the chronic ambivalence of the obsessive handicapper can be explained, once again, by the fact that so many variables are involved. Some variables we've never figured out in any sport, let alone a sport involving nonhumans. Hawk Harrelson, the former baseball player and announcer for the Yankees, is a talented scratch golfer. When he retired from baseball, before he took up broadcasting, Hawk joined the pro golf tour for a while but rarely made the cut. Yet he was a terrific golfer. So I said to him, "If you can shoot seventy-one at Doral today, why can't you shoot seventy-one at Doral tomorrow?"

He said, "When Nicklaus is playing next to you, Doral ain't the same."

And that's what they've been trying to figure out about horses and "class." Horse fanciers argue about class versus speed. If a horse can run six furlongs in 1:09 today against an ordinary group of horses, why will he run it in 1:12 next week against a better group of horses? Where does that three seconds' difference come from? What we've never been able to explain is, why does that intrinsic difference of class make past times unimportant? I know that horse can run it in 1:09. Why should the competition make him run *slower*? If you can shoot Doral in 71, what do you care who's shooting next to you?

Every so often you might see a track event where the leader sets a new world record and the next three or four finishers all set personal bests as well. It doesn't work that way in horse racing, though, because there is such a thing as class. When you go above your class, you don't run as well. Does the horse know who the horse next to him is? Secretariat could *humble* other horses. When he won the Belmont by thirty-one lengths in 1973,

those other horses were running five, six, and seven seconds
slower than they could run it any other day. Are you going to
tell me that they gave up, that they knew enough to give up?
They saw that this horse was so much better than they were,
and so far ahead, that they just gave up? But how do you explain it?

Willie Shoemaker swore to me, for example, that Forego, who
was a great horse, knew when he won, knew *how* to win, knew
what a winning line was, measured it, and was depressed when
he lost. If Forego didn't go back into the winner's circle, Shoemaker said he was depressed. He knew what he was doing and
when he was doing it. He knew how to move between horses.
He knew what the game was about.

Some horses don't know anything. Jockeys have told me that
some horses get into the lead and then play around. Some horses
think they're supposed to run in a pack; they don't want to run
away from the other horses. Some very good horses play like
that. Then there are some horses that intrinsically want to kill
you. They want to run you down. But those other horses . . .
are they really thinking, Hey, wait a minute, I don't want to
be ahead, I want to run with my friends here? In a sense you're
making them run away from the people they know. Are these
horses having fun—with *our* money?

The information that appears in code on the *Racing Form*
adds another color to this picture. Often you'll see abbreviated
forms in the sports section of your daily newspaper. Next to a
horse that's running that afternoon at Aqueduct, for instance,
it might just say, "likes the mud." Or more likely, in track par-
lance, "loves the slop." That's another fact that we don't have
any scientific reason for. We know that some horses run better
in the mud. But is that because the mud bothers them *less* than
it does other horses? We have come to call such horses "mud-
ders." So you will actually see an intelligent handicapper write,
"If it rains as forecast, Echo Lake will love it tomorrow." You
mean Echo Lake is going to look out from her barn and say,
"Ho, wow! Rainstorm! Get me out there, man!" Or is Echo
Lake so dumb that the rain bothers her less? Or does she run
faster just to get out of it? Does she think, If I run fast today,
I'll get back to my nice dry barn sooner?

It's a baffling game that keeps you guessing about all the aspects involved. The fine jockey Julie Krone, for example, thinks that in a lot of ways women suit horses better—especially younger horses, especially female horses—just by the way they hold the reins. Hartack also thought that. He forecast the coming of a Julie Krone. "Someday there'll be a great female jock," he told me. "And when she's good, she'll be very, very good, because horses respond well to females. It's their touch. The horse knows it's a girl."

Bill didn't say *how* horses know, but they know. That doesn't surprise me, though, because horses are just plain strange. Frank Whitely, who is a great trainer, thinks horses love the snow. He thinks the snow is good for them; he thinks they like being out in the snow and that it's a good conditioner. Why? How the heck do I know? The horse might hate the snow. But thoroughbreds are a quirky bunch. Hartack told me once that you can never trust them. He says he's never totally relaxed around a thoroughbred, because anything can spook them.

So what kind of person bets more than he can afford to lose on such a beast? I ought to know, since I spent years doing just that. But all I can tell you is that, for racetrack people, it's their life. A common statement at the track is "I hope I break even, because the rent's due."

Here's a true story that happened years ago at Aqueduct, told to me by a good friend. A guy goes up to the window at Aqueduct and says, "I want five thousand dollars to win on the 3."

The clerk starts to punch lots of tickets. One hundred dollars was the top ticket then. Now they're all on computers, so you can punch that on one ticket, $5,000 to win on the 3. But back then, the tickets came only in certain denominations: $2, $5, $10, $20, or $100. So he had to punch fifty $100 tickets. The clerk is punching all these tickets right up to post time. The horses are about to go off when the guy looks at the tickets and says, "Hey, I didn't say the 3. I said the 5. I don't want to pay for these tickets. I said the 5."

The teller says, "You said the 3."

Now the horses are going in the gate. "I said the 5," he says. "I want five thousand dollars on the 5 horse."

"You said the 3," the teller says. "I punched the 3. Take your tickets."

The guy says, "I don't want the 3, man, I said the 5, and I ain't got time to wait. That's it."

Now they look up, and the 3 horse is 20 to 1. They're standing there. The tickets are lying there. The teller won't touch them, the bettor won't touch them.

"I ain't taking those tickets!" the bettor says.

"They're yours!" the teller says. As they're standing there arguing, the race goes off. And the 3 breaks on top. They're transfixed listening to the call. The 3 is ahead by five lengths, then ten lengths. When he turns for home, they're both grabbing for the tickets. "They're mine!" the teller yells. "You didn't want 'em!"

"They're mine, you motherfucker! You woulda made me pay for 'em!"

The teller's screaming, "Fuck you, you wanted the 5!"

Finally the teller calls the management down, and they end up splitting the money.

Unlike Vegas or Atlantic City, where you're playing against the house, at the racetrack you're playing against each other, because of a unique system of betting. It was devised in France more than a century ago by a Parisian businessman named Pierre Oller, and it's called the "parimutuel pool." It's a form of betting in which all the people holding winning tickets divide the total amount bet in proportion to their wagers, less a percentage for the management and taxes, which in America is usually 17 percent. In other words, if $1,000 total is bet on a race, then out of that, $170 would go to the track and taxes. The remaining $830 would be divided among bettors holding tickets for the first three horses to finish: win, place, and show. The odds are determined by how much or how little had been bet on each of those three horses.

The only time a track can lose with the parimutuel pool is when they don't draw enough people, and overhead exceeds income; or, since the track must pay at least a nickel on a dollar, if everybody in a race bets the same horse and that horse wins, the track would have to pay all of them ten cents on each two dollars bet. That's the law, and its called a "minus pool."

Sometimes the horse that everybody, or almost everybody, has bet will finish out of the money, and then the track has lots of money to distribute to very few winning tickets. In that case, a horse may pay several hundred dollars on a $2 bet. Those races are known as "bridge jumpers." When a horse is so odds-on to win—so favored to win—that everybody bets him, and then he loses, the bettors wait on line to jump off the bridge.

A good bridge jumper story is the one about Native Dancer in the Kentucky Derby. Some guy desperately needed $5,000, so he took $50,000 from his grandmother's vault and bet it on Native Dancer, who couldn't lose. The horse was such a favorite that he'd only pay a dime on a dollar to win, but with a $50,000 bet the guy would still win $5,000 and give Grandma back her $50,000. But Dancer lost. That's a bridge jumper.

Perhaps the most common phrase at the track is "Who do you like?" It's the buzz phrase of the serious bettor and it transcends all other lines of communication. A couple of months before my bypass surgery, in October 1988, a camera crew from the CBS show *West 57th Street* followed me around for a few days for a feature they were doing on me. One idea they had was to take me out to Brooklyn and walk around the old neighborhood with me. They miked me and my brother, and I thought we came up with some neat stuff, although they didn't use it on the show. But I had a good time seeing my old neighborhood in the Bensonhurst section of Brooklyn, where I hadn't been in twenty or thirty years.

I noticed that in the spot where a pants store used to be, there was now an OTB parlor. I walked in. A lot of people in the neighborhood recognized me just from my being on TV, and some recognized me from my having grown up there. Much of that neighborhood is still there. When I grew up, it was mostly Jewish and Italian, with a few blacks mixed in, and it wasn't anything like it is today, the Howard Beach of Brooklyn.

So I went into this OTB parlor with the camera crew following me. A guy I didn't know said, "Hey, Larry King."

Another old guy came over to me and said, "Hey, Larry, I knew you when you were growing up."

"Hey, good to see you," I said.

And he said, "Who do you like?"

Eight days after my heart operation, on December 9, I left
the hospital. News of my operation had been in all the papers.
I stayed at my brother and sister-in-law's place for a week, and
then my brother went back to work. My sister-in-law walked
me down to the pharmacy to fill my four prescriptions. I was
feeling pretty good and I wanted to walk around some more
but she had to go on a casting assignment. So I strolled over to
OTB by myself and walked in.

The first guy who came over to me said, "Hey, didn't you
just have heart surgery?"

"Yeah," I said. "That was eight days ago. I'm feeling fine
now."

He said, "I love the 2 horse in the fourth."

That's it. Heart surgery conversation is over. He loved the 2
horse in the fourth.

Sam "the Genius" Lewin looked like Batman's foe, the Penguin.
No matter how hot it was, he always wore a black hat and black
suit with a little black string tie and a long black cigarette
holder. While Sam was at Harvard Law School, he went to the
races one day at Rockingham Park in New Hampshire and hit
nine out of nine winners. He never went back to law school.
He never got his degree. Someone explained the *Racing Form*
to him and for the Genius it was love at first sight. He spent
the rest of his life at the track. He owned some horses and he
bred some horses, but mostly Sam the Genius—who got the
nickname because of that one great day at the track—was a
tout. A tout is a racing expert, a personal handicapper; he's like
an investment adviser for bettors. He has accounts and clients.
Sam would give people horses he picked to win; they would bet
and give him a cut of their winnings. He had some pretty successful clients, and he was certainly known as a guy who knew
the game of racing. But his life was really sad, and he ended
up tragically. I don't know where he's living now, but I hear
he's a recluse. He doesn't go to the track anymore. He got married late in life, at age forty-five. He had a child when he was
fifty, but then his wife ran away with another guy and took the
kid. That destroyed him.

At one low point in his career as a tout, Sam the Genius had lost thirty-seven consecutive races, touting the wrong horse. But a true tout never loses faith in his ability to pick winners. So they're running a race at Tropical Park in Miami, and he likes a horse that's a prohibitive favorite. The odds are 1 to 2, which means on a two-dollar bet you'd only win a dollar. But that's his pick. And there's another horse in the race, a long shot at 40 to 1. Both these horses come down to the finish line together. It's a photo finish. They have to wait five minutes for the official results. It's so close they have to keep blowing up bigger prints of the picture. Finally they put it up, and his horse wins by half a nostril. Sam taps the guy next to him and says, "Do I know this game? Did I tell you?"

If handicappers and jockeys are a breed apart, my friend and surrogate father Duke Zeibert is part of a dying breed. His kind of restaurateur is no longer in fashion. Today a lot of popular restaurants are owned by chefs, like Wolfgang Puck at Spago. Duke works the room. He takes care of his customers. He goes to every table. If he knows you, he'll sit down, he'll talk, he'll hover, he'll make sure that everybody's comfortable, that you've got everything you need. I'm not just talking about the food. Duke cares about you. And besides, Duke is a character in his own right, a really colorful guy. He's a horse fancier and a serious gambler, a guy who likes the big action at Vegas and Atlantic City. Duke says that he's lost the equivalent of two buildings by gambling, and he's probably being conservative. "I'll tell you something about gambling," Duke once said. "The only thrill in gambling is to gamble for more than you can afford to lose. If I didn't gamble in my life, you could fill this room up with hundred-dollar bills. You could paper the walls with them." *The only thrill is to gamble for more than you can afford to lose.* That line ought to be etched in marble over the gateway to Las Vegas, that's how true it is. And how sad.

More than anything, you get addicted to the danger and the thrill. "I can't go to the ballgame these days," Duke said recently, "even though I love the Orioles. For me to sit there and watch them without a bet on the game, how can you do that?" Duke's rationale is illuminating. The reason he can't bet is that he's sitting in the owner's box. A true bettor doesn't bet with his heart; he bets with his head and his gut. In Duke's heart, he wants the Birds to win. But his gut may tell him the other team is a better bet. Or his head may tell him to take the points. But then he'd be rooting for the visiting team to win while he's sitting in the Orioles' box, and Duke's too much of gentleman to do that. So he doesn't go.

I know all too well what Duke means about betting more than you can afford to lose. Not long ago, I was at Santa Anita racetrack in California, as a guest of the management. I was having lunch with Cyndy Garvey at the Turf Club. They were treating us really nice, bringing over their best food and wine, running my bets for me. It was "Mr. King this," and "Mr. King that." Suddenly it brought back a memory of an earlier time, fourteen years before, when I had been at Santa Anita under very different circumstances. At that time I was out in California looking for work. I had all of $12 on me and my return ticket to Miami. Parking at the track was $4, so I parked on the street, a mile and a half away. I had called and somehow managed to wangle myself a press pass, so I didn't have to pay the gate admission. All I said was "Larry King, *Miami Herald*." They didn't know me, but the guy said, "Okay, Larry, come on ahead."

Even so, when I got to the track all I had was twelve bucks to bet. I was limiting my wagers very carefully, placing two-dollar bets here and there. I had a bet going on one race that came down to the wire. It was a photo finish involving one of the horses I had bet for an exacta. We stood around waiting and waiting for the picture, and finally they announced it was a dead heat. Jacinto Vasquez rode my horse—I remember that. Anyway, I got half the winnings and ended up with seventy-two bucks. So there I was, out of work, dead broke, with a daughter to support, walking a mile and a half because I can't afford the parking. But I had seventy-two bucks, and I was saying to myself, I'm going to a movie tonight! I'm gonna go to Bob's Big Boy, and I'm gonna come back here tomorrow! I was probably more excited winning that seventy-two bucks than I would be winning ten or a hundred times that much today. It's just like Duke said: the thrill was there because I couldn't afford to lose.

Now that I can afford to lose plenty, I have to take my gambling thrills where I find them. One place I can usually find a good time is the horse room at the Sands in Vegas, which is a bettor's seventh heaven. That's the room where they beam in by satellite horse races that are going on in tracks all across the country and show them on large wall screens. There's a race going off every few minutes, so you can bet the third at Belmont, the fourth at Arlington, the first at Santa Anita, the fifth at Pimlico, and so on. I was doing just that one day, really enjoying myself and having a good time. I also had twenty silver dollars on me, and I was playing the slot machines in those rare moments when there was no race to bet or nothing to watch on the screens. As the afternoon was winding down, I had three silver dollars left, and I had bet the last race at Arlington. The race was about to be shown on the screen right above the slot machine I was standing at. Meanwhile, I was idly watching a black man playing the machine next to mine. He'd been there a long time, steadily pumping in dollars without winning any back.

The horses were going into the starting gate, and I said to myself, I'm going to play these three silver dollars as soon as the race is over. Then I noticed that one of the horses was acting up in the gate and backed out, meaning there was going to be a delay of ten or fifteen seconds while they got it back into the gate. So, not wanting to be out of the action for that long, I dropped the three dollars into the slot and pulled the lever. As the horses broke out of the gate, I looked down and saw the three wheels on the machine light up: 7, 7, 7.

The horses are running and suddenly all these lights and bells start going off. People come running over. One of the guys from the casino runs over and says, "Ah, Mr. King, you've won a thousand dollars." The black guy looks up from the machine next to mine with a grimace of real anger. And all I can think of to say is "Hold it! I want to watch this race."

They all freeze, the people running over and the Sands people. We're standing there watching the race, which I lost—got beat by a neck. So then I go back to the machine: 650 Sands silver dollars—tokens actually—have come pouring out of the machine. They give you 350 real dollars and 650 tokens, and they have to write down the number of the machine. You know how long it takes 650 coins to come out of a machine? The idea of the tokens is to get you to go and play them all again. But I just wanted to cash them in, so the Sands casino guy says, "Okay, Mr. King, we'll have somebody come over and help you."

Two guys come over and start stacking the silver dollars for me. Just then the guy who's been playing all day at the next machine looks over and says, "So you lost the race, huh? Tough."

Now I'm embarrassed. It's an embarrassment to be well known and have something good happen to you. The only thing I can think of to say is "I'm going to give it to my foundation, the Cardiac Foundation." Like he gives a shit. As I'm about to leave, the casino guy says to me, "Drop one in so we can get the machine rolling again." I looked at him a moment. Is this like tipping the croupier or something? I felt like saying, "Why don't *you* drop one in?" But just to be a mensch, I drop three in and I lose. The black guy turns to me and says, dead serious, "Hey. Ya lost again, huh?"

The wonderful thing about gambling is that it's an equal opportunity destroyer. My favorite joke in this regard was told by Shecky Greene. A guy is driving back to California from Las Vegas when he hears a voice from the heavens that says, "GO BACK TO LAS VEGAS!" The guy ignores it and keeps driving, and again this deep, booming voice seems to come out of the sky saying, "GO BACK TO LAS VEGAS!" He keeps driving, pulls into a gas station, gets out to get gas, and he hears the voice again: "GO BACK TO LAS VEGAS!" He says to the gas station attendant, "You hear anything?"

The attendant says, "No." Now the guy figures God is talking directly to him and him alone. He gets back in the car, makes a U-turn and drives straight back to Vegas. He hits the strip and he's driving around when he hears the voice say, "GO TO THE SANDS HOTEL!" He looks around and nobody else is looking up. He is the only person hearing this voice. He pulls up and goes into the Sands. It's mobbed. Now the voice says, "GO TO THE ROULETTE WHEEL!" Holy Christ, he thinks, God is directing me. He goes to the roulette wheel, and the voice says, "PLAY THE BLACK!"

The guy goes over to the pit boss and changes all his cash for chips, gets all the credit they'll extend him, calls home and has his wife wire him their life savings. He takes all his accumulated wealth and goes back to the roulette wheel. Again he hears the voice: "PLAY THE BLACK!" The wheel spins, the croupier throws the ball in, and it comes up red.

And the voice says, "SHIT!"

5

Politics, Sex, and Power

Washington is a very sensual town, a sexy capital city. For one thing, it's on the water. By law, there are no billboards to mar the surrounding countryside, and no neon signs, which makes the stars seem brighter at night. Standing on the balcony of my apartment in Arlington, I can watch the lights on the Potomac from the cars streaming over the bridges linking the District of Columbia with Virginia. I can see the Lincoln Memorial, the obelisk of the Washington Monument, and the dome of the Capitol building, all lit up in a line against the night sky.

Not more than a hundred yards from my front door is Arlington Cemetery, the Iwo Jima Memorial, and Fort Myer. I can also see the Watergate and the Kennedy Center. So I have a view of the panorama of American history from the beginning to the present, all in one glimpse. Smack in the center of that I can watch planes landing and taking off at National Airport. This way, I can check on whether the Trump Shuttle is *really* on time, or if the Pan Am Shuttle is doing better.

A geologist on my radio show once explained to me why the weather is often so foggy in Washington. When you build on swampy ground, he said, no matter how much you fill in and how much you build over it, the topography and weather remain the same. Washington was built on swampland, and in summer when the sun shines on swampland, you get fog and haze. If you stand in Washington and look toward Virginia, you won't see the haze, because Virginia isn't swampy. But there will be days when, from Virginia, you can't see Washington because of the fog. "In other words," I said, "what you're telling me is that the weather doesn't know there's a building there."

"Right," he said.

They never thought people would live here. The reason the District of Columbia doesn't vote for president is that no one actually lived there when the law was made; they all went home at night to their plantations in Virginia or Maryland. A historian I had on my show told me that they assumed people would go to work in the capital and live in Virginia or Maryland. It seems obvious now: who would want to live in a swamp?

That said, I have to admit that Washington is one of the cleanest and most beautiful cities in the country. Many people don't realize that the reason there are no billboards in Washington is Ladybird Johnson's beautification program, enacted back when LBJ was president. It makes for unobstructed views, but on the other hand, sometimes billboards can be helpful. If you want to find the Key Bridge Marriott in Rosslyn, for instance, you may have a problem.

Washington is all about power and sex. Money is third. There's plenty of money here, but this town still has fewer millionaires than a lot of cities. The big, big money lives elsewhere. We have Forest Mars and Jack Kent Cooke. Most people know Cooke, who owns the Washington Redskins. Few know anything about Mars, who is one of the richest men in America. Mars lives in McLean, Virginia, near Tyson's Corner, but no one ever sees him. He owns the Mars candy company. It's not a public company; he owns it outright. But as far as I know, he doesn't show up at parties and social events, so he never makes the columns. But there's no Rockefeller in the Washington area, no Lee Iacocca, no major industrialists, none of the top twenty-five other than Mars. The top-earning CEO here, Bill Marriott of the Marriott Corporation, pays himself $700,000 a year. Money isn't the thing here. For example, if I'm perceived as having clout in Washington, it has nothing to do with my salary. It's because I'm on television and radio every night. If I can get a front table at Duke's, it's for the same reason.

Ultimately, the perception of power translates into sexual attractiveness. If you work in the White House, you'll make out better than the president of Woodward and Lothrop, whether you're a man or a woman. That's power perceived, and in an odd way it's one of the things I like about Washington. Money doesn't talk here. It may show up in the form of influence peddling and areas like that, but in terms of social prominence it's secondary at best. When you live in Miami or L.A. or New York, you hear about how much this one makes and how much that one's home is worth. I almost never hear that here. We wouldn't have a conversation in which someone says, "Do you know what Ted Koppel makes?" Here it's, "Can you get me on *Nightline?*" That's the way this town is. It's a fascinating place, and there definitely is something called Potomac Fever.

Washington exercises a hypnotic attraction in another way. A lot of politicians who retire or are eventually defeated stay here long after they're out of politics. It's hard for many of them to go down to the 7-Eleven in Cedar Rapids after they've been to the Palm or Duke's. Something draws them to it. It's a big small town.

Conventional wisdom says that sexual attitudes have been changed by the impact of the women's movement and AIDS. I'd like to add a quirky theory of my own, which is that the sexual atmosphere in this country is affected by the aura of the White House. Neither Reagan nor Bush gives off any sexual charge. Jimmy Carter did, and he admitted it. If you happened to be with a woman in Carter's presence, as I was a couple of times, you definitely felt he was sexually turned on and, were it not for his religion and his wife, would have responded. Kennedy's sexuality is now legendary, but Lyndon Johnson was also a major womanizer. He wasn't as suave as Kennedy. He pawed at women; he grabbed them. But nowadays it almost seems as if, for all the talk about sex, we've entered a period of sexual retrenchment, and Reagan and Bush have contributed to that.

Right now in Washington you hear fewer stories about womanizing than about homosexuality. I've heard rumors about several major congressmen for years, but nobody ever backed them up. It used to be taken for granted that the one thing that could ruin a political career was an allegation of homosexuality. That may or may not be true today, but one thing *is* clear. An allegation might hurt you, but an admission probably won't. If I can get just one message across in this chapter, it's this: beat them to it. If there's some secret about you or your past, once you admit to it publicly of your own volition, you take most of its destructive potential away. Barney Frank got in a lot of trouble in 1989 for paying a male prostitute for sex and then giving him a job and a room in his condo. But back in 1987, when he first came out, he short-circuited rumors that he was gay and successfully defused any problems he might have had at the time.

I don't read the gossip columns much, and it's hard for me to feign curiosity over something I don't care about. A lot of things may be wrong with me, but I never liked gossip, especially behind-the-scenes gossip at radio or television stations where I've worked. I never enjoyed the conversations at lunch about who the general manager was sleeping with, and I take that with me on the air. I don't care if George Bush ever slept with another woman or not; I care what he said today about the environment. Adultery would affect his ability to govern only if a scandal erupted. I think John Kennedy was improving every day on his way to being a great president. In *The Kennedy Imprisonment,* Garry Wills attacks Kennedy's whole presidency based on the moral principle. I don't buy that. I think you can be a womanizer and a great CEO. I think you can be a promiscuous woman, or a lesbian or a gay man, and be an effective head of a corporation. Unless someone can blackmail you, why should what you do off the air, so to speak—other than harming people—have any effect on how you do your job? I'm not saying married people *should* have affairs; I just don't think it has to affect their work.

The thing that puzzles most people in Washington about Kennedy is not how he could do his work and still be getting laid all the time. The question really is, How did he do it with no one reporting it? I asked Barry Goldwater that. "How did all this go on?" I said. "Even you said it in your book: 'Hey, I wasn't the salt of the earth.' And Kennedy obviously was fooling around like crazy. Senator Smathers was famous for it among his colleagues. Why wasn't it in print?"

"Different time, different circumstances," Goldwater said. "What enters your mind now just didn't enter your mind in those days. Even when the press knew categorically about something, they wouldn't dream of printing it."

The reason I'll go along with that is that when I first went on the air in the mid-fifties, you couldn't say the word "pregnant." We had to say "with child." Back in the sixties, I wrote a column in the *Miami Herald* favoring abortion. We got annihilated. It was almost on a par with saying I was in favor of legalized drugs. John Knight, the publisher, called me before the column came out and said, "You know we'd never stand in the way of your opinion. Are you sure you want to say this?" I can still remember the vitriolic tone of the letters attacking me and the newspaper for daring to run such a column.

I later asked Walter Cronkite, "What did you think about the fact that there were no women in the news department in the early days?"

He said, "I never thought about it."

The same principle held true for a president's sex life. No reporter thought of going back to his desk and writing, "An unidentified lady entered the White House today, was shown into the president's private quarters, and left at 2 A.M." The reporters knew what was going on because John Kennedy wasn't a secretive guy. What maneuverings and secrecy he undertook were not so much to escape the press as to avoid having Jackie find out. He didn't want to harm Jackie. But I don't think he ever went to sleep at night worrying whether the *New York Times* was going to carry a story about him and some young starlet. Certainly Bobby stopped him from going on with some of the women who were Mafia-connected, but that was probably because he was more afraid of blackmail than of the press.

Kennedy did show a modicum of concern about the possible repercussions of his activities, but only the most perfunctory sort. The story is that Frank Sinatra got mad because Kennedy didn't use his house in Palm Springs for his assignations. But the supposed reason he didn't use Sinatra's house—he used Bing Crosby's instead—was that if something had happened with a woman and it was also Sinatra's house, that would only double the problem for him. Bobby's theory was, If you're going to have a problem, have it at Crosby's house. That was how concerned anyone in the White House was.

Gary Hart told me that he was upset at the vast inequity in the reporting of his extramarital affair and the many affairs that Jack Kennedy had had. "I didn't do near what he did," Hart said with some exasperation. "He became president, and nobody wrote about it. Now it's front page all over America."

The unfairness of it mystified him. He said he just couldn't believe it. We now accept Kennedy's daily dalliances as common knowledge. Hart, on the other hand, had been separated from his wife in the past. He never tried to pretend that they had a happy marriage. They knew they had problems, and so did the press.

"I don't want to knock Kennedy," Hart said. "He was a fine president. But what are you doing to me?"

Some observers have said the difference is that Kennedy was already in the White House, and once someone is already president, the press is a little more hesitant about skewering him. Nobody wants to believe that the guy running the country is a moral degenerate. Look at the level of incompetence that Reagan got away with for eight years. Even the so-called liberal press was loath to dwell on his inadequacies and shortcomings.

But that argument doesn't hold up fully in Kennedy's case, because he was screwing around as a senator and was already known as a ladies' man before he entered the White House. In fact, it was one of the reasons he was a lackluster senator. As John Kenneth Galbraith told me, "The thing you have to give Kennedy greatest credit for, which few did, is his continual growth. He was growing in that office every day."

Galbraith thinks that by the end of 1968, JFK would have been one of the all-time great presidents. But as a senator? Bobby was a much better senator. Teddy is the best senator of the three, ten times more effective than John was. Yet Kennedy was making great strides in terms of growth in understanding, in taking the pulse of the country. He was learning to have a little more guts. He was learning from his mistakes.

Ben Bradlee of the *Post* knew about Kennedy's flings; the whole town knew. But as David Brinkley says, "The whole town knew Roosevelt was in a wheelchair and never printed it. America knew that they had a president who had polio, who occasionally had to use a wheelchair, but they did not know they had a president who couldn't walk." In other words, no one ever wrote about "the crippled Franklin Delano Roosevelt." Why not? The reporters certainly saw him. Brinkley would describe a scene at a press conference: "And now the president is entering the room." He didn't say, "And now the president is rolling in his wheelchair." When photographers took pictures, FDR was seated behind his desk. They knew he liked to sit because he didn't want to put pressure on his legs. But no one thought this man could not walk. In 1928 when he nominated Al Smith at the convention, they stood him up, propped him up by the elbows; he took two steps and hit the podium and spoke. He was never seen walking. Once again, I have to believe that the members of the press themselves didn't want to dwell on the fact that their president could not walk. And there were other things. Roosevelt was a chain smoker. You never read that.

I'm a little surprised that more stories don't come out about the shenanigans in Washington. Sometimes I think it's just a matter of chance, what comes out and what doesn't. Duke Zeibert used to date Elizabeth Ray before the scandal broke about her being what amounted to a paid "companion" on the congressional payroll of Wayne Hays. She wasn't a call girl, but she went out with a lot of guys, and Duke was one of them. One day Duke had taken her to New Haven to see a Giants football game, and they were coming back on the train when the train got stuck for some reason. A reporter from the *Washington Post* who happened to know Duke came over and was just making idle conversation to kill time while they waited for the train to get going again. Duke was known as a man about town, and Ray was introduced as a woman he was taking out. Duke went to get a drink, the woman from the *Post* started talking to Elizabeth Ray, and that's how the story was broken. *Who do you work for? Wayne Hays. What do you do? I don't do anything. You don't do anything? I mean, some days I go in, some days I don't go in.* If the train doesn't get stuck, there's no story. It was just one of those things.

It kills me that so many people expressed shock over Ralph Abernathy's disclosures that Martin Luther King, Jr., had ex-

tramarital affairs. I knew those King stories for years and so did
everyone else in Washington. King implied to me several times
that if there was a weakness in his life it was with regard to
relationships. But he never preached sexual morality. He wasn't
like Jimmy Swaggart in that respect, and that's why J. Edgar
Hoover couldn't have gotten much mileage out of the photos he
supposedly had of King. Someone once told me that when Hoover called Lyndon Johnson to tell him he had incriminating
photos of King in bed with a woman and then came over and
showed him the pictures, Johnson had two responses. The first
was that King went up a notch in his estimation. And the second was, "These pictures could have been of anyone I know."

I think LBJ was more concerned that if Hoover was getting
photos of people in bed, then Johnson or some of his friends
could be next. Now we're in the age of total disclosure. If I
were running for public office, on the day I announced I might
have to mention at my first press conference that I began to
masturbate at age eight. Because you never know.

Someone who understood the convoluted relationship between
politics, ethics, and personal belief was Edward Bennett Williams. Williams was a liberal Republican who became a Democrat and a close friend of Teddy Kennedy. It was one of his
principles that his law firm would never turn down a case because of notoriety. As a result, they ended up defending Oliver
North and John Hinckley. We were having dinner at Duke's
once and talking about the North case. "You know what we're
becoming?" he asked rhetorically. "We're the firm of the fruitcakes. Hinckley, North—fruitcakes. Not much difference between the two. Zealot fruitcakes. But they can pay."

Hinckley's father paid a ton, he told me. And North had a
barrel of money going in, according to Ed. That business of
Jerry Falwell raising money for North's defense was a joke. People contributed millions. Former Marine colonels were giving
him money. The firm's retainer was paid before they ever
started work on the case. But once Ed had a client, he fought
like mad. I was with Ed the night before the Hinckley verdict.
He said, "We need a smart jury tomorrow. Because this guy's
really nuts, but they've got to accept the fact that he's nuts."

He won. He didn't try that case himself, but he knew about

every case going on. When they were on trial, all partners knew the strategy for all the other cases and who was assigned to what case. Ed didn't assign lawyers to a case because they shared the client's convictions. A lot of people think the fellow who represented North at that trial must be a raving conservative warmonger. Remember Brendan Sullivan, the lawyer who said, "I am not a potted plant"? Brendan Sullivan is a moderate Catholic Democrat, a major figure at Georgetown University. Ed liked to do that. He knew that if he put a conservative Republican on that case, the guy would get emotional. So he put a moderate Democrat in. Because then all Sullivan wants to do is win. He's not thinking about some abstract political principles. The winning is all that counts.

In a sense, Sullivan is going to do a better job for you than a guy who believes in your cause. He doesn't have to believe in your cause; it's enough that he believes you've been unduly charged. The son of a bitch subpoenaed Ronald Reagan. Would a diehard Reagan conservative have been able to do that with conviction? They put Reagan on the stand, in effect, and that's why they won on most of the counts. They're not stupid. Do you think for a minute that Ed Williams liked Ollie North or approved of what he did? All Ed wanted to do was win.

But then North stayed one day too long. North will fade. He'll be a postscript because he went out and made too much money. He went all over the country and made all those speeches, and he'll fade with the contras.

In a way, it's not that hard to understand the American public's momentary fascination with Oliver North. Among other things, the country had been suffering from a lack of charismatic figures and seemed happy to latch on to North as someone who at least held strong convictions and had the chutzpah to act on them. The fact that he was, in his own words, "a loose cannon on the gun deck of State" didn't dampen their desire to believe in someone. That makes it all the more lamentable that a genuinely charismatic leader such as Mario Cuomo should remain in the wings of the national political theater. But it may also explain why another politician, who only a few years ago was considered to be on the radical fringe, has been able to work his way into the core of America's heartland through sheer charisma.

I've known Jesse Jackson a long time, and I've come to believe that he is one of the best public figures at dancing his way through racial politics in America. The first time I met Jesse was when I interviewed Martin Luther King, Jr., in the 1960s. He was just another guy in the movement then. He stood out a little because he had a lot of hair, and most of the blacks around him, like Andrew Young, did not wear their hair in a big Afro. But that was the only thing I remembered about Jesse. Other than that, he could have been an Israeli secret service agent. Martin had seven or eight guys around him, and Jesse was one of them. He was taller than the rest and built like an athlete. I thought he was a very good-looking guy, but when he first started to become well known, he had an image a little like Al Sharpton's.

Jesse is a genuinely charismatic political figure who, were he white, could be president. Jesse has changed a lot from the days when people used to hate him when he walked into a room. I've noticed this change taking shape since the '88 campaign, going back to the way he brought his candidacy to the farmers in Iowa. The white perception of Jesse now is almost that he is old hat. He's become familiar, so no matter what he says, he is perceived as less of a threat today than two years ago, even though he's saying the same things. For the same reason, he is in less danger of being assassinated. Television is partially responsible for this development. Viewers have grown accustomed to him. Jesse is now a television personality who has become one of our accepted left-wing political figures. Bush invites him to the White House and no one is shocked. It's good politics. If Jesse goes into a restaurant, the white bigots go home and say, "Hey, I met Jesse Jackson today!"

Once you become accepted as an American personality, then you have to do something very crazy to go back to your old status as fringe weirdo. During the 1988 campaign, more people would go to shake Jackson's hand than Michael Dukakis's hand. Dukakis was the nominee, but during that campaign you would rather have been in a room with Jesse. And he dances well through tough questions and challenges. You think you know where he's going, but then he's not where you thought he was. What Gary Hart couldn't handle, he handled brilliantly. He was never thrown by a question like "Jesse, are you seeing other women?"

"It's none of your business," he'd say to the reporter who'd been rash enough to ask. "It's really none of your business. It has nothing to do with the strong issues that matter, the issue of people starving, of drugs, of the homeless in this community." Jesse knows how to do three minutes on hunger, drugs, and the homeless until the guy asking the question looks like a schmuck. Jesse's just talked about people starving, and the reporter has to go back to "Yes, but do you have a girlfriend?" He puts those questions away. He's the most adroit politician I've ever seen at that, and he never gives in. He never humbles himself. I get the impression that if Bush invites Jesse to the White House, Bush is more excited than Jesse. If the two take a picture together, you look at Jackson.

During the campaign there was a lot of talk on both sides about the foregone conclusion that a black man couldn't be elected president in America at this time. If you were a liberal, you were supposed to be outraged at this notion because it was prejudicial. And yet, from where I sit as host of two national call-in shows and from all the phone calls I've taken and everything I've read, it's safe to say that, at the very least, a black politician starts off eight percent down. That's not bad, because twenty years ago he would have been thirty percent down. Still, about eight percent of the voters in America will not vote for anyone who is black, under any circumstances. Call it the hard-core bigot factor, or fear, or whatever you like. The political reality is that you can't start off eight percent down if you're running for national office. So at this point, a black could be vice-president—maybe an extremely popular person who is not perceived as being especially black. But I don't think he can win the presidency today, starting eight percent down. The only question is whether the eight percent will shrink by 1992 or '96.

If that wasn't so, then Tom Bradley would have been governor of California. He lost by four percent, which means he really did a hell of a job. Deukmejian should have won by at least eight percent, so that means without the hard-core bigot factor Bradley would have won by four percent. (I haven't taken scientific polls and surveys on this, but as someone suggested to me, I probably talk to more people nationwide in a week than anyone else. Local talk show hosts may talk to as many people, but in a narrower area.)

The only way we might have a black elected to national office today is if a Republican administration is on the downfall or if we have a major economic crisis and a popular white shining knight runs with a moderate black vice-presidential candidate—and it wouldn't hurt if he was once a successful athlete. Jesse Jackson, however, would never be a vice-president. It's just not in his nature. And since he can't win the presidency and would never accept the vice-presidency, Jesse disrupts the party. Why does he do that? I've talked to him about it. He answers, "Do you want me not to have a philosophy?" His answers are all logical, but they miss the point.

There's another point we're all missing. If it were back in the old days, when the back room system of party politics ruled supreme, the Democrats would be in the White House now. Mario Cuomo would be president and Sam Nunn would be vice-president. Jesse Jackson would be a key figure in the party. But Jesse would have been told, "There's no primaries to get into, Jesse, because the primaries don't matter anyhow. Here's who the nominee is. What do you want? Okay, now here's where you go out to make speeches."

I'm not sure that the days of Mayor Daley, Sam Rayburn, and those guys didn't produce better candidates. The back rooms gave us Eisenhower, Roosevelt, Wilson. Back rooms gave us Lincoln. There were only ten primaries when Kennedy ran. Back room guys were pretty sharp. Since the fifties, we've never had anything approaching the Eisenhower-Stevenson races, in which two individuals of outstanding character were vying for leadership. Stevenson may have had more intellect, but Eisenhower was a genuine leader. And for a Republican, he was certainly wary of the military-industrial complex. Eisenhower looks better all the time. Those back room guys knew what they were doing. Can you imagine the back rooms coming up with a Bush-Dukakis election? They would have swallowed their cigars first.

Here's how the old system worked. There were committee
men from power groups in each city, like Tammany Hall in
New York. When the party had a convention, delegates came,
but they were the delegates of the power groups. So Sam Rayburn might call in the guys from Oklahoma who were delegates. "Listen, guys, here's who we're going with," he would
say. "Here's who we like. This is the push. Get your guys on
the block here."

And sometimes they went forty ballots. Maybe the back room
guys couldn't decide on a candidate, or rival factions arose. But
what we have now is public participation. And when the public
participates, Jesse's always going to get twenty-five to thirty
percent of the delegates. That *sounds* very democratic. But in
the old days, the enemy was the other party. Now, in the Democratic party, the enemy is other Democrats. Primaries are ex-
hausting, so the incumbent has an automatic advantage. By the
time Dukakis realized he had to go on TV to get back in the
race, he looked like a beaten man. Maybe Bush was smart not
to do interviews after all. And in the primary process with all
its debates, rivalries become public. Dukakis and Jackson became enemies, and the party had to reheal itself constantly. The
Republicans seem to be able to handle this better now. For one
thing, their delegates are less representative of all of America;
they have fewer women, minorities, environmentalists, workers, or farmers. They're more homogeneous. The Democrats
have an almost utopian mixture of delegates, but they end up
picking a consensus candidate, the least offensive guy in the
field. The irony is that the Democrats used to be better than the
Republicans at sifting the candidates. They waged their own
little internecine wars, but when they ran a national candidate,
they'd run you under the rug. Why?

It's not that difficult to explain, especially if you accept the
dictum that politics makes strange bedfellows. Roosevelt could
have both the blacks and the Bilbos running around screaming
for him because they all knew what it meant to win. Bilbo was
a white senator from Mississippi, a noted racist, a supporter of
Roosevelt but also of Jim Crow, segregation, and lynching.
Bilbo was tolerated in the party not only because he delivered
votes but because he also supported all of Roosevelt's social pro-

grams. Claude Pepper often said that, to his dying day, the worst vote he ever cast was against a law to ban lynching. He voted for the poll tax for the same reason: his constituents expected it of him, and he needed their support to get his own socially progressive legislation through. Remember, Pepper was a guy who was called a Communist in his day, and now he is remembered mostly as one of the country's greatest advocates for the aging.

But through this system the party got the best people and nominated the best people, and they put their resources behind them. In the old days, a guy like Jesse Jackson would have been a key, but he wouldn't have run as a maverick. Under the old system, someone like Cuomo wouldn't have refused to run. First of all, it was a lot easier then. Why would anyone say no? You didn't have to go to Iowa. You didn't have to stand in the snow. You didn't have to sit with the farmers. The party heads told you: "You're the nominee. Here's the money. Here's what we'll do. Here's what we'll give you if you lose." But under the current Democratic system, it's the survival of the blandest—whoever can hold on the longest by taking the most centrist position. That pretty much ensures a string of boring candidates.

I voted for McGovern, but he ruined the Democrats. His 1972 campaign set down new rules. They're wonderful rules, including minority participation. But there are a few drawbacks. Being a member of Congress doesn't guarantee your being a delegate. Tip O'Neill wasn't a delegate in 1976. He had no vote. Tip O'Neill had no say in selecting his party's nominee. The last four or five Democratic party conventions were the most democratic of all. They were racially mixed. They were everything I like about America. That system can elect congressmen on the local level, but it can't win the presidency.

America watches both party conventions. And that eight percent factor sees the Democrats: Jesse's at the podium, and forty percent of the delegates are black or minority. That mentality thinks if they vote Democratic they're voting for a black party. And all you need to win (or lose) is eight percent.

I was at both conventions in 1988, and I broadcast from both, so I got a pretty good idea of what went on there. I didn't do my usual TV show during that time but instead did inserts into the news coverage and talked to guests.

To begin with, the conventions were in the wrong cities. The Democrats would have loved New Orleans, as the Republicans would have loved Atlanta. Atlanta is white bread and highly technological. New Orleans is a fun-loving, sensual, racially intermingled place where the accent is on spicy food and jazz. The Democrats are always much more fun, much more interesting at a convention, whereas the typical Republican convention is a lot like an Amway gathering.

One thing I noticed, covering both conventions, is that the media people seem to exist there as a world within a world. We walk around together, we have lunch with ourselves, dinner with ourselves. We have parties for ourselves. The *Atlanta Constitution* threw a great party at the Atlanta art museum, and the walls were covered with the headlines of all the campaigns the newspaper has reported on. *USA Today* threw parties at both conventions. There were mayors' parties and governors' parties. Ted Turner put on a huge party at CNN headquarters in Atlanta. The city of New Orleans threw a party at which all of its famous restaurants had booths and handed out the specialties of the house. But the media included a group of about 150—types like Art Buchwald, Abe Rosenthal of the *Times*, Ted Koppel—who might be called nationally known. We went to all the parties. We were a traveling group, always asking each other, Where are we going today? What are we talking about today? Rumors were always rife. Dukakis is meeting with Jackson. He's *not* meeting with Jackson. What are we going to say? What are we going to find? Is it going to be here?

The conventions had their share of poignant and humorous moments. Of the poignant moments, two stand out. The first was watching Gary Hart walking alone in Atlanta's Omni, covering the Democratic convention for some Soviet newspaper. I walked with him, and he came on the air with me for a few short interviews. He definitely felt wronged, and hard as it may be to feel sorry for someone who did something as stupid as Hart did and then handled the upshot so badly, I still felt sad seeing him. He said something to the effect that it should have been him up there on the podium, and that was the saddest

part of all. The other poignant sight was of Tip O'Neill, stuck
in a bad seat, up in the bleachers. No longer Speaker of the
House, he was there as a guest of the convention. I watched a
lot of young delegates go right by him as if he never existed.

The humorous scenes had to do mostly with security. I walked
the New Orleans Superdome every day with the Secret Service
guys to get in my workouts. We did our exercise together. Every
morning, we walked around the dome ten times, two and a half
miles. In Atlanta *U.S. News & World Report* took over a health
club and then made a hundred VIPs their guests for the week.
But Jack Valenti and I were the only two to take advantage of
it. Not one other guest used the club. It was so cold in the
convention arenas and so hot outside that my glasses fogged up
every time I walked in. The security was beyond belief. Passes
changed daily: brown pass good on Sunday, not good on Monday; yellow pass good on Monday, good until Wednesday, and
not good on the floor.

There was a bulletproof screen in front of the podium in Atlanta. If someone wanted to assassinate a candidate, he'd have
to be shooting from above. Security didn't have to watch the
crowd because no one could do any damage from the floor. So
instead they waited for peculiar movements and antics by people in the seats above and around the podium. They acted as if
there were no metal detectors at the doors to the convention
center. You couldn't get in without going through the X-ray
machines and metal detectors, but the Secret Service working
the crowds inside acted as if there were no machines. They
know what delegate's supposed to be in what seat. But they also
know there's a lot of roaming. They take a lot of faces into
account. They have books and pictures of all the network cor-
respondents. The Secret Service don't waste time looking to see
if Dan Rather or Larry King has a badge. If they recognize you,
they assume you have a badge. They don't watch people they
know. You can be lunging for the president, and if you're Dan
Rather they're going to let you lunge because they'll be watching somewhere else.

On the other hand, the security people at the doors don't give
a damn who you are. Sam Donaldson doesn't get in without
a badge. Of course, there's always a way. My friend Herb

Cohen's theory is that it's all your attitude. He was at the Democratic convention in Madison Square Garden in 1980. You had to get special passes to go on the floor. Herbie was in the Garden visiting me at the Mutual setup, and he wanted to go on the floor. Wearing a gray business suit, he just walked up to one of the entrances where a security guard was posted. Then he walked right by in deliberate, authoritative strides, as if he owned the Garden. And as he went by the security guard, Herbie just rapped him on the shoulder and said, "Great job!" The guy smiled proudly, and Herbie was on the floor.

In Atlanta, the Omni uses those magnetized cards instead of keys to let you into your room. But the metal detectors at the convention center wiped out the card's magnetic code every time you carried it through with you. A mass of people went through the security machines during the day, and that night none of them could get into their hotel rooms because the cards didn't work anymore. So the hotel had to reprogram the whole key system. You had to tell them what room you were in so they could issue you a new card. But naturally, a lot of people forgot their room number, which for security reasons isn't printed on the card. So the desk clerks were looking up room numbers for a couple of hundred people, most of whom were yelling, "I've got to go to a fucking party!"

The next day to get into the Omni center you had to pass your room card around to the attendant, like you would keys or a camera at the airport, so it didn't go through the machine with you. This took much more time, and there were huge lines to get in. And, inevitably, every so often you'd hear an anguished groan: "Oh shit, I went through, and now I gotta get a new key!"

When I came back from the conventions, I was sitting in the broadcasting booth at an Orioles game, just for fun. Jon Miller, the Orioles broadcaster, asked, "Was it more like a World Series or a Super Bowl?" That's when I realized that the one thing conventions don't have is suspense. In a big sports event, you don't know who's going to win. But at today's conventions, you already know; it's more like a coronation than a contest. Conventions used to have suspense when they went to a second ballot. But we haven't had a second ballot since Eisenhower and

Taft in 1952. It's been nine conventions since we've gone to a
second ballot. But other than that, the drama is wonderful if
you're a political freak. I certainly am, and I wore three hats
every day—broadcasting radio and TV and writing for USA
Today. Somebody said I was the quintessential convention person. What they didn't know was that I was still living in the
days of smoke-filled rooms. When I went into the USA Today
headquarters to write my column, all they had were computers.
I don't know how to write with a computer, so they had to get
a manual typewriter for me, and they put a sign on it: LARRY
KING'S ANCIENT TYPEWRITER.

The convention is a traveling circus. The media, the elected
representatives, the candidates are all a part of the show. But
let's be honest, it's a media show. They may be the players, but
we're the stage crew and directors. Where are the cameras?
How's the lighting? And of course, there's plenty of comic relief.
Bob Dole said to me early in the Republican convention, "When
he announces me as vice-president, do I do the humble thing?
How would you make your entrance? What if it's my wife?
How am I going to handle that? How are we going to handle
going to parties if it's my wife? Do I come in behind her or in
front of her?"

The American Truckers Association threw a nice party for
Dole. Ted Koppel and Sam Donaldson were there. I got up and
said, "Before we even go on with this, Senator Dole, what is
your basic position on trucks?"

Dole picked right up on it. He said, "Trucks consume a great
deal of my waking hours. I am concerned about trucks. Indeed,
I got my start on trucks. Trucks have always been close to me.
Trucks are as American as apple pie. When I think of America, I think of its trucks." He had everybody laughing.

After watching Donaldson and Chris Wallace for years, I'd
always wanted to have the adventure of reporting from the
floor. CNN said, "Okay. Third night of the Democratic convention, you can take our regular reporter's place on the floor, with
the headset."

They positioned me, told me what camera to speak to, and
what time I'd go on. Comes the day, I'm standing on the floor,
in the middle of the Illinois delegation. I'm going to talk to the.

mayor of Chicago when a delegate comes up behind me. I turn around and see that he's wearing moose ears. Did I say it was a traveling circus? I meant a zoo. I turn around and the guy says, "Hey, Larry King, you're down in our delegation. Can I get your autograph?"

They're coming to me with the camera now. In my ear I hear, "Okay, let's go to Larry King in the Illinois delegation." As they come to me, I'm signing an autograph for a guy dressed like a moose. I'm also holding a microphone and I have the mayor of Chicago. I say to Mayor Sawyer, "Hold this mike." He puts the mike in front of me, and I say, "This is Larry King at the Illinois delegation." They start to crunch in on me, because I'm a celebrity to them. They're delegates, just ordinary people. They probably got Sam Donaldson's autograph the day before. Meanwhile, the mayor of Chicago can't manage to string two sentences together. He was subsequently defeated in the election, and it's no surprise why.

There were twenty cameras up in the rafters, and only one of them was the CNN camera, the one I had to look at. You don't want to be talking at the ABC camera. The only way to know when they're coming to you is to listen to the director, who is talking to you in one ear while you're hearing the program in the other ear. But it's like listening to a radio dispatcher in a taxicab. You can hear what he's saying to everyone. He'll say, "Larry, you're second. We're going to go first to the Montana delegation. Wait a minute, Bill's got someone over in Missouri. We'll go to Bill. Larry, you hold."

I'm holding. Now another guy comes over for an autograph, and the moose head is really bothering me. Finally I'm on with Mayor Sawyer. "Mr. Sawyer," I say, "Jesse Jackson wants a poll of the delegates for the vice-presidency." Remember, Jackson was a little ticked that he wasn't asked to be vice-president. "Do you favor this?"

Sawyer reaches deep and says, "Uh, I'm thinking about it. And I'm talking to my delegation about it."

"I understand, Mayor Sawyer," I say. "But I mean person-ally. I realize your delegation may vote against you. But *personally*, do you think the delegates should vote for the vice-presidential nomination as Jesse Jackson wants, or not, as Michael Dukakis requests?"

"I've spoken to Jesse about this," Sawyer says, "and I intend to speak to Michael about this, and I'll have an answer then."

"In other words," I say, "you have no opinion."

"I'm not saying that," Sawyer says.

Meanwhile, a guy dressed as a grasshopper is standing next to me, and somebody with a SUPPORT THE TEAMSTERS banner is hanging over my left ear. I say to myself, "Never again."

I don't think it's any secret how much I admire Mario Cuomo, both for his serious political views and for his wit. I've interviewed him often, but one time in particular those two facets of his political style came together more brilliantly than I've ever seen before—and very few people witnessed it.

It was at a gathering of the New York State Broadcasters Association in Saratoga Springs in the summer of 1989. I generally avoid broadcasters' conventions for a very good reason: they're boring. Most of the people who attend these functions are not talk show hosts or radio announcers—referred to in the trade as "talent"—but rather station owners, managers, syndicators—the business crowd. I know that deep down inside, these people feel they are as quick-witted and drop-dead hilarious as anybody who works for them. But put them behind a microphone and suddenly the room begins to resemble nothing so much as an American Legion pancake breakfast in Cedar Rapids. That gets my juices flowing, and after a few minutes I'm itching to get hold of that microphone and show them why they have to pay "talent" a lot more than they pay themselves.

I was there to be part of an interview "face-off," as the program notes described it, between Mario and me. Beforehand, we met over coffee and Danish to discuss the format. The meeting had been arranged by Mario's aides, a bunch of bright young people who, I think, go to entirely too much trouble to protect Cuomo from whatever members of the media they think may be out to sandbag him. For one thing, Mario doesn't need protection; anyone who tries to sandbag him is liable to end up on the floor. For another, it isn't Cuomo's style. I had been informed by these aides that the purpose of the meeting was to determine exactly what I would be asking the governor in front of all those radio people. And the first thing Cuomo said to me was, "I don't *want* you to tell me what you're going to ask me.

I want to be able to go out there and say we haven't arranged anything." Which tells you a lot about Mario Cuomo.

So when I got up in front of the audience, I duly announced that Mario and I had just had coffee together and that the rules were that there were no rules. But, I said, it felt strange for me to sit with an Italian and have no rules. I proceeded to tell the story I've told many times about growing up in Brooklyn in a neighborhood where there were only two kinds of people, Italians and Jews. (That's true, by the way. I never knew a Protestant in Brooklyn. The first Protestant I knew was John Lindsay.) I told the audience about the ritual we had—every Thursday afternoon at four, the Italians would line up the Jews and punch them out, saying, "You killed our Lord." Until one day Herbie said, "Hey! Let's stop all this. We'll admit we killed your Lord. But the statute of limitations has run out."

The story got the usual laugh and we moved on—but to what? I got an inspiration. It was risky, but it would certainly get things going. "You know," I said, "I'd like to make this like the presidential debates. And make it very controversial. So my first question, Governor Cuomo, is this: Your wife is raped and murdered. What do you do?"

Everybody remembered Bernie Shaw's infamous question to Dukakis during the 1988 presidential debates and Dukakis's failure to give a convincing response. My friends and I had all agreed that if it had been Mario instead of Mike, he would have answered it with the perfect mixture of passion and intellect. But now Cuomo sat there and rolled his eyes, looking exasperated. The first thing he said was, "Now I think I understand the rules. Let me make it clear—at least I wouldn't worry that it was going to be done by a Jewish guy, because that couldn't happen."

Mario was matching me jab for jab. Then he said, "I also thought you should know that Larry King *did* support John Lindsay. But not until he told everybody in the old neighborhood that Lindsay was Jewish but changed his name for business reasons."

Things were threatening to get bloody, so I moved on. I asked Cuomo if he thought his stand on the death penalty would hurt him, and if he hadn't misread the mood of the people, which has swung in favor of capital punishment. That's when he became serious. "After thirty-five years of studying the issue," Mario said, "of representing people who were sentenced to the electric chair, and of being there in Ossining, not only am I more convinced than ever that the death penalty is a terrible surrender to primitivism, but recent Supreme Court decisions have absolutely convinced me that the present lust for capital punishment is a sign of great weakness in this country. When you can reach the point where the Supreme Court of the United States of America, in an opinion written by Antonin Scalia, says that we are allowed to execute mentally retarded people because there is no consensus against that, that's not a sign of strength. Because what you're really saying is that we can't deal with drugs, we can't deal with crime, so let's do the most barbaric thing we can think of. Nobody else in the world does it. The only two industrial countries that use the death penalty the way we do are South Africa and the Soviet Union, and *they* don't kill the mentally retarded. So I am more opposed to capital punishment than ever. And I think it's worse than ever because we are weaker than ever."

Cuomo then dealt with the perception that American public opinion is currently leaning in favor of capital punishment. "We have to be careful, first of all, not to make a god of public opinion," he said. "And yet, on the other hand, we have to be careful not to be guilty of the reverse elitism and snobbishness that says, 'Well, if that's what everyone else wants, then I'll prove I'm smarter than they are by going the other way.' You need to have a decent respect for the opinions of people, and you need to listen to them because they are very, very smart. The consensus view is normally very good. But having listened to it, you then have to bring to bear your own intelligent experience, wisdom, and logic. And I do that. I read the editorial writers. I watch television. I try to get a sense of where the people are going, to see if perhaps I've missed something. I try to represent them because they selected me. But in the end, especially on the questions of abortion and capital punishment, you have to bring to bear your own judgment."

Cuomo reminded us that, although the American Catholic bishops, including Cardinal O'Connor in New York, are now opposed to capital punishment, they were not always so outspoken. "In 1977 when I was debating Ed Koch," he said, "and a woman in Brighton Beach came up to me and spat in my face because I told her that I was against the death penalty, there were no cardinals, no bishops, no priests standing up in their pulpits saying, 'We're with Mario.' " Conservative as that audience of broadcasting executives was, I think Mario had them in his pocket, emotionally if not ideologically.

On the subject of how he could square his stand on abortion with his Catholic faith, Cuomo again turned the issue on its ear and said that the case could be made, indeed had been made by some Catholic theologians, that although abortion is a real moral issue for the woman having the abortion, the outside world has no right to make a judgment *for* the woman in the first five or six months. "This is based," he said, "on the old moral principle that society ought not to make a rule where it has no power, and the only person who has power over the fetus in the first five or six months is the mother." As Cuomo put it, "There is argument even within the Church on the subject of abortion. Not on the question of whether a woman commits a sin when she has one performed, but whether you, Larry King, or I, Mario Cuomo, or the state of New York, or the federal government, has the right to order that woman to act any way at all."

He then reduced it to an even simpler level. "It's not a moral question," he said. "It's not a religious question. For example, if you belong to the club called the Catholic Church, and the Church says it's wrong to use birth control devices—which it still does, saying that it's a matter of natural law at the same level of gravity as abortion—then if you want to remain a member of the club, you have to live up to that rule. That's different from saying that I have to make *everybody in this room* live up to that rule because I happen to be a Catholic."

In other words, since the Church is opposed to birth control, do Catholics have the right to, say, ban the sale of contraceptive devices to those who don't believe as they do? His observation was rendered all the more timely because not long after that, right-to-lifers began to appear on talk shows insisting that contraception be outlawed along with abortion. That was so patently absurd and so grossly out of phase with the public consensus that those people haven't been heard from since. As for federal funds being used for abortion, Cuomo said, "We believe that if there is a constitutional right, whatever your personal discomfort with it, the poor have a right to share that right with nonpoor women. And so we will continue to offer Medicaid funding for abortion as long as that federally recognized constitutional right exists."

At that point the audience burst into spontaneous applause. Then we came to the inevitable subject of whether Cuomo was a candidate for president. I asked Mario if he would think about running for reelection as governor in 1990 while at the same time announcing that he was also thinking about running for president in 1992. He said, "Let me think, then, about running for governor and saying I'm thinking about it."

To which I responded, "In other words, you will think about thinking about it."

"I will think about thinking about it," he said. "But I won't think too much."

Now the place broke up. "At a certain point you have to end the speculation," he added. "But that's surely not going to happen this morning."

"But couldn't we have a scenario," I added doggedly, "where you're running for governor and you say to the people, 'I am thinking about it'?"

"So then the question is," Mario replied, "Could you have a possible situation where, when I announce that I'm running for governor, I attach a coda that says, 'However, while I'm running for governor, I'm also thinking about not serving the four years'?"

"Correct."

"Could that happen?"

"Right."

"I don't know."

It was like some Abbott and Costello routine, but it played great to that crowd. Then, as Mario does so well, while the crowd was still laughing, he segued into a serious statement. "I believe you have to feel in your heart that there is nobody else out there who can do it as well as you can for the good of the whole country," he said. "People seem surprised if you don't exhibit a mad lust for the presidency on the ground that, 'Gee, I got to be vice-president of the company, shouldn't I want to be president? I got to be good at WNBC, shouldn't I want to go network?' The whole assumption in this country is that you should keep going until you go through the roof, and if you don't there's something wrong with you. I hear this all over the country. I have actually overheard people saying, in reference to me, 'Well, let's face it. If he was as good as all that, he'd want to be president of the country. I'll bet you anything it's his family. There's some kind of mob ties. His son did something wrong. He *did* beat up Jewish kids in the old neighborhood. . . .' "

Suddenly he had them howling again. Sometimes Mario is alternately so eloquent and so off-the-cuff funny that you have to be like a bulldog to nail him down. Finally I just said, "Are you open to the possibility?"

"You're obliged to be open to the possibility if you're in public service," he said. "If you're in public service, then your whole purpose is to help as many people as you can, so of course you have to be open."

"Suppose key Democratic party people asked you?"

"That doesn't count," he said. "It's what you say to yourself. Do they need me? Can I win? If you concluded that they needed you and that you could win, then you'd *have* to run. But that's like saying, If I had a little ham and a little cheese and a little lettuce and two slices of rye bread, I would have a ham and cheese with lettuce on rye. It's all speculative."

The entire hour swung wildly from outbursts of laughter at lines like those to moments where the audience strained to hear every word Cuomo had to say. When a TV crew that was taping parts of the exchange made a little too much noise, I noticed irate audience members turning around to stare them into silence. It's worth repeating that this was a crowd of owners and executives, people who are not among the most liberal in the country. If they didn't always agree with the governor, they appeared at least to be mesmerized by the balletic movement of his logic and softened by his sense of humor. I don't know whether Cuomo won any votes that day, but he sure captured a few hearts.

Edward Bennett Williams told me that Cuomo made the most remarkable speech he'd ever heard, at a Holy Cross commencement. Williams was on the board of trustees at Holy Cross, and he'd asked Mario to speak there. "I've been in courtrooms around the nation with some of the best trial lawyers in America," he told me later, "but that was the best speech I've ever heard."

In the speech, which lasted twenty minutes, Cuomo talked not to the graduates but to their parents. According to Williams, Cuomo said, "I don't remember who spoke at my graduation. I only remember that I knew he was going to speak for twenty minutes, and I kept looking at my watch because I wanted to get out of there. You're not going to remember me. So I'll tell you what—you indulge me. I'm going to be fourteen minutes, and I'm not going to talk to you. I'm going to talk to your parents who are sitting behind you."

And he never looked at the students again. He took his sight line up beyond them. And by the end of the speech, he had the students all turned fully around, looking at their parents. It was as if he and they were talking to their parents together. He was talking about letting go, letting them find themselves.

"They've graduated from this school now," Cuomo told the parents. "You've paid a lot of money. Some of them are going to be doctors and some are going to be artists. And some aren't going to make it. We'd all love to make it, and in society we all can make it. But what we really want is the opportunity. What Holy Cross has given you today is that opportunity. Give them the opportunity. Don't tell them what to be."

And when Cuomo finished, the parents and graduates applauded each other.

It was the kind of touch I've come to expect from Mario, who is a master at turning situations around, usually to his own advantage. Lew Lehrman once told me a story over lunch at the Palm that shows just how much of a down-and-dirty politician Mario can be when he wants to. Cuomo was running against Lehrman for governor in 1982, having defeated Ed Koch for the Democratic nomination. It was a tough race, and both candidates knew it was going to be close. Oddly enough, the Italian voters were going for Lehrman because he was tough on crime, but Cuomo was getting the Jewish votes because he was more liberal on social issues. Lehrman, meanwhile, had eighty zillion dollars to spend on his campaign. They were in a Rotary Club debate that was being telecast statewide. The rules of the debate called for the candidates to alternate making statements and answering prepared questions. For the last part of the debate, each candidate could ask the other any question he wished and then could respond to the answer.

When they got to the final question, Lehrman went first, and Lehrman's question was something like, "Can you promise the people no new taxes? Can you say that in a Cuomo administration you will promise not to raise any taxes? Be honest." So Cuomo answered, and Lehrman responded. Then it was Cuomo's turn to ask the question. And Cuomo's question was, "How much is that watch you're wearing?"

The audience seemed surprised. Lehrman said, "That's not germane."

"I was told that the rules of this debate are that the last question could be on any topic," Cuomo said. "Lew, I've been admiring it all evening. It's for my own interest. How much does that watch cost? That's my question."

The moderator affirmed that the question was within the rules of the debate. And Lehrman told me, "I'm not a liar. I had to answer. The watch was a Rolex."

So he answered. "Thirty thousand dollars."

Mario gave him a withering look. "Thirty thousand dollars for a watch," he said. "Well, you earned it, Lew. The man earned it. He started with nothing, and he could buy a thirty-thousand-dollar watch. That's marvelous. But thirty thousand dollars for a watch? A jeweler friend of mine told me that after five hundred dollars, you're just paying for the ornamentation. All watches run the same. Why not a five-thousand-dollar watch? Twenty-five thousand dollars could feed a whole family for a year."

It was calculated and surprising, and it devastated Lehrman. Lew said it was unbelievable. Then Cuomo looked at his own watch and said something like, "My watch says nine o'clock. . . . Here are my closing remarks."

When you're talking about low-ball politics, of course, the name Richard Nixon quickly comes to many people's minds. But he told me a spooky story once that transcends politics. I had become friendly with Nixon through Bebe Rebozo. Bebe used to bring dates to my radio show when I broadcast from a houseboat called *Surfside 6* in Miami Beach. Rebozo and Nixon were tight, so after Nixon lost for governor of California in 1962, he spent a lot of time in Miami, and Bebe would bring him on my show. I was interviewing Nixon on TV one time when he told me the strange story of where he was the day Jack Kennedy died. That story got such a great response from my audience that I started to do a whole series on where famous people were when Kennedy was shot. I would ask that question at the end of my TV interviews, and then the station put them together into a half-hour special and aired it as a tribute on the fifth anniversary of Kennedy's death, November 22, 1968.

Hubert Humphrey told me he was speaking at a luncheon sponsored by the Chilean embassy. When he got word of the assassination, he left immediately, went to his office, and locked the door. Then he turned on a tape recorder and taped every remembrance he had of John F. Kennedy because he thought that it might be of historical interest someday. If you go to the Kennedy Library in Boston, you can hear the tape of reminiscences that Humphrey made that afternoon.

Tony Randall said he was somewhere in Europe—I forget which city—and he ran to the American embassy. He didn't know what else to do. It was evening, and everyone was just standing around. There were thousands of Americans just standing around the embassy. They watched the flag being lowered to half-mast and they didn't know what to do.

Bob Hope got a phone call, although he still doesn't know who it was from. He picked up the phone, a little groggy because it was 9:30 in the morning in California. A voice said, "Turn on your TV." He hit the button, and there on TV was a reporter talking about Kennedy dying. And right on top of the TV set was a picture of him and Kennedy that he'd received the day before from the White House, framed. He'd been at a dinner with Kennedy, and that was his memento. It was eerie.

But it all started with Nixon, and Nixon's story was absolutely the eeriest. I asked him at the end of an interview in late 1964 where he was when Kennedy died, and he said, "You know, I've never talked about this publicly. And oddly enough, you're the first person who ever asked me. My friends know the story, but no one has ever asked me on the air. I'll be happy to tell you. I was in Dallas."

I took a deep breath. "Dallas?"

"Well," he said, "I was leaving Dallas. There was a convention of the Pepsi-Cola bottlers, and my law firm represents Pepsico."

On November 22, 1963, Nixon was at this Pepsi-Cola convention in Dallas, and he left that morning. He had spoken and then was driven to Love Field. As he was taking off from Love Field, he saw all the flowers being set up for Kennedy's arrival and the band rehearsing. And the guy sitting next to him said, "You know, a couple of thousand votes the other way and that could be you coming here today."

Nixon took off about a half hour before Kennedy landed. He was only a former vice-president at this point, traveling alone, no Secret Service protection or anything. He was just another corporate lawyer. He flew to New York and got off the plane at La Guardia Airport. The firm was supposed to have a limo meet him and take him to the law office. But when he got off the plane, no limo was there. (Later he found out the limo driver had the wrong airline.) So Dick Nixon hailed a cab.

He got in the cab, and the driver made a wrong turn trying to get onto Grand Central Parkway. Instead, they ended up on a side street, and the driver had to go around the block to get back to the parkway. They were now on a residential street in Queens, just the cab driver and Nixon. So they went down the street to turn around and they had to stop at a red light.

It was a sunny, chilly November afternoon. Nobody was on the street. As they were waiting for the light to change, a woman came running out of her house screaming. She was obviously very distraught, and Nixon thought maybe there had been an accident, so he rolled down the window of the cab, stuck his head out, and said, "Can I help you?"

She looked up, saw Nixon, and fainted.

Nixon got out of the cab, and people started coming out of their houses. The cab driver got out to help him, and they revived the woman. The woman came to and said, "I just heard on the television that President Kennedy was killed. I didn't know what to do, so I ran into the street and the first person I saw was Richard Nixon, and I thought the world was coming to an end."

Nixon rode the rest of the way in silence.

It's been a long time since we put that show together, but it's hard to forget some of the stories we used in it. Jim Bishop told me he had asked Kennedy about a week before he was killed if he ever thought about assassination, and Kennedy said, "If somebody wants to kill me, they're going to kill me. If you want to kill a president, and you're willing to give up your life, anybody can kill any president. I don't care what the Secret Service says or how much protection they can give you. If you want to kill somebody, you can kill him. So I never think about it."

Senator Spessard Holland, Democrat of Florida, was sitting in the Senate the day Kennedy was killed. Ted Kennedy, a freshman United States senator, was running the Senate that day. When the vice-president isn't there to preside over the Senate, freshman senators take turns running it so they can learn all the procedures. Teddy just happened to be running the Senate that day when Spessard Holland's page came in the door and handed Senator Holland a note that read, "John Kennedy is dead. Recess the Senate."

Holland went up to Ted Kennedy and said, "Recess."

"Why?" Kennedy asked.

"Just recess," Holland said.

"We've only got a couple of minutes left till lunch," Kennedy said.

"Your brother has been shot," Holland said. Then he had to hold on to Ted while he recessed the Senate.

Some years later, during the 1968 primary campaign, John Siegenthaler, a campaign aide for Bobby Kennedy who now writes for *USA Today*, was driving in a cab with Ted Kennedy up Nob Hill in San Francisco, and they had the radio on when Ted learned that Bobby had been shot. Ted was in San Francisco that night because he had handled Northern California and he was up there with the campaign. They had just listened to Bobby's speech, jumped into the cab, and were going up Nob Hill. They told the cab driver to turn on the radio to see what kind of reaction the speech was getting, and then they heard the bulletin.

Captain Eddie Rickenbacker, the World War I flying hero

who made Eastern Airlines a commercial success, was a diehard conservative who hated Roosevelt and felt that Truman
was, by contrast at least, "forthright." He admired John Kennedy because even though he was a rich man's son, as Rickenbacker put it, "he worked his way into politics to the degree
that he took an advantage of an opportunity. Nixon was a sick
man when that campaign was on, and if he hadn't gotten into
those television debates with Kennedy, Nixon would've won
hands down." When I asked Eddie where he was when Kennedy died, he remembered clearly.

"I was in St. Louis, Missouri, talking to the state chiefs of the
Chambers of Commerce at their annual luncheon. Just as I was
introduced and was about to get up, someone handed me a note
that said, 'The president has been shot.' I told the audience the
contents of the note and asked them to rise in a silent prayer in
his behalf. During that silence I thought to myself, What do I
do now? Because I knew that in my speech I would be lam-
basting his administration. I decided that since I'd never started
anything in the past that I hadn't tried to finish, I should go
ahead. About halfway through, another message was shoved
under my nose, saying that the president was dead.

"I stopped my talk and said to the audience, 'I'm sorry, but
our president is dead. May we have another silent prayer for
those he left behind.' And during that silence I thought again,
Will I go on or won't I? And again the good Lord came to my
rescue and said, Go on and finish. So I did."

6

In the Green Room
with Ol' Blue Eyes, and
Other Celebrity Tales

It's been said that the real business of America is celebrity. Over the years I've heard a lot of attempts to explain why we are so obsessed with celebrities and how we define celebrity, but without going over them all, I can say one thing for certain. We think of a celebrity as someone who is not only different from us but also different from anybody we know personally. When a celebrity walks by, people turn and stare, no matter how they feel personally about him or her. If Brando or Sinatra or Nancy Reagan walks into a room, you look, even if you can't stand the person. And although it's part of my business to talk to celebrities, and even though I've begun to enjoy a certain celebrity status myself lately, I'm still susceptible to the same awe of celebrities as anyone else. So when I learned that Frank Sinatra had agreed to an hour's interview on my CNN TV show, I was naturally pretty excited.

I got to the CNN studios in New York early on the night of the interview and was surprised to find only Frank and his pal Jilly Rizzo—no hangers-on, no bodyguards. That was a good sign, and I began to feel that maybe I'd get to see another side of a man who is often thought of as one of the most protected and isolated celebrities of our time. It was a Friday night in May, and the first thing Frank said to me was, "Do you know where they want me to spend this August? In the Hamptons.

The Hamptons! Larry, can you picture me in the fucking Hamptons? Sinatra in the Hamptons. Who are they kidding? The only thing they do that I like to do is drink."

Frank couldn't see himself, the ethnic Italian, in white-shoe country, but that was where his wife wanted them to go. He wound up not going. As we continued to sit around and chat, Frank suddenly grew wistful. The last time I'd seen him, I'd apologized to him because I was smoking and he was not. I had asked him if he wanted me to leave the room when I wanted a cigarette. He said, "No, it doesn't bother me." So the first thing he said to me this time was, "Now we have role reversal, Larry. Do you mind if I smoke? Do you want me to step outside?"

We were in the green room, and people were walking back and forth outside the room, looking in. As I said, Sinatra is one of those people who, if you know he's sitting in a room, you have to look in. It doesn't matter what age you are. He just is larger than life. But he was ready to step outside in the hall because I think he genuinely felt bad. I asked him why he went back to smoking, and he told me he had been sitting around the house in Palm Springs one day, all alone. No one was home. The chauffeur was away, Barbara was shopping. And there was a pack of cigarettes on the table that somebody had left from a party the night before. He hadn't smoked in two years and had had stomach surgery. He said to me, "I just looked at the mother, and I didn't know what to do with my hands—and I lit up. And I've been back to smoking Camels full time ever since."

"It's okay," I said, "that doesn't happen to me." I could still sense an air of melancholy about him, so I asked how he was feeling. As he answered me, I began to understand why he works so much even at his age; I think he needs it more than the audience does. Sammy Davis once told me that Frank wants to work all the time. Sammy said an Australian promoter offered Sinatra something like a million dollars for one night, but he doesn't like Australia because he had a bad run-in with the press there once. So Frank got on his private jet, flew down, and flew out the same day. Jilly told me, "Frank was in Australia for three hours." He had it timed. They landed at eight, he went on at eight-thirty. He did encores. He said good-bye to the promoter. They left the airport at eleven, and he slept all the way back. Frank was in the sky thirty-six hours because he didn't want to stay in Australia.

A few nights before we did the interview, Frank had called me on the phone. I was walking out the door to go to Duke's for dinner. A woman came on and said, "Mr. King, do you have a few moments for Frank Sinatra?" Can anyone say no to that? Frank said, "Hey, Larry, how you doing?"

"Fine."

"Looking forward to seeing you," he said.

"Same here, Frank."

"Hey, can I say on your show 'pimps and whores'? Is that allowed on television? Can I say that?"

"Referring to what?" I asked.

"These writers, these pimps and whores who write those things about me. I can say that, can't I?"

"Yeah."

"Good, that's all I wanted to check on. So, how's it going? How you doing?"

But now, as I was sitting next to him in the green room, he was totally relaxed and started talking about songs. He had performed at Irving Berlin's one-hundredth birthday party the night before, where he'd sung "Always." Someone else, he didn't know who, had sung "Remember." Sinatra was saying that the older he gets the more acutely he realizes that the genius of so many songwriters, the genius even of the Beatles or of Elvis, is simplicity. To him, the genius of good singers and the genius of great writers—especially lyricists, because he loves lyricists—is that they don't get involved. They keep it very simple. And he dissected the whole song, Irving Berlin's "Remember." He took the lyric, line by line: " 'Remember the night, the night you said "I love you." Remember?' "

He was singing it to me, and I got goose bumps. Here was the all-time master interpreter of lyrics, taking a lyric, breaking it down for me, and explaining why it was great and how he sings it. Like that first line, which is a throwaway. He said, "Look at that. 'Remember the night, the night you said "I love you." ' Pause. 'Remember?' Ain't that terrific? Berlin broke a couple of rules there. He paused, and he had an aside line, a throwaway, a repeat of the title. 'Remember you vowed by all the stars above you.' You could sing that sort of angrily. Or you could sing it tenderly. You could be very hurt or very disappointed and bitter."

Sinatra laid it right out for me. You can play it a lot of different ways, he said, and he explained each choice. He did that for the whole song. Other singers and musicians, from Ella Fitzgerald to Louis Armstrong to Count Basie, have said to me on different occasions that there was no one who could interpret a lyric like Sinatra. That's high praise coming from Louis and Ella, because no one has ever done it like they did, either. But sitting there listening to Frank analyzing that one simple Irving Berlin song, and doing it so simply and elegantly, I realized the genius in his own simplicity of approach to interpretation. That was what Louis and Ella—either one of whom could tear a lyric apart eight ways from Sunday and swing it mercilessly—must have dug about Frank: that simplicity, that economy of expression.

Sinatra ended with a little anger in his voice as he sang, " 'You promised that you'd forget me not. But you forgot . . . to remember.' " Then he just said, "Jesus Christ." I wound up humming and singing that song for a month. And he had me thinking about it, hearing all kinds of nuances in it that I'd never known were there.

When Frank wants to be nice, he can really pour it on, and he did that day. He doesn't understand the Kitty Kelleys of the world. Before the show, he was saying to me, "Forget them. Hey, I'm a big boy. I got kids, grandkids. What are people like that accomplishing? Is it adding to the culture to write about what my mother did when she was twenty-five?"

Frank reads the papers, but he doesn't put much stock in them. "How's the fucking *Washington Post?*" he asked me. "Fucking piece-of-crap newspaper that is."

As I said to him, "You know, Frank, you may be the only person who would not return a call from the *New York Times.*"

"Why should I?" he said. "Who the hell are they?"

That anger comes from his early experiences with the press over the Ava Gardner affair and the breakup of his first marriage. When Sinatra had it all, the press loved him. He was selling out at the Paramount, and he was going on all the radio shows. But what he never realized, I think, is that sometimes you start believing that they will love you forever. Teddy Kennedy thought that because Roger Mudd was a liberal and the *Washington Post* was liberal, it somehow meant they would play down Chappaquiddick. What none of these people has ever learned is that the first thing the press is after is a story. And when you, as a public figure, entertainer, or politician, fuck up—that's a story. So when Frank met Ava Gardner and left his wife, that was a story, and no matter how much the press may have loved him, they loved a story more.

Sinatra's distaste for the press reached such an extreme that he refused to fight back, even to this day when more than one untrue story about him has become embedded in the public imagination. Frank has been bum-rapped about how he got the role that won him an Academy Award in *From Here to Eternity*, but he had never publicly explained the true story. He hated *The Godfather* when it came out because everyone said that the singer who got a part in a big movie because the Mafia threatened the studio heads was based on him. Everyone remembers the scene in which the studio owner wakes up to find his favorite horse's head in bed with him. A lot of people are under the impression that the mob got Frank Sinatra the role in *From Here to Eternity*. He was down and out, wasn't performing much, wasn't doing any TV or movies, and had no hit records. He was suffering from bad press because he was the guy who'd left his wife for a sexy movie star and made a fool of himself. But after he got the part of Maggio in *From Here to Eternity*, he won the Academy Award, got a Capitol recording contract, and never looked back.

Frank resented *The Godfather* and all it implied. Mario Puzo, who didn't know Frank, was supposedly writing about the story everyone had heard all these years. And Sinatra had never done anything to defend himself against that story. In other words, he never said, "It's untrue!" He just said, "Those motherfuckers!" I probably believed the story, too, because it sounded plausible. We've seen the photos of Frank with some Mafia capos, but that works both ways, I suppose. If the mob wants you to sing for them and be their entertainer, are you going to say no?

Anyway, one night I was interviewing one of my favorite

actors, Eli Wallach, and I asked him that question of mine, "Did you ever turn down a part that you later regretted?"

"Yeah," he said. "But I knew it would be a good role, so I can't say I turned it down because I didn't think it would be any good. But it was a strange set of circumstances."

"How's that?" I asked.

"I got the part as Maggio in *From Here to Eternity*, and—"

I immediately stopped him. "Wait a minute," I said. "*You* got the part?"

"Oh, yeah," he said. "They tested about five people. They liked Sinatra a lot, but they thought I had a little more theatrical experience for that kind of role, and I got the part. It was only fifth or sixth billing in the movie. But I liked the script and I sure liked James Jones. So I was all ready to do it. I flew out to the coast, and they were doing wardrobe, fitting me for my uniform. And all of a sudden I get a call from New York. It's Tennessee Williams. And he says, 'Eli, can you open in *Camino Real*?'

"Well, I would always jump at a chance to do something with Tennessee, because he's an actor's dream, and I always liked the stage better than films anyway. So I went to Harry Cohn, who was producing, and I said, 'Look, this is crazy. I love this movie and I'm under contract to you. Is there any way you can let me out? I'd like to do this play, but I don't want to hang you up.'

"And Cohn said to me, 'Well, it's a key role but it ain't the major role. And Sinatra's test was pretty good. So you owe me one, Eli.' They called Sinatra, who had already been told he didn't get it, and said, 'Wallach can't do it, would you do it?' Sinatra was there in two minutes."

Wallach went on to tell me that every time he opens in a new play, whether he's on tour or on Broadway, roses come from Sinatra. This has been more than thirty-five years. The roses come with a note that says, "You dumb actor. Thanks, Frank."

"Of course I was dumb," Wallach said. "I mean, that was a dream role. He won an Academy Award. But I did it of my own volition."

I was dumbfounded. "But all these years, Frank has taken this rap that hoodlums got him the part."

Eli started to laugh. "Hoodlums! I was all signed. We had auditions, and I got it."

When I asked Sinatra about that, I said, "Why didn't you respond? You'd read the innuendos. You could have called a favorite writer of yours who writes in *Time* and said, 'Listen, let me tell you—' "

"Oh, no, no," Frank said. "I don't call nobody for favors. You print a lie, fuck you. I don't deny. I don't say 'No comment.' I say nothing."

So I said, "You've let this go on for more than thirty-five years, people thinking that the mob got you this part. A guy writes a piece of fiction, a movie comes out based on it, and everyone thinks they're all writing about you. Now we both know that ain't the way it happened, and you got a guy who will certify it ain't the way it happened. Eli Wallach had the part."

"Nah, they don't want to hear about it," Frank said.

I told Sinatra that I'm surprised he doesn't get offered movie roles these days. I said, "You don't get any movie roles? Not even as a detective?"

"Nah, too old," he said. "I don't see parts."

I said, "I can't believe you don't see parts."

"I don't see parts. And I like doing a detective. I'm very comfortable doing a detective. I'm a one-take guy because I like to work quickly."

That last statement was verified for me by a very reliable source. Tom Selleck, who is one of the most intelligent actors to work on TV, told me that Sinatra was the best guest star he ever worked with on *Magnum, P.I.* He was impressed by Sinatra's spirit of cooperation and the fact that he was always on time and always knew his lines.

A couple of months after the CNN interview, I ran into Frank in Hollywood. He said, "Hi, Larry, how are you?" He gave me one second and just walked on. But then when I won an award as Broadcaster of the Year, I got a congratulatory letter from him, which I never expected. So this is a strange, complex man. Somebody once told me that Tony Bennett was in a private plane on his way to a singing engagement when they ran into a bad rainstorm. The plane was flopping around in the sky, and everybody was getting pretty nervous. And Tony said, "Why didn't we call Frank?" Like Frank would have made the sky clear. Frank will make everything okay. That's the way other people in the entertainment world think of him. At the same time, Frank is complex enough that he can let a myth linger for years that the Mafia got him a part in a hit movie. And I have to find out it isn't true, not from Frank but by asking Eli Wallach, "Did you ever turn down a role?"

If celebrities are different from anyone else we know, then Frank is one who happens to be different from just about any other *celebrity* we know. And if there's a noticeable downside to celebrity, it's that out of a need to protect their privacy, certain celebrities become removed from the world to some extent. For instance, Don Rickles and Sinatra were in Monte Carlo watching TV one day, and they happened to be tuned in to CNN, which is carried worldwide by satellite. An exercise program came on, one of those short items they repeat throughout the day called a Fitness Break. Sinatra said to Rickles, kind of disgusted, "They showed this thing twice already."

Rickles said, "What do you want me to do, Frank?"

Frank said, "Call Larry King."

"And what's Larry King going to do?"

Frank said, "Hey, he's got clout there. Tell him they're running the same fucking thing three times in a row."

"In other words, Frank," Rickles said, "if you don't like something that Tom Brokaw does, I should call Johnny Carson?"

"Yeah," Frank said, "call Carson. You call anybody who's got clout. You don't call Ted Turner. That's dumb. You call Larry King."

Rickles said, "Frank, I don't mind it three times a day. Why don't you call?"

And Frank said, "I call no one."

On top of everything else, that story shows you the kind of wild life that Sinatra leads, sitting in Monte Carlo, one of the most glamorous cities in the world, watching television in his room all day.

Just how far are celebrities removed from the real world? I don't consider myself a big celebrity, but my face is on the tube often enough, and because of my two shows and my newspaper column I have enough clout that I'm frequently treated like one. People are nice to me, probably nicer in many cases than they are to other people they don't know personally. My ex-wife Sharon used to ride me about this. "Everybody's nice to you," she would say. "You don't see the real world. Celebrities hardly ever see the real world."

That's probably true. The ordinary person who comes in contact with a celebrity is nice to him or her because they usually want something, even if it's just an autograph or the chance to tell their friends, "Hey, you'll never guess who I met at the 7-Eleven today." Other celebrities are nice to you because you have a standing in the business, and they don't want to make enemies. But the bigger the celebrity, in many cases, the larger the break with reality. I firmly believe that Frank Sinatra sees no part of the real world. Nobody says to Frank, "You're out of your fucking mind!" Maybe they perceive they'd be dead if they did, but it's also possible that they *could* say things like that to Sinatra and that he might just say, "Yeah, you know, you're right. What the hell was I thinking about?"

But if you're perceived as having a lot of clout, you have to let people around you know it's okay to be honest with you. One of the things I appreciate in my life is that people are free to say to me—and often do—"You're out of your mind, Larry." Tammy Haddad, my executive producer, gives me that perspective. I make allowances for people to tell me when they think I'm off base. But from the general public, I don't get much in the way of flak. I had the new president of El Salvador, Alfredo Cristiani, on my show, and he said, "I watch you all the time, Larry King. I'm one of your biggest fans." He knew the names of a lot of my guests and talked to me about specific shows he'd liked. "Come on down, Larry," he said. "We'll give you the run of the place."

When you always get a good table, you don't know that people stand on line. And my clout is fairly limited. Imagine what kind of treatment Sinatra gets. I don't mean from flunkies, but just from people who deal with him. Is the elevator operator at all rude to him? Is the hotel clerk? Who's nasty to Gregory Peck?

Someone may ask me, "How do you like the Plaza?" I'll say, "Boy, they're terrific."

"You like that place? Shit, they were surly to me."

I don't know that. And it's not a question of Donald Trump giving the word that he wants me treated better than the rest because he likes the exposure he can get on my show. Most service people take a deferential attitude toward celebrities anyway, and they know that if they *are* nasty to someone with clout, they'll be gone in a minute. So the real world may seem at times like a very hazy, distant place to Frank Sinatra. How removed can someone like that become? Let me tell you a story with a slightly different slant that may give you some idea.

Richard Condon, the author, was on my radio show a few years ago, plugging his latest book. I happen to like the way he writes, especially his book about Kennedy, *Winter Kills*. Richard Condon also wrote *The Manchurian Candidate*, the book that the film was based on. So I said to him, "Why don't we see *The Manchurian Candidate?* It's never on television, you can't get it on videocassette, and it doesn't play at the revival houses." I hadn't seen it since it was originally released in 1962, but it was still imprinted in my memory. I couldn't forget those astonishing, surreal brainwashing scenes, the assassination plot, the cold war backdrop, the character based on Senator Joseph McCarthy. Judging solely from memory, I'd have insisted that the film contained the finest screen performances I'd seen by Angela Lansbury, Laurence Harvey, and Frank Sinatra. The director, John Frankenheimer, had been on a roll then, too. His film of William Inge's *All Fall Down*, a critical success, and *The Birdman of Alcatraz*, a box office hit, were released that same year.

But Condon couldn't answer my question. "I don't know," he said. "We were sure happy with the film. Frankenheimer did a great job directing, and we got wonderful reviews. Maybe it was because Kennedy was assassinated soon afterward. Maybe that's why they took it off. But jeez, it's been over twenty years. Somebody ought to bring it back."

"Did you ever write to Frank?" I asked.

"I don't really know Frank," Condon said. "I mean, I met him when they were making the movie, but I couldn't write to him." The guy wrote the *book*, but he doesn't feel comfortable writing a letter to someone who acted in the film, because the someone happens to be Sinatra.

I later discovered that around the time of my interview with Condon, Frank had just changed lawyers. As chance would have it, Sinatra's new lawyer was listening to my show and heard the exchange with Condon. So at his next meeting with Sinatra, he said to him, "Frank, you know any reason why *The Manchurian Candidate* is not shown?"

"I don't know," Frank said. "I never see it. I thought it was a good movie."

The lawyer checked and found out that Sinatra owned it. The deal was that, because he had taken less money for appearing in it, after five years the rights reverted entirely to Sinatra. His lawyer had made a hell of a deal for him, but apparently no one bothered to tell him. So when Sinatra found out, he said, "Release it. I love that movie." That's a true story. And when they finally rereleased the film, it got even bigger raves than twenty-five years earlier because it had held up so well over time. So here's a guy who all these years didn't know that he owned the rights to a classic film.

When I talked with Sinatra, I asked him, "How could you not have heard about it?"

"I don't know," he said.

But he didn't hear about it because he never sits around in restaurants with normal people who might say, "Hey, Frank, whatever happened to *The Manchurian Candidate?*" He did remember the producers' coming to him and saying, "Look, we've got Laurence Harvey and we'd love you to do this part. We can't pay you what you're used to getting paid, but maybe we can work something out."

We watched a scene from the film together on the air, and during the break he told me what a good actor he thought Laurence Harvey was, compared to himself. I like Sinatra's work because he's a reactive actor, but Frank was a little dismissive. He talked about the scene in which he thinks he's on to something and he confronts Harvey's character, Raymond. As we were sitting there, Sinatra said, "Watch this." On the screen, Sinatra goes over to Laurence Harvey, grabs his shoulder, and says, "Raymond, what's wrong?"

Raymond gives him the all-time withering look, and Sinatra

takes his hand away. Frank said to me, "Now look at this scene. I'm the one who's excited. In fact, I'm the only one talking. But you're watching him. That's how good he was, he just needed that look to nail you. Jesus, I didn't have that subtlety."

Sinatra may be capable of that kind of perspective on himself and his talents, but I still say that he doesn't see much of the real world. Even people who have a good reason to get angry are generally not surly to celebrities. I once cut off a guy when I was driving. The guy got mad, hit the horn, and stuck his head out the window. His face was beet red. He was glaring at me, and all of a sudden he recognized me. So he apologized for freaking out. *I* cut *him* off, and he said he was sorry. But I try to live a regular life. CNN offered me a limo to work and back every day in my new contract. I don't want that. I like driving.

Like almost everything else in society, celebrity has its levels of hierarchy. Meeting a major movie star is a much bigger kick than meeting a major political figure. It's much more of a thrill for me to sit next to Burt Lancaster than George Bush. That's because film is larger than life. Even the athlete has become so commonplace that we know him like a brother. We feel as if we've known Magic Johnson and Pete Rose for a hundred years. But when we were kids, sports figures were truly magic. We didn't know what baseball players did in the dugout. Before television, we'd sit in the stands and wonder what they were doing in there. Isn't that true? Now you know what they do. You know exactly how Tony LaRussa looks. We watch Tommy Lasorda checking out the lineup card, drinking from the water fountain, making faces at a bad call. When we were kids, we had a sense of wonderment about all that.

There's nothing about celebrities' lives that people don't know, and that's because they're always being watched.

Alexander Hamilton High School in Los Angeles is a magnet school for outstanding music students from all over L.A., similar to Stuyvesant or Bronx High School of Science in New York City. It happens to be Norm Pattiz's school. He's president of Westward One, which owns Mutual Broadcasting Systems, which carries my radio show. Norm recently donated so much money to Hamilton High that when they redid the auditorium

they named it after him. Norm asked me to come out to emcee
the opening, and since it was the same week I had to be out
there doing a book tour, I agreed to go. This was shortly after
my heart attack, while I was seeing my ex-wife Sharon and
trying to make that relationship work for the 1,743rd time. I
decided to spend the week there with her and see what happened. We had a suite at the Beverly Wilshire, all expenses
paid, so what the hell?

The week started off with a bang. A very nice crowd attended
the auditorium opening. Mayor Bradley was there, and Doc
Severinsen played. It was glitzy but kind of low key. Then suddenly, Don Johnson and Melanie Griffith arrived. They got out
of the car, and the paparazzi went wild. Those guys never
quit—eight thousand flashbulbs went off in a matter of minutes. Don and Melanie were both red hot at the time; Melanie
was a smash in *Working Girl*, and they had announced they
were getting married again. The photographers followed them
into the auditorium and to their seats. At that point, Don Johnson spotted me, and he came over to say hello. Don was standing there with Melanie, and Sharon and I were next to them
chatting away. He was trying to have a normal conversation
with me, saying things like, "Saw your show last night. When
did you get out here?"

Meanwhile the paparazzi were going, "Don, turn this way.
Don, turn that way. Don, over here, please!"

Don was doing his best to ignore them, and he said to me,
"Are you two going to get married again?"

I said, "I don't know."

He said, "We're going to get married again. Because I love
Melanie, and because she's pregnant."

Through all of this, people were literally breathing down his
neck. So I said to him, "How do you live like this?"

"I've learned to act as if it isn't there," he said.

Then someone handed Don one of those supermarket tabloids
with a picture of him and Melanie on the cover. The audience
was being seated, and thirty photographers were hovering
around them. Don said, "I don't remember this picture."

Melanie didn't remember it either. "We never took this picture together," she said. It turned out it was a superimposed

photo. She remembered the outfit she was wearing, which she'd worn only once, to some all-women affair.

"Now here you are," I said, "looking at a superimposed picture of yourself on the cover of a tabloid. Thirty photographers are shooting you, and you're trying to have a conversation. How can you live like this?"

Then Don said to me, "Why don't you come down to Miami?"

I said, "Yeah, we'll go to Joe's Stone Crab."

He said, "Oh, no, no. I can't go to Joe's Stone Crab. But they'll come to me. I'll have them bring over anything you want. Are you kidding, Larry? I can't go out."

Paparazzi are a wild bunch. You could be getting assassinated and they would be popping flashbulbs as your body was falling to the ground. "Larry, this way, please! Can you give us a little more blood, Larry?" Angie Dickinson knows them all, and she chooses to handle it by being nice and friendly. "Hello, Michael. Hello, Phil. Hello, Tim."

And they play to her, too. I've watched them. "Oh, Angie, you look great tonight. I love that dress, Angie. Can we get one more, please?"

But then they step over the line between professionalism and rudeness. When I went someplace with Sharon and they started taking pictures, they would go over to her and ask, "Who are you?" The other person is always "Who are you?" I remember walking into Spago with her once, and a photographer asked her, "Who are you?"

She said, "Sharon."

"Sharon? Oh, I read about you. More pictures!" She went berserk.

It usually takes people a while to get used to it. I took my daughter, Chaia, to the Tyson-Spinks fight in Atlantic City. They had a VIP lane, and I pulled right into it. We got out of the car and there was a crowd of fans waiting to see celebrities. As soon as we got out, they started taking pictures. That was the first time Chaia had seen that kind of manic behavior. She said, "Dad, this is crazy. They could shoot you." Then she whipped out her sunglasses.

Not long after that we went to my nephew's wedding in

Houston, and as we were walking through the Houston airport, people were stopping me. So Chaia said, "I'll be your bodyguard, Dad. If I spot anyone suspicious, I'll throw my body in front of you."

I said, "Chaia, I don't think you'd throw your body in front of me."

"You're probably right," she said. "I'd probably run to the ladies' room."

Aside from a few moments with friendly but obnoxious fans, I've never had any serious problems, though. Still, there is one fan who calls me all the time for no apparent reason. She told me recently that she moved to Virginia from California. I didn't ask why—I was afraid she had moved to be near me. The whole thing started when she wrote me a letter about four or five years ago, and I made the mistake of answering it. I knew from the first phone call, though, that I had no personal interest in her, no romantic interest. When I went out to Los Angeles to do a show, she appeared at the studio, and I met her briefly. She was not attractive, not unattractive, just an ordinary lady of about forty. Then I started getting little packages of baked goods in the mail. She was calling me on my home phone, little calls asking how I was doing. I still don't know how she got the number.

One day she called and said, "Oh, by the way, I'm moving." I asked her where, and she said, "Arlington." I said, "Where in Arlington?" She said, "Right near the Iwo Jima Memorial," which is near where I live. I didn't ask why. She told me that she'd been to my show at the Jefferson Hotel twice, although she never came up and introduced herself. Every so often she calls and says, "Can I talk to you now?" I usually say, "No, you'll have to call me later." She's very polite and just says, "Okay, fine." I never encourage her, although I'm not about to change my number just because of her, either. I'm never rude to her and I don't hang up on her, and I'm afraid to say, "Never speak to me again. Don't you dare call me here." Because you just never know.

But celebrity takes its toll in other, more subtle ways, too. For instance, when I asked Sylvester Stallone how he felt about the fact that now everybody knows him, he insisted that he does pretty much everything he wants to do, despite the recognition factor. "It sometimes causes havoc," he said, "but I make a point of doing things anyway." One thing, though, had become a serious problem.

"I entered this business as a writer," Stallone said, "and now I've lost my ability to be anonymous. I can't go out and observe people. I can't eavesdrop. Everybody eavesdrops on *me*. So the writing I do now is second and third generation."

And sometimes the effects of celebrity are so mundane they sound comical. When I asked Dan Rather if being a celebrity prevented him from doing the things a normal person does, like Christmas shopping on Fifth Avenue, he said that he does go shopping there. But he also told me that he likes going to baseball games and not just watching them on television. When he goes to the ballpark in Baltimore, say, it's not that much of a problem. "But in New York," Dan said, "sometimes I wear my baseball cap and sunglasses and pull my collar up. Then I buy tickets for two or three different seats and I move every couple of innings. That way I can concentrate on the game and enjoy myself."

During the week that I saw Don Johnson and Melanie Griffith in Los Angeles, everyone was telling me I should go to Mateo's in Westwood. Mateo's is a popular Italian restaurant where the locals hang out. Tourists hadn't discovered it yet. Sharon and I pulled up in a limo with my friend Sid Young, with whom I'd grown up and gone to Lafayette High School. As we got out of the car, Art Modell, owner of the Cleveland Browns, was walking out. Art said to me, "How you doing? I had the same surgery you did. Nice crowd in there." That covered all the bases.

We walked inside and took up a position at the bar. Dane Clark came by and asked how I was doing, and I had an immediate emotional reaction. Dane Clark hasn't done a lot of acting lately, but he has always reminded me of my father. Clark is built like my father, looks like him, talks like him, moves like him. It was like watching my father again. As the maître d' was leading us to our table, the first person we passed was Lee Iacocca. He grabbed my arm as we went by. "Larry, how are ya?" So we started talking. "We've got a new Chrysler coming out," Lee said. "I'm going to have you drive it for a week, see how you like it."

I didn't have the heart to tell him I love my Lincoln Town Car and wouldn't think of switching. When we finally got seated, Red Buttons came over to the table and started doing shtick. At the next table was Sidney Sheldon, whom I've interviewed many times. Not far away I saw Mike Douglas. My first thought was, God, this room is packed with celebrities. My second thought was, Whatever happened to Mike Douglas? About twenty yards away, on the other side of the room, Frank Sinatra and Gregory Peck and their wives were sharing a table. All this in one Italian restaurant on a Sunday night, eating pasta and talking across the room at each other. There was no gaping, no autograph hunting, because it was all locals, so the atmosphere was genuinely relaxed.

I counted three Academy Awards in the room (Buttons, Sinatra, and Peck), arguably the major industrial CEO in America, one of the best-selling pop novelists in history, the ultimate pop singer, and a talk show host out of the past. I had to admit I was impressed. I went to the men's room, and as I walked past the bar, two guys were sitting there taking in the room just as I'd been doing a moment before. And one was saying to the other, "Did you see who's here tonight? Frank Sinatra, Lee Iacocca, Larry King."

I couldn't believe it: I had just been saying the same thing, except these guys were including me. It's hard not to let that go to your head. But the truth is, I was more concerned about why Sinatra and Iacocca didn't say hello to each other. Was something going on there? I suddenly felt like Liz Smith. Is this a column item? Barbara Sinatra said good night to Iacocca and his daughter. Frank did not. Gossip fans, read into that what you will.

Before we leave Southern California entirely, let me give you one more example of how celebrities can't do simple, ordinary things. I was walking down Rodeo Drive and Tom Selleck was walking on the other side of the street. He waved and yelled out, "Hey Larry, how you doing? I'm on your show tonight."

That's a very natural thing to do when you see someone you know. And yet the moment he said it, heads started swiveling.

You can't miss that voice. Selleck had inadvertently called attention to himself, and people began to run over and surround him, asking for autographs. From across the street, I could see that look of chagrin on his face. He had forgotten himself just for a moment, forgotten where he was, and had done something totally natural. The result was that he got mobbed.

Not long before my trip west, I'd had a somewhat more pleasant experience in New York City, involving another actor I admire a great deal, William Hurt. Two days after I left the hospital following my bypass surgery, I was at my brother's place in Manhattan when Albert Brooks called me from Los Angeles. "Larry," he said, "we're having a screening of *Broadcast News*, and James Brooks insists that you come."

"But I'm just out of the hospital," I said.

"I know. But it's this Monday, it's in New York, and the whole cast is going to be there. I'm flying in, Larry, so you're coming."

It was my first major adventure outside the hospital. I had gone to dinner with Angie Dickinson, and I had been walking outdoors every day, but this was going to be a big media extravaganza. The surgery had been December 1, and this screening was December 12. We went to the theater, and Mike Wallace and Diane Sawyer came over to tell me how great I looked. I felt like I was onstage. The whole cast of the film was there, including Holly Hunter and Bill Hurt. Albert, meanwhile, was scared of what all these people were going to think of him.

"These are real broadcast people, Larry," he said to me. "I'm not a newsman."

Albert was literally hiding in the back. I kept turning around to look for him during the movie and I could see him shrinking down in his seat. He'd get a big laugh and he'd cover his face with his hands. The minute the movie ended, Albert started to run out of the theater. James Brooks had to yell out, "Albert, you come back here!" He sounded like his father. Albert stopped and came back with a sheepish look on his face.

"Albert," James Brooks said, "here's Larry. You called Larry. You made him come. Now you're running away?"

"I don't want to know what they think about it," was all Albert would say.

"Albert, they loved it," James pointed out. "They applauded for ten minutes. These are broadcast people. They laughed at every line."

"I'm not sure."

When they started to come up to him and shake his hand, Albert would hang his head and say, "Oh, thank you, thank you."

He was so cute. Finally we started to file out, and someone tapped me on the shoulder. I turned around to see William Hurt standing there with his girlfriend. "Do you remember where we met?" he asked me.

"Of course I remember," I said. "It was backstage at *Hurly-burly*."

"Right," he said. And then he said to his girlfriend, "You see, I told you I knew him."

I felt like eighty million bucks. My sister-in-law said, "Boy, did your stock just go up!"

Charles Schulz isn't the kind of celebrity anyone would recognize on the street, but because his *Peanuts* comic strip has exerted such a hold on the American imagination, I've always assumed that he *is* somebody people would love to meet in person. I met Schulz in San Francisco when we did a remote there, as we do about once every two years at the Four Seasons Clift Hotel, one of the world's great ones. I expected the audience to be reverential toward their hero, but a strange thing happened. The celebrity of his comic strip creations had surpassed his own fame. When Schulz took questions from the audience, he found that a lot of people were pissed off at him. They were angry because he allowed the *Peanuts* characters to do commercials for Metropolitan Life, both print and television. Charlie Brown has become a symbol for Met Life, and these people all felt that Charlie Brown should never be commercial for any reason. Schulz took great offense at this. For one thing, he found nothing wrong with a life insurance company. His kids weren't doing anything out of character. But he couldn't change people's opinions. Much as these people worshiped him for the pleasure he'd brought them, they obviously felt that he owed them a certain responsibility and that Charlie Brown and Lucy belonged to them more than to their creator.

But that exchange also showed how we bring our own inflated notions of meaning to what are often very simple things. Schulz has no idea why people identify so much with *Peanuts*. He says that he never reads larger meanings into what he does. He draws what he draws. Lucy takes the football away because she takes the football away, because Lucy is a brat and Charlie's a nice guy. And Charlie's going to miss the football. Schulz is not trying to say that life is a bitch, and we all miss the football. If you read that in, according to Charlie Schulz, that's your problem. I know that people have written long scholarly papers about how *Peanuts* is somehow an extension of all of us. And I guess I'm guilty of some of that same attitude. I used to read *Peanuts* regularly and find great meanings in it that Schulz is saying he didn't put there.

When I was writing a column for the *Miami Herald*, the *Peanuts* distributor, King Features, decided to up the rate the *Miami Herald* would have to pay for the strip. The editors of the *Herald* said, "Nah, they're asking too much. Let's test how popular it is. We'll leave it out tomorrow." The next day the switchboard was out of control. Editors couldn't get calls. Eventually the switchboard became overloaded and broke down. The phone company came on three separate occasions to try to fix it. All because people wanted to know where *Peanuts* was. I told that to Schulz, and he said, "That's what papers do. When they feel a cartoon is slipping, they don't want to pay more. And they leave it out as a test."

As the late John S. Knight, publisher of the *Herald*, told me, "We will never forget this day in our history. We did not need this. We're talking twenty-five dollars a week here."

But that's the power of celebrity—even in a cartoon strip.

7

Celebrity II: Presidents, Billionaires, and Others

When you're talking about celebrity, you can't go very long without acknowledging that the ultimate celebrities in America are the president and First Lady. The first time I met Ronald Reagan was in 1982 at a party in the Rose Garden for the President's Council on Physical Fitness, of which I was a member. George Allen, the former coach of the Redskins, had put me on the President's Council, something I found hilarious. At the time I still smoked three packs a day, I was twenty-five pounds overweight, and my exercise consisted of walking to the mailbox in the morning. But George said to me, "You'll be a big help with media advice." I went to a couple of meetings, after which they sent me letters asking for advice, and I wrote answers back, although I can't tell you what useful suggestions I could possibly have given them. It's a good thing I didn't get paid for this advice, or right now I'd probably be up in front of some congressional investigating committee trying to explain myself.

Ultimately, though, we did get some reward for all this free consultation. They threw a big party for about a hundred members of the council, where we got to meet the president. We all gathered in a room in the White House and proceeded into the Rose Garden, where cocktails were served. Reagan mingled for an hour as George Allen walked around introducing him. I was standing off in a corner of the garden, smoking furiously, when

Reagan caught my eye. He said in a loud voice, across the lawn, "You're a member of the Council on Physical Fitness?"

He used that theatrical, quizzical tone of his, and half the people at the party suddenly turned to look at me. And I said, "I'm the poster boy." Reagan laughed, and I could see that the laugh was genuine. Fortunately, he took the remark in the same humorous vein I'd said it in. I saw him again on a couple of other occasions, and then in 1988 Marvin Hamlisch, who had been conducting a series of concerts at the White House that were taped for broadcast on PBS, asked me if I'd like to be invited to the final one. It was to be given outdoors, and I said, "Sure, I'd like to be invited. And I'd like to take Chaia."

It was held on the White House lawn. A few cabinet members and the head of the FAA were there, along with some heavy hitters from out of town. They had about eight hundred people on the lawn, and afterward we were invited to a small gathering for about twenty people. The bandstand was set up on the lawn, and they put on an all-Broadway show. Nancy got up at the end and sang a little with Hamlisch, and Reagan spoke. Ron and Nancy were seated directly in front of me and Chaia, and as they marched in to "Hail to the Chief" and then sat down, Nancy turned around and grabbed my hand. "How are you?" she said. "You look so good. You've done so well, and I'm so happy for you. We saw your show in Brussels."

Then she reeled off a list of foreign countries where they'd seen my show by satellite. I didn't know what the hell to say, so I said the dumbest thing that came to mind. "Do you watch me in the United States?"

"Sometimes," she said tactfully. "Although at nine o'clock we sometimes have our other programs. But when Maureen was on, we watched." Throughout the performance, she kept looking back at me and winking, just to say, Isn't this terrific? Aren't you enjoying this? Reagan was sitting there, very relaxed, having a good time. He had some lady on the other side of him who obviously bored him to tears, but he was enjoying the show. Afterward we went back inside for the reception. A navy guard took Chaia's arm—all the women had navy guards. Then each person in this group of twenty got to have a picture taken with Ron and Nancy in different parts of the room. Chaia and I were standing to one side with Hamlisch when Ron and Nancy came over. I heard Reagan ask Chaia what she was going to do after college. Chaia said, "I don't know."

"Why don't you be an actress?" Reagan said. "You're pretty. It's easy. Who can't do it? If I can do it, and Nancy can do it, you can do it." Meanwhile Nancy was talking to me about favorite guests and who I'd like to have on my show. It all seemed so genuine that it never occurred to me that maybe they were well prepped or just acting. If they really watched my show as much as Nancy said they did, they had to know that I was no fan of the Reagan administration. But that was the Reagans' charm, I suppose. Either he was a consummate actor who could pretend to like you if he wanted to, or he was just having so much fun being president and working a few hours a day that he didn't care if you were for him or not.

At any rate, Chaia was thrilled. She started saying things like, "Hey, he ain't so bad." Then we stood on the lawn, and some aide said, "Did you know that on the roof of that building"—he pointed to the Office of Management and Budget, that gingerbread house next door to the White House—"there's an antiballistic missile?" The aide wasn't kidding. He explained to Chaia how it works. If a missile is coming at the White House, that ABM goes up. But as he was talking I couldn't help thinking, That's just a mile from my home. What if it went off by accident? I don't think it's nuclear, but still. So now I drive through the tranquillity of Washington thinking about that ABM on the roof. He also told us that there are always two men stationed on the roof of the White House. Just in case.

Ron and Nancy were both exceedingly nice, and they had to be led away from the party. Someone came over and said, "Mr. President. . . ." They didn't duck out of it. But for all Reagan's charm—and he genuinely does make you feel that he likes you—I found a lack of curiosity that was disturbing. Let's just say he's more personable than intellectually impressive.

In contrast, I found Nancy not only surprisingly attractive but also far more interested in things than Ron was. He's a guy you can't hate, but he's not a character. She strikes me as having the capacity to be a true Shakespearean character, full of guile and bile, the power behind the throne, so to speak. Russell Baker recently described Lyndon Johnson to me as one of the great modern figures equivalent to those of Greek or Shakespearean drama. He said, "Lyndon Johnson was King Lear." He was the only president Baker would put in that category. LBJ was larger than life and extremely complicated, driven and manic, and, Baker believed, suicidal. He believed that Johnson went back to smoking after the Vietnam War in a wish to die. Don't forget, Johnson had had a heart attack and surgery and had stopped smoking in 1954. But he went back to smoking the day he returned to his ranch after leaving the White House.

Reagan boasts no such complications. You never got the impression that Reagan would have said during his presidency, "God, what a dilemma. What are we going to do?" It's hard to imagine now, for instance, that George Bush is calling him for advice. Nixon, yes; Carter, yes; Ford, maybe; Reagan, never. Oh, maybe for advice on how to handle a meeting with the families of servicemen who died or something like that—the emotional show. But "How should I handle this crisis with the Russians?" No way. You can gather all that in the five to ten minutes you spend chatting with the man.

But I could see why people said, "Boy, is he a nice guy." I'll tell you what he didn't have—guile. You knew Nixon had guile, and Johnson was heavy on guile, and even Kennedy could screw you over pretty good. Reagan had none of that. I would never worry that Reagan might be up at two in the morning saying, "Get me Larry King's income tax returns. Let's see what we got on this guy." I'm sure he had no enemies list.

When I say that the president and First Lady are the ultimate celebrities, I'm also talking about the most desirable of celebrity perks—convenience. People always say that money isn't everything, that it can't buy you love, peace, or happiness, and they're probably right. But one of the things money *can* buy is convenience: first-class airplane tickets, limo service, preregistration in hotels, that sort of thing. You never have to sign anything; they just bill you. You don't see the little vagaries of life. What most people imagine about that part of celebrity is true. Maybe you can't buy love or serenity, but when you're going to New York, there's a room for you at the Plaza. There'll be a limo waiting at the train station or the airport, so you don't have to worry about standing in line for a cab. Your hotel room will be ready and someone will hand you a key the minute you arrive; you're upstairs and you're in. There's a certain serenity in all that.

When you get used to the conveniences, you can sometimes forget what it was like when you had to do everything yourself. Even though I still carry my own bags at the airport, I'm under no illusion that I lead a "normal" life. But there are levels of celebrity convenience way beyond mine, even further removed from what it's like for the rest of the country, not to mention the world. These hierarchical levels rise like a pyramid, with the president and First Lady occupying the uppermost, gold-encrusted apex. The president of the United States is the only American who lives without any inconvenience at all. (I say American, because I'm assuming that the Sultan of Brunei has it even better, but who knows for sure?)

Even Frank Sinatra and Donald Trump don't get clearance at the airport. They may have their private jets, but they have to wait in line for takeoff like everyone else. The president doesn't have to wait. In fact, he doesn't even leave from the airport. The president flies from Andrews Air Force Base. I wasn't surprised to hear those stories about Nancy getting depressed in her last days at the White House. She was beginning to realize that the incredible convenience of the previous eight years was not going to continue. No amount of money or Galanos gowns and no amount of well-heeled friends in Beverly Hills could give her and Ronnie that luxury. All of this, of course, raises one obvious question. If someone of my celebrity status can sometimes seem removed from the real world, and if a Frank Sinatra is even further removed, then why is it that the man who is entrusted with running the country and looking after a couple of hundred million people is the furthest removed from reality of anyone in America? Just thought I'd ask.

If you can't be president, maybe the next best thing is to have dinner with him. In May of 1989, I was invited to a state dinner in honor of King Fahd of Saudi Arabia. I invited my executive producer, Tammy Haddad, to accompany me. Fahd then canceled, and the dinner was rescheduled for September. By that time I'd met Julie Alexander and had become engaged to be married, so Tammy suggested I take my fiancée instead. I asked Julie, but she wouldn't hear of Tammy's not going. Then Fahd canceled again, and the White House decided to invite everyone who had been invited to the Fahd dinner to a dinner for the president of Mexico, Salinas de Gortari, in October. The security arrangements for a state dinner are almost comically severe. No matter who you are, you have to bring identification with your picture on it, such as a driver's license or passport. The night of the dinner, Tammy and I got to the East Gate and the three guys there—the one checking the IDs, the one in charge of security, and another guy—all said to me, "Hey, Larry, how are ya?" The security head said, "Man, we're up late at night a lot here, and you're our savior."

"Gee, thanks," I said.

And then he said, "Okay, ID please."

You walk into the grand foyer and proceed downstairs where fifty violinists are playing cocktail music while news photographers take pictures and reporters ask you questions. The big question for me was, "Where is your fiancée?" A Marine guard escorts each woman into the cocktail room and into the dining room. In fact, you can't go to the bathroom alone; a Marine guard escorts you to the door of the restroom. It was the day of the failed Panamanian coup against Noriega, and none of the heads of state, including Baker and Bush, seemed the least bit perturbed. Baker said this was only the first of several coup attempts we might see over the next year or so, and eventually Noriega would be ousted.

On entering the room, you are formally announced, and you mingle. Barbara Walters and her husband, Merv Adelman, came up to me. Then we got on a reception line, and we approached Bush and Salinas and their wives, as an aide whispered into the president's ear the name of each guest. In my case, Bush recognized me and gave me a nice introduction to the president of Mexico, who happens to be a Harvard graduate.

Then you go into the main room for the dinner party. There was no dais, just fourteen tables with ten people at each table. Dan Quayle was the host of my table. I sat next to Merv Adelman and Alma Powell, the wife of General Colin Powell. A marching band played the American and Mexican national anthems, the president gave a brief toast, the Mexican president gave a very long toast, about ten minutes, and after that it was a party. And as a party, it was everything you've dreamed of. Strolling violinists, wonderful food, great wines and champagne (all domestic, naturally), and great conversation. Also at my table was a lawyer named John O'Connor, a really nice guy who began the conversation by mentioning that the wife of my namesake, the playwright Larry L. King, is one of his law partners. Then we got to talking about greed. O'Connor said that the downside of capitalism is evident in how greedy America has become. "These punks on Wall Street are stealing from people, selling short," he said. "They deserve to go to jail." It was an interesting conversation, and as we were walking out I said that I'd like to say hello to his wife. At these dinners they split everyone up. You don't sit with your spouse or whoever you came with. "Sure, she's right over there," he said, pointing to Sandra Day O'Connor. It had never occurred to me the whole time we were talking to ask what his connection to the dinner was. I'm just glad I hadn't started talking about what a mess the Supreme Court was in.

Merv Adelman, who founded Lorimar Pictures, told an amusing story. We assume that famous people in the same line of work all know each other. We think Angie Dickinson knows Lee Remick, that Oprah knows Donahue. Adelman had been having lunch that day with Dick Munro, the chairman of the board of Time Inc., and at the next table was Mort Zuckerman, chairman of *U.S. News & World Report*. But Adelman had to introduce them to each other because they'd never met.

You don't table hop during the dinner, but afterward there's plenty of time to talk while you're having coffee on the veranda with the president. The Secret Service is pretty much absent by then, so it gets very convivial. That's when James Baker told me he watches my show all over the world and uses it to set his watch as he changes times zones. He said that when you travel as much as he does, you have to pick a time zone and live in it for a couple of weeks at least, or else you go bananas. That week he was on central time.

I also had a talk with Colin Powell, the new chairman of the Joint Chiefs. He said, "I live next door to you." I couldn't believe it. I said, "You live in my building?"

"No," he said, "I live in Fort Myer. I'm in my third house there." For Myer *is* next door to where I live. I forgot for a moment that generals don't live in private homes. Every time he got a promotion, they moved him into a different house in Fort Myer. Powell told me he never thinks about being black in relation to his job, although he's always aware of it outside of work. For instance, he frequently talks to Jesse Jackson, which surprised me a little. Powell is not what you would call active in civil rights, but he gives Jackson advice on anything he can. "I believe in the military, and defense of this country is my number one job," Powell said. "I'm not a black man in this job. I'm Colin Powell, and I love it. I love parades. But I can never forget I'm black."

I also chatted briefly with Brent Scowcroft, the president's national security adviser, who had been on my show when he was in Ford's administration. He was violently opposed to SDI in the early days, so it's interesting to me that he's now Bush's security adviser. I told Scowcroft that I'd seen Bud McFarlane that very day, walking all alone down Connecticut Avenue. McFarlane had come over and said hello to me, and no one recognized him or went over to him. So I said to Scowcroft, "Doesn't that give you pause for thought?"

"Yeah," he said. "It tells me a lot about where *I'm* gonna be in a few years—walking along Connecticut Avenue with no one saying hello to me."

Tony Quinn, whom I had interviewed on TV only a few weeks before, was there with his wife, Iolande, and we talked about acting and interviewing. But when Douglas Fairbanks, Jr., joined us, it turned into a very emotional moment. When I'd interviewed Quinn, he'd talked about how he had been born to a dirt-poor Mexican family and had grown up in East Los Angeles. He described how he had become interested in drawing. From the time he was seven, Quinn had drawn pictures of celebrities from movie magazines and mailed the pictures to them, asking if they would like to buy them. None of the stars had ever bought one, except Douglas Fairbanks, Sr., who'd sent him $25 for his drawing. That was as much money as Quinn's father earned in a week, and it had flipped Tony out. So when he told Fairbanks the story at the dinner, and what his father's gesture had meant to Tony and his family, they ended up embracing each other. Then again, Tony was hugging a lot of people. He kept putting his arm around me and saying, "Hey, a Mexican boy, a Jewish kid, what are we doin' here? I mean, Lincoln ate in this room. Who woulda thunk it?" Meanwhile, what was going through my head was, Who woulda thunk it that I'd be standing here trading stories with Tony Quinn?

Later we went into yet another room where Judy Kaye sang show tunes for about twenty minutes, followed by dancing in the main hall of the White House, right behind the Pennsylvania Avenue entrance that you always see in photos. I was dancing with Tammy, and Bush was dancing with his wife, and we were the only four people on the dance floor. That's a heady feeling, to be dancing in the White House and the only other couple on the floor is the president and the First Lady—even if they are Republicans. As I was watching all this, Joseph Reed, the chief of protocol, cut in on the president, and then Bush cut in on me.

As Bush cut in, he asked where my fiancée was. Bush knew Tammy from when I'd interviewed him on CNN, so I went through the whole story about why she wasn't there. Then as he was dancing, I grabbed him by the shoulder and said, "You're the kind of guy who would do this. Julie's home alone in Philly. She could've come here tonight, but she insisted that Tammy come. Would you call her?"

"You bet," he said. I gave him the number, and Julie told me he called at about 11:30 and talked to her for ten minutes about her job as a legal headhunter. Julie is a Republican, although more of a Rockefeller or Scranton Republican than a Reaganite, and Bush asked her if she thought that between the two of them they could convert me.

The whole evening had the kind of relaxed atmosphere that made that scene on the dance floor seem almost normal, which was kind of surprising to me since I'd expected more formality. I talked about that with Bonnie Studdert, whose husband, Stephen, had been Reagan's assistant for special activities. This was their last state dinner. She told me they had found Washington so strange when they first arrived, and now that they'd finally gotten used to it, they were going back to Salt Lake City. They're Mormons, but after eight years in D.C. they would have to readjust to life in Utah.

Bonnie explained to me the difference between a Reagan state dinner and a Bush state dinner. Under Reagan, these affairs were much more formal, more likely to be white tie than black tie like this one. You could order hard liquor during cocktail hour under Reagan. With Bush, there was no bar setup; they just served you wine. The table settings were different, too. Reagan always occupied the most prominent table. At this dinner, Bush was at table 12; I was at table 1. It didn't matter that much. The atmosphere in the room was different because the tone was set by the Bushes. Barbara was having a good time, whereas, Bonnie said, Nancy would have been much more conscious of where everyone was in the room, how they were seated, whether the protocol was just so. Maybe it's the difference between old money and new money. The old money Bushes are much more relaxed in those situations; they don't need the show. The new money, Hollywood Reagans lived for the show, the pomp, the imperial presidency.

This was all confirmed by the chief of protocol, Joe Reed. With Bush, anything can happen at a moment's notice. One afternoon they were sitting around and Bush said, "Aw, let's go out for dinner." That day in the Oval Office, a friend of Bush's had told him about a new Italian restaurant in town called I Ricchi, so now Bush wanted to try it out. It was four in the afternoon and suddenly Reed had to call the Secret Service and make arrangements to eat at I Ricchi. And the press had to go along and wait outside, because ever since the Kennedy assassination someone from the press corps goes wherever the president goes in case he's killed. They don't leave the White House until the president retires for the night.

Reagan never would have done that on the spur of the moment. Nancy might have gone to the Jockey Club once a month, but that would have been planned a month in advance. Most of the time Reagan preferred to stay home and watch movies, which somehow doesn't surprise us. But Bush just hops up and out the door, which, come to think of it, is what Jack Kennedy used to do. I know there's a famous Lloyd Bentsen line in here someplace, but since George was nice enough to call my fiancée at home, I won't use it.

Maybe I just have a soft spot for people who are nice to me and my loved ones. Most of my friends don't understand why I like Donald Trump, but for one thing, I know I could count on him in a pinch. That said, though, I also like Trump because he is what he is. I don't know him that well, but as big a celebrity as he may be, I think he's still a straight guy. Once when I was in Atlantic City, I asked the guy who parks cars at the Trump Castle what he thought of Trump and he told me he was a terrific guy to work for. He said he paid fair wages, treated the help well, and it was a good place to work. What more can you ask from an employer? I know he has an enormous ego, but so did Sam Goldwyn and Louis B. Mayer, and we still love the movies they made.

I'm also certain that Trump must be a vicious competitor, yet the public loves him. Although Americans tend to elect wealthy, aristocratic presidents, they often display a general hostility to the rich. Iacocca was okay until Chrysler closed down its plant in Wisconsin. His second book didn't sell nearly so well after he put five thousand people out of work. Yet for all Trump's billions and all his cockiness, people love him. They love his yachts, his excess. He's the ultimate yuppie fantasy: born rich, he just gets richer and richer. But not only yuppies identify with him. Blacks like Trump; Puerto Rican cab drivers *love* him. Why isn't he disliked by the working class? I have to believe that Trump is tuned into some frequency of the popular mind-set that is inaccessible to most of the people I know.

And I'll tell you one thing, he doesn't take himself as seriously as you might think. One night Don Rickles walked on my show in Atlantic City, and he tore up Trump on the air while Trump sat in the audience laughing.

"Donald Trump, I think, is a moron," Don said.

"A what?" I asked weakly.

"A moron," Don said. "I met Donald Trump. He's a thirty-eight-year-old guy. His father is fantastic. His dad, God bless him, owned property in Brooklyn and said to me, 'Don, I'm so rich, I gave it to the kid.' I came up to New York with my wife and I said, 'Let's see if I can get an apartment at Trump Tower.' This is true. My wife and I came up to the office where you look for apartments. And every apartment in Trump Tower is two million six, seven million nine, forty million. It's so great, your tuchis starts to hum. The place was unbelievable. And Trump is saying, 'Don, for nine million six, you and your wife can see helicopters go past the room while you're making love.' And I threw up on him.

"Come on, Donald," Rickles said to Trump's face, "you inherited money. Your father built all this stuff. He left you some money, and now he's somewhere in Queens, and he don't even know there's a Trump Tower. It's his name, Donald, not yours. They got your old man in a room somewhere, feeding him a little cheese. He's dribbling his milk, and they tell him, 'Your son's doing okay.' "

It was borderline tasteless, as always with Rickles, but Trump never looked offended. Maybe that was what made him trip over the thin line between bad taste and good humor one night. Donald can take a joke, but as for making jokes, well. . . . I was interviewing him on TV and he suddenly said to me, "Do you mind if I sit back a little, because your breath is very bad?"

I gave him a blank look. "It really is," he said. "Has this been told to you before?"

"No," I said.

"Okay," Trump said, "then I won't bother."

I had been talking about his phenomenal success and his book and his board game, and my last question had been, "How do you do all this?" So although his answer took me completely by surprise, after a moment I recovered and realized what he was trying to do. "That's how you get the edge, isn't it?" I said finally.

"Okay, Larry," Trump said, smiling. "Your breath is great."

Then on the break, he asked me, "Larry, was that funny?"

"I don't think it worked," I said.

Trump looked concerned. At the time, I thought he had been trying to show me how he gets the edge over people. Maybe he was, but he also thought he was being funny, which shows a lack of judgment. That remark caused some uproar. It was reported the next day in the *New York Post*, which incorrectly stated that I was fuming over the exchange. All sorts of people came up to me after that show and told me how angry they were at Trump—people I would not expect to have noticed or cared, like Gloria Steinem. Penn Gillette of Penn and Teller mentioned it on the air when they were on my show, referring to him as "that rat bastard Donald Trump." Fortunately we were taping at the time and were able to bleep it.

I didn't have a problem with it myself because I knew Trump didn't mean it. He probably thought it would be a funny way to make a point.

Still, Trump has done something that is no mean feat: he has become a well-liked billionaire. Then again, as Herb Cohen says, Donald Trump may have no money. We don't know. These guys don't know when they have money. Remember Everett Dirksen's great line? Someone said that a new project would cost a billion dollars, but that wasn't really a lot of money. Dirksen said, "No, that's not a lot. But a billion here, a billion there, pretty soon it adds up to real money."

For all Trump's money, though, it's clearly not enough. More than just being rich, Trump wants something else as well—he wants to be famous. That's why he wrote those editorials, why he wrote that book, why he talks about running for president. That's why he surrounds himself with as much celebrity as possible. When Trump threw a party at Trump Plaza the night of the Tyson-Spinks fight, it was his way of saying that he wants to be the next Malcolm Forbes. Among the guests were Stephen King, who was there with his son. King's son is a double for him, a fourteen-year-old with glasses, a little bow tie, and a dark suit just like his dad's. Jack Nicholson was at the party, and Warren Beatty was sitting right next to him. They both said hello to Chaia, who was twenty-one at the time, but Warren Beatty didn't mean a thing to her. After Nicholson shook hands with her, she ran out into the hall and telephoned her mother to say, "I just shook hands with Jack Nicholson!" That's the relativity of celebrity. Jackie Mason, who was at the height of his recent popularity, was wandering around with nobody paying any attention to him. He looked as lonely and melancholy as he did when I interviewed him in Miami in 1968. Then Jesse Jackson walked in, and the room lit up for a moment as people surrounded him.

And Donald Trump lit up right with them. Here were all these people at his party, *his* party. He was a success.

Money is a funny thing, though. I recently encountered what may be the most lavish hotel suite I've ever seen. After Henri Lewin took over the Sands in Vegas, he invited me out to spend a weekend in the presidential suite, the same one that the Reagans had used in 1982. The suite was so big that, although I shared it with Chaia and my friend Joyce Downey, it would have been possible for the three of us to spend the entire three days in the suite and never see each other—or anyone else in the hotel, for that matter. We had our own private entrance. We had our own pool and our own garden. There was a concert grand piano and a billiard room in the suite, and a limo was always parked outside our private entrance so that we could go anywhere undetected by the masses. Unless we chose to go to the casino, we never had to walk through the hotel lobby.

Although I make a lot of money, I don't consider myself a wealthy person. Yet I think this is the way rich people live most of the time, and it was very new to me. I certainly could have afforded this kind of treatment for three days, although I didn't have to pay for it since it was a gift. But all I kept thinking was, "Where were these people when I needed them, when I was really broke?" On the other hand, it's hard to keep my daughter from believing that this is the way life is. As Joyce said, "This *is* the way life is for her. You can't make her a coal miner's daughter."

I haven't talked about it much, but if celebrity has its funny moments, it certainly has a dark underside too. In the past couple of years, I've met the ex-wives of two well-known athletes, Shari Theismann and Cyndy Garvey, and it's kind of chilling to hear horrifying stories about your former sports idols. We all know that Babe Ruth had a drinking problem and Ty Cobb was a racist, but their vices seem to dim with age while their accomplishments rise higher in the mind's eye. But Steve Garvey and Joe Theismann are athletes I often watched in their playing days and admired as much for their skill as for their guts and poise. In Joe Theismann, we all saw a football hero and a doting father. But according to Shari, he was not interested in his kids at all. He was never in tune with them and didn't have time for them. He was so caught up with his girlfriend, Cathy Lee Crosby, that he lost all touch with his family.

Shari found out about it only through Chuck Conconi, the columnist with the *Washington Post.* Conconi called the house to get a comment on the impending divorce, and she answered the phone. She talked to Chuck, hung up the phone, and said, "Joe, what is he talking about?"

"Oh, yeah, honey," Theismann supposedly said. "I gotta talk to you. I'm filing for divorce."

Cyndy Garvey said that Steve had no interest in the team, only in himself, his stats, where he stood in the individual rankings, how he felt, what counted to him. She said that Steve would rather go three for four and lose than go one for four and win. Dodger blue didn't mean anything to him. That was so unlike the image that at first I thought she was just bitter. But after a while it started making sense. She said he was screwing every woman in sight. After the Wade Boggs–Margo Adams case hit the papers, this kind of thing didn't seem so bizarre, but back then it was strange stuff, especially considering what Steve Garvey represented. He always signed every autograph; he always said the right thing; his hair was always combed. He was always conscious that the camera might be on him. And everything in his life pointed to the same conclusion. Take a look at Steve's career stats: .312, .319, .317, .316, .315, 33 homers, 21 homers, 28 homers, 26 homers. He was a model of consistency. Except off the field.

Speaking of Wade Boggs, in 1988 I did a live broadcast from the All-Star Game party, a two-hour TBS special the night before the game. Peter Ueberroth and Bart Giamatti were my guests. The party was held at the Cincinnati Zoo and it was the best sports party I ever attended. I used to think Super Bowl parties were great, but for the All-Star party the whole zoo was opened up, with food served in a special area. All the people who participated in the All-Star Game—players and team officials—were walking around the zoo. The camera kept moving, so one time I might be in front of the gorillas, and then they'd cut away and come back to me in front of the rhinos. They built a little set by the center of the zoo for me to work from, and we were doing everything as it happened. We had runners going around the zoo looking for players to come and do brief walk-ons with me. They'd see Dave Winfield and ask him, "Hey, Dave, wanna come on with Larry King?" And they'd bring him over.

It came off as a happening. Then the runner found Wade Boggs, and Wade said, "Sure, I'll come on."

I could see Wade coming toward me, and I said, "And now, Wade Boggs is coming to our microphone." Boggs had a woman with him, walking just in front of him. As he got closer to me, he started pointing to her from behind and mouthing words for me to see. I couldn't make out what he was trying to say, until he got close enough for me to read his lips. *"Wife!"* he was mouthing. "It's my *wife.*" I guess he didn't want me to get her confused with someone else.

But if he weren't such a sports celebrity, would anyone have cared who he was carrying on with? Would I have cared about Joe Theismann's callousness or Steve Garvey's self-absorption? Nope, but that's the price you pay. You get the perks and you also get the pain.

Here's one final story about the privileges of celebrity, although in this case it was kind of a mixed blessing.

Bijan is a well-known clothing designer and perfumer born in Iran. He has a store in New York and a store in Beverly Hills, and I've had him on the show a couple of times. We've talked after the shows, although really nothing more than that. Then one day just before Christmas 1988, I was strolling down Fifth Avenue with my ex-wife Sharon. As we were walking past his store, Bijan himself happened to be in the window, fixing the window display. He tapped on the glass, and when we looked up he waved us into the store, which is open by appointment only. He showed us through the store himself, and my eye was caught by a gorgeous black leather jacket, suede on the outside, leather on the inside. The chain on the back that you hang up the jacket with was pure gold. It had lots of detail, little coils and loops and leather straps everywhere. I tried it on, and it felt great. I said, "How much is this?"

Bijan said, "Six thousand dollars."

I sort of laughed. I thanked him, and we left the store. Then about a week before Christmas, a package was delivered to me by UPS. It was a Bijan box, and inside was the black leather jacket. The card said, "Merry Christmas," signed Bijan. I couldn't believe it. I tried it on. It looked even better than it had looked in the store. I was supposed to go to the Palm that night. Chaia was coming in from school and we were going to have dinner together. I said, "Wait till Chaia sees me in this!" As I was walking out of my apartment to meet Chaia, I went to zip the jacket up. The zipper broke in my hand. Broke right off its hinge. I couldn't even zip the jacket shut.

So, I thought, what do I do? I mean, he *gave* me the jacket. Do I take the jacket that Bijan gave me back to the store and tell him that his zipper broke? That didn't feel right. So I went to my tailor, Arthur Adler, in Washington. I asked him, "Can you please fix the zipper?" I left the jacket, and Arthur called me a couple of days later. "Larry," he said, "to fix it the way it was, we have to remove the zipper, replace the entire thing. It requires undoing a lot of intricate leather work. It's going to cost you seven hundred and fifty dollars just for the workmanship."

"That's a lot of money for a zipper, Arthur," I said.

"Look," he said, "there's another way we can do it. It'll require changing the original design of the jacket a little. But it'll be simple to do and we'll only have to charge you two hundred and fifty."

"Fine, let's go for that."

When I got the jacket back from Arthur, it looked okay, and I couldn't tell the difference. Then one day I noticed that I'd gotten it dirty. I couldn't get the dirt off. I didn't know what it was. I sprayed a little suede cleaner on it, brushed it, and it suddenly started getting spotty all over. The suede cleaner just made it worse. And, of course, all my friends had different opinions. Somebody said, "Maybe it's reversible. Turn it inside out, you won't see the spots."

No such luck. Then Sharon told me, "I don't like that leather strap around the collar. It would look much better without it."

So I took the strap off, I put it away somewhere, and now fifteen different people were telling me, "Hey Larry, the collar looks weird. Looks like something's missing there. You can see the loops, but there's no strap." So I went to put the leather strap back, but I couldn't find it. Wherever I put it, it's lost for good.

Then I went out to California. Whenever I'm in Los Angeles, I like to stay at the Beverly Wilshire and walk around the Beverly Hills High School track. It's a great place to do workouts. But a lot of celebrities walk there and you never know who you might run into, so you want to look good. Naturally, I wear my Bijan jacket. So I'm doing my walk in my leather jacket, not thinking, and as I walk I start to sweat. When you sweat in a fine leather jacket, it really hurts the leather. It gets stained, and it starts to smell.

Not long after that, I was in New York and I decided to go over to Nate and Al's in Brooklyn wearing my jacket. All my friends from Lafayette High School were there, and I started telling the story of my Bijan jacket. I asked my friend Sid Young, "What do you think this jacket costs?"

Sid said, "Boy, Larry, that's some nice jacket. That's probably two seventy-five."

I said, "That was the zipper."

By now I was beginning to think of this jacket as some kind of curse, and it was really starting to look bad. Back in Washington, I decided to bring it to a dry cleaner. There was a big sign in the window that says, WE SPECIALIZE IN CLEANING LEATHER! It cost $37 and took a couple of weeks. When it came back I noticed that the elastic that holds the jacket around your waist had lost its elasticity. I could also see that they cleaned the stain but somehow ended up discoloring the whole jacket. I now had what could best be described as a fairly ugly $6,000 leather jacket.

The next time I was in California I thought, The hell with it, I'm bringing it back to Bijan. Maybe they can tell me what to do with it. So I took it to his store in Beverly Hills, and fortunately Bijan wasn't there. The store manager, though, was horrified. She cried out in physical pain at the sight, "Oh my God, and with our Bijan label on it."

The jacket had a Bijan insignia, so the whole world could see that this Bijan product looked like a piece of garbage. "You've ruined our jacket!" she said contemptuously. So now it was my fault. She proceeded to read me the Rules of Bijan, which state that when you buy anything at Bijan, if you need it cleaned, repaired, or altered in any way, you send it by Federal Express, collect, to the Bijan store nearest you. They will fix it, clean it, and Fed Ex it back to you, free of charge. That's all part of the Bijan service. I said, "But I got it free."

"It's still part of the Bijan service," she said. "It's still free. We'll be happy to clean and repair this for you."

Three weeks later, I got it back, and frankly now it's a very nice, ordinary-looking black leather jacket. I still love the way it feels, because it's wonderful soft leather. But nobody ever came running over to me and said, "God, what a beautiful jacket!" Which is all I ever wanted to hear.

Now Bijan will read this story or someone will tell him about it and he'll hate me for the rest of my life. Sounds like an Alan King story, but it's all true. That's the mixed blessing of fame.

8

The Writing Life

In my previous books, I've written at some length about what makes a good guest. But all my expertise must not count for much, since I'm still not allowed to book my own guests. My executive producer on television, Tammy Haddad, believes I have so much natural curiosity about people that I think *everyone* is interesting. "The problem with television," she tells me, "is that the audience won't wait. You've got to deliver within a minute. Some guests might start telling wonderful stories once you get them warmed up. But they won't work on TV because you don't have those extra five or ten minutes to warm them up."

I love to interview smart guests. To me, the more articulate, the better. But as Tammy has said to me more than once, "Articulate is for PBS, it's for MacNeil-Lehrer. This is prime-time TV. People aren't going to stop what they're doing to watch articulate. They want someone who's going to emote, who's going to be able to tell the story in dramatic terms." Once when I asked her what she and Randy Douthit, my senior producer at CNN, were aiming for with their bookings, she told me bluntly. "Larry," she said, "we're trying to beat that clicker. We sit there in the control room sometimes, saying to each other, 'Did you hear that sound? It's the sound of millions of people changing the channel.'"

For Tammy, literary people make prime candidates for the clicker. "We have a philosophy," she told me, "that, as a rule, writers make lousy guests because they're better at writing than they are at talking about it."

Well, I can't agree with that altogether, and in this chapter I'm going to give you some reasons why.

Take Matthew Lesko. You may not remember his name, but if you happened to catch him on either my radio or television show you'd remember his voice and enthusiasm. Matthew Lesko is wild, excitable, passionate, and funny. He comes on and talks about all the bargains and deals you can get from the government but that you probably never heard of.

I never expected his wild personality. Off the air, he is as calm as can be. The first time I interviewed him was on the radio, back when I was doing my show from midnight to five. I had arrived at the studio feeling really tired. Matthew was going to be on for three hours, and the title of his book was *Getting Yours: The Complete Guide to Government Money*. It was a huge tome. He was sitting there with his wife, both fans of mine but both very quiet. I went into the control room and said to the producer, "This is going to be a long night. This guy is sort of laid-back and boring. He's got this enormous book about the government, and I'm really not looking forward to this." The producer tried to reassure me, without much success.

Then I went on the air. "Good evening, ladies and gentlemen. Welcome to the *Larry King Show*. My guest is Matthew Lesko. Mr. Lesko has written a book called *Getting Yours: The Complete Guide to Government Money*. How did you get this idea?"

"How did I get this idea, Larry? I'll *tell* you how I got this idea!" He started rattling off information so fast he blew me off the chair. The night went by like two minutes. Among other things, he told the story of Mr. Potato. "Someone hired me to find out whether he should invest in Maine potatoes," Lesko began. "He was willing to pay me twenty-five thousand dollars if I would be his consultant and answer his questions about potatoes as an investment. But where do you start? Well, did you know there's a man at the Department of Agriculture who sits at the Potato Desk? In fact, they call him Mr. Potato. There's also Mr. Tomato, Mr. Carrot, and so forth. Do you know what his job is, Larry? Forecasting. He's available to the public, absolutely free. Every bit of information on the potato and potato farming is sent to him—weather information, productivity, sales and profits in potato farming, everything. Mr. Potato publishes pamphlets on the subject, and any citizen can visit him at any time."

It sounds crazy but it was fascinating. Lesko is not one of these get-rich-quick-through-real-estate guys, and he's not into government auctions or that kind of thing. But he'll tell you how you can get a scholarship or how the government will help you do your income tax—not just answer questions on the phone, but actually sit down with you and help you do it. You don't have to go to H & R Block. So I loved Matthew from that night, and now I look forward to having him on.

Stephen King probably has had more of his books transferred to the big screen than any author besides Ian Fleming. He is one of the most popular guests I've ever had, and one of the most down to earth. It's hard to believe he's sold so many millions of books, because he shows up at the studio wearing a beat-up flannel shirt and jeans and carrying a six-pack. In the course of two hours on the radio, he finishes the six-pack and is as relaxed and articulate as when he walked in.

One night I began by asking him about the five other books he has written under the name Richard Bachman. I asked him if these were manuscripts he hadn't published before he got popular, and he told me they were. "I've been writing since I was about six," King said. "And the first novel that I ever wrote, I wrote in college. I was nineteen, and it was called *The Long Walk*. I submitted it to a first-novel competition, got a form rejection slip, and never sent it out again. I probably still have four novels in the trunk even now. They just happen to be DOA. They're not good books."

"So how do you judge your own manuscripts?"

"My definition of how you know when a book is a bad book," he said, "is that even if you're drunk you can't read it and say, 'This is a good book.' It's just a bad book. But there were several books from that earlier time that I thought were all right. And so, after I became successful, I had a chance to publish them under a pseudonym as paperback originals. A lot of the books that I read and loved as a kid were paperback originals by unknown writers like John D. MacDonald, Elmore Leonard, and Ed McBain, who have since become better known. I got away with it four times, and then I stopped because I felt that Richard Bachman was dead.

"Then I had this book called *Thinner*, and it read a little too much like a Stephen King novel, so it didn't quite hold water. What finally happened was that a guy who works in a Washington, D.C., bookstore and also in the Library of Congress went back and looked up some old copyright information, and it was the *Smoking Gun*."

I asked Stephen if this was the last of the Bachman books, and he said, "Yes. I think he died—cancer of the pseudonym."

"And the picture on the back of the books?"

"He's a tire salesman from Minneapolis," Stephen said. "He's a friend of my agent's."

"Does he get a cut?"

"I think he got five hundred dollars and a trip to New York out of it. But he's a great-looking guy. Some of the people who are listening to us out there will have that hardcover book, and to me he looks like the guy who could be the second lead on a really good soap opera—the older man who's sort of the gay deceiver."

Later I asked Stephen if he had a ghost in his house, because I had heard this. But he said it was just a rumor. "Are there lots of rumors about you?" I asked.

"Yes, sure," he said. "Because you get the persona as Ghostmaster General, so to speak. You live in an old Victorian house; ergo there must be a ghost. I think once in my life I saw a ghost. I'm pretty sure that I did. And it's not a story that I've ever told except to friends. I'll tell it if you want to hear it. It'll take about two minutes."

He could have had all the time he wanted.

"I'm sure this must be the way ghosts appear to people," King began, "because it was so utterly prosaic. My wife and I went to a political fundraiser. It was wintertime, and it was one of these things held in an old house, where somebody takes your coats and puts them upstairs in an empty bedroom. You know, the fabled room upstairs where everybody's coat is on a bed, and when the party's over, you have to go find your coat. We had dinner reservations somewhere, so we stayed about an hour. At the fundraiser we met Senator Muskie and all the rest of it, and we gave our fifty dollars or whatever. My wife said, 'Gee, we've got to make it to dinner because it's getting late.'

"So I went upstairs to get the coats. I wore fairly heavy glasses, and I was upstairs rummaging around through the coats trying to find ours. And over the top of my glasses, where things get kind of fuzzy and vague, I saw an old man in a blue suit with a bald head, sitting in a chair in the corner, looking at me. I started to feel very guilty, because I thought, This man thinks I'm looking to steal things. I was just a young guy who was going through the coats, and I didn't know what to say or how to react.

"I found my wife's coat, and I found my coat, and I looked up and there was nobody there in the corner at all. It's one of the things that I've faced again and again in my books. What I did was to take the coats and go downstairs. My heart didn't race. My blood pressure didn't go up. I thought about it and thought about it, and my first inclination was to say I didn't see anybody. And then later I said, Be serious with yourself. The guy was there and you saw him. And then you looked down for a minute to pick up the coats, and when you looked back up again, there was nobody there. That was all."

"But you saw him?" I asked.

"Oh yeah, he was there."

"You didn't invent him."

"No. But it's the kind of thing that is very hard for me to tell. For instance, if Stephen King reported a UFO to the air force, they would laugh themselves into a hernia. It's as simple as that. Once you get that reputation, you're like the little boy who cried wolf."

Then I asked Stephen if he liked to scare people, and he said, "Yeah. I do."

I guess that comes as no surprise. My daughter, Chaia, has been such a fan of Stephen King for so many years that when she heard he was going to be on my show, wild zombies couldn't have kept her away from the studio. So after a while I asked her if she had any questions for him.

"Often your novels and horrifying tales center around the evil and dubious side of human nature," she said, very much the professional interviewer. "Is this the most terrifying thing to you?"

"Yes," he said. "The worst thing is the unexpected. Holes in the middle of things. You have an ordinary life, you have a routine, you have familiar scenes, places you go, people you know. Nothing out of the ordinary. You're not dealing with some strange setting in Africa or anything other than a perfectly middle-class American family or situation. And all of a sudden, one thing happens that's out of the ordinary, and little by little the whole fabric of reality gets torn apart."

"So you don't deal with vampires out of the sky," she said.

"No, not out of the sky. If I deal with vampires, they're the kind of vampires who might hide in the freezer case at the Food King during the day."

Then Stephen told me a funny story about something that happened while he was working on *Salem's Lot.* "I grew up in Maine," he said, "and I've always lived there. My wife and I were living in a house on Sebago Lake, which is in the western part of the state. I used to write in a little guest house that was separated from the main house, because I always crank the music loud and at least there I wouldn't bother everybody else.

"One night I was out there writing away, and the wind was high, and branches were knocking on the walls. I was writing about a vampire crawling up the wall or something, and I was really into it—it is a little like self-hypnosis when I write. I was bent over the typewriter, working away on this thing.

"All at once, there's an awful scraping noise at the window, and I look up and I see this white face peering in at me. And I am out of the chair, I'm grabbing carpet . . . and it's my wife. She crept out there to scare me, and she's laughing hysterically in the window, like it's so funny she can't believe it. I said, 'You do that again, I'll kill you.' "

Later we took calls because the phones were lit up with people wanting to talk to a guy who likes to scare them. One caller wanted to know why his favorite Stephen King novel, *The Stand*, was set in Boulder, Colorado.

"Because I lived there," King said. "It's a funny story in a way. I'd written *Carrie* and *Salem's Lot*, and they were both set in Maine because that's where I'm from. So I said to my wife, 'I think it's time to set a book somewhere else. This looks like it's going to be a career, not a hobby.'

"She said, 'Where do you want to go?'

"I said, 'I don't know. Just someplace where I can see something else and get a feel for some other part of the landscape.'

"She got out the Rand McNally road atlas and opened it to the map of the United States and said, 'Come over here.'

"I said, 'What are you going to do?'

"She had a neckerchief and she put it over my eyes and said, 'Point.' So I pointed and it was somewhere in Colorado, close to Boulder, and that's where we went."

Another caller said that *his* favorite short story of King's was "Gray Matter," and he wanted to know where Stephen got the idea for it.

"I used to play poker with a bunch of guys Thursday nights," he said. "And there was one guy who had once bought a six-pack of Budweiser with one can that was totally white. There was no writing on it or anything. He thought this was the most fantastic thing, like a great artifact or something. This can had been in his refrigerator for five years. He used to bring it out and show it to people. So we got after him one night: 'Come on, open it.'

"Finally the guy opened it. And all this gray goo like oatmeal or something just sort of spurted out, and it got all over his hands and everything, and the guy went totally crazy. And a friend of mine said, 'Well, you opened it, now drink it.' So the story came out of that."

Another very successful author who can be surprising on the air is James Michener. He is an enormously charming and witty person and knows how to play an audience. I interviewed him on the radio once at a remote from San Antonio, and he had the crowd in stitches much of the night, something I think most people don't expect from James Michener.

First, though, I wanted to learn about some serious things, such as how he began to write in the first place. He said he didn't do anything concrete about it until after he was drafted during World War II, already in his mid-thirties.

"I was one of the oldest men drafted in America," he said. "I had a very tough draft board, and there were a couple of people on it, I think, who wanted to get me. Little did I know that they were doing me a favor by throwing me into uniform. I was thirty-five. They chose me for my knowledge of the Mediterranean. I had been an able-bodied seaman in the British merchant fleet, so I knew the Mediterranean intimately, every corner of it. America thought the major naval war was going to be fought there. By the time they got me into uniform, though, the Mediterranean was pretty well locked up. So instead of going there, I was shoved off to the South Pacific.

"I must say it was a most vivid experience. I was in naval aviation, which allowed me to see the great carriers and the land bases. I saw some action, but I usually got to an island about three days after the tough fighting had ended, because I was bringing in material for the aviators. I was on three landings, but not tough ones. On Monday, Wednesday, and Friday they would hit Tarawa and Saipan and Okinawa, three of the most hellish fights there ever were. And on my days it was just like going to a Sunday school picnic. The Japanese were always on the other side of the island by then, and we just walked ashore."

"So where and when did you start writing?' I asked.

"I wrote the first book on a small island south of Guadalcanal, where I was stuck away on a backwater. We had pretty well cleaned out that part of the ocean. I was there doing almost nothing, and so I would go to a movie every night. We all did, around seven o'clock, and the movie would be over at nine. And then I would go to a warehouse and I would work until two in the morning.

"I served on forty-nine different islands during the war, so I knew the South Pacific as not many people knew it. And as I would listen to the men beef and bellyache about the war, two things impressed me. For one, we never had it as tough in the South Pacific generally as the troops had it constantly in Europe, where the Germans had those great artillery barrages. We never had that, although we had other things. Japanese troops were first-rate, and oftentimes in a one-to-one deal they did us in. And they had the suicide squads. We would have these flaming moments at Tarawa and elsewhere, but not what the fellows in Europe had in Italy and the Bastogne, and so on.

"And so it used to irritate me to hear men bellyaching about it. It occurred to me that fifteen or twenty years from then they would look back upon that experience as one of the crucial experiences of their lives. And when that happened, I wanted them to have a record of what it was really like, as far as I could depict it. I lived to see many men write to me in later years and say that they were so glad I had put it on paper because that was the way they now remembered it. It was written as fiction, but I had no great ambitions for it except that it be an honest record. I sent it to the publisher under a nom de plume because the company I was working with after the war, Macmillan, had a rule that they would not publish any books written by their employees. It was accepted immediately."

"You then told them?"

"Yes, and there was quite a brouhaha when I did, but they finally gave me a legal ruling that I wasn't really working for the company when I had written it. They figured out a way to make it all right."

Much to my surprise, Michener told me that *Tales of the South Pacific* was anything but a best-seller when it came out. "The book was published almost in secrecy by Macmillan," Michener said. "Several critics of great repute saw it immediately as a winner, but it never sold any copies. And then at the very last moment that it would be eligible, it won the Pulitzer Prize. There was a big flurry of news, but no sales. Then about two years later, it became this great musical. It was well spaced out. It was no overnight sensation at all."

Speaking of *South Pacific*, I said that I'd always felt that one of the greatest songs in it was also one of the great unknown songs—"You've Got To Be Taught to Hate."

"Let me tell you a story about that," Michener said. "Prior to the first real performance in New Haven, I was invited to the home of some distinguished people in Connecticut. We all went to see the show, and the next morning, as I was about to get on the train, two of the men took me aside. They said that they thought Rodgers and Hammerstein really had something, but it was all spoiled by the song of the young Marine when he was in love with a Polynesian girl, 'You've Got to Be Taught to Hate.' They said, 'Why don't you ask them to take it out?'

"I must say that as a guy without a nickel in my pocket and everything riding on this, because I'd even borrowed money to invest in it, I still practically told them to go to hell. I said that that was what the play was all about. Some of the critics later said that this song marred the beauty of the show. Well, by the standards of that year, it did. But I took their objection to Rodgers and Hammerstein and the three of us just laughed. We didn't even discuss it."

That song is a classic in attacking the insidious ways in which racial prejudice is passed on and unquestioningly accepted: "To hate all the people your relatives hate, You've got to be carefully taught." In that sense it was well ahead of its time.

I asked Michener if at that point, with the Pulitzer Prize and a smash Broadway musical under his belt, he didn't wake up and say, "I am now a full-time writer."

"I have not coined very many good phrases in my life," he answered, "but I coined a good one when some people asked me about that. I said, 'I'm kind of like Lord Byron after the publication of his great poem "Don Juan," when he said he went to bed unknown and woke up in the morning famous. I went to bed unknown and woke up to find Ezio Pinza famous.' And that's about the way it was. I kept my job at Macmillan and kept writing."

An enormous amount of research and study goes into each of Michener's books, through what he calls the "iceberg principle." You see only ten percent of the actual work or research involved in the final product. "I try to do everything I write about," he said. "I go oystering in the Chesapeake. I go crabbing. I fly everywhere. I climb mountains, and I've gone across deserts. I've had a wonderful life. What I do is construct a little universe in which the reader can live for two or three weeks and get to know it as well as I knew it."

"You are in that universe as well when you're writing?" I asked.

"Oh, yes, absolutely up to my ears," he said. "I think that I should be viewed as a literary Baptist. I believe in total immersion. I think that unless your head is underwater, you really ain't been baptized."

"How much research before the first word is written?"

"At least a year. We move into a place, rent a house, set up housekeeping. It is our home for the next two or three years. Fortunately, I have a wife who is one of the most congenial and active people on the block. By the end of the first week, everybody knows she's in town, and they suspect I am. And by the time I need to interview people, she has them lined up at the door."

He was revising *Texas* at the time of my interview. "Why did you live in Austin while you were working on this book?" I asked.

"When I decide to do a big book like this, which is going to take three years," he said, "I need a city with good libraries and an airport. It's as simple as that. I find that when I work away from those conveniences, I'm very unhappy and uneasy, and I spend my time trying to get places and so on."

When I asked Michener how he liked Texans, he told me that he found them to be more forthright and responsive than most people. I asked him to elaborate. "Oh, they take you into their homes," he said. "They laugh with you. They can laugh at jokes at their own expense. And they can tell you some fantastic jokes. I was with a man the other day who graduated from Texas A&M, which is the great agricultural school here—it's a science school now. He was from that school, and he asked me whether I'd heard about the graduate of A&M who was bitter about the fact that people were always sort of downgrading him. It seems this graduate asked for advice, and a woman told him, 'You know, the thing that gives a man cachet above everything else is if he's able to speak French. That moves you up several grades on the ladder right there.'

"So the fellow goes to Paris, takes a crash course, comes home, goes into the principal store in Dallas, and says, 'Monsieur, I would like some chicken *cordon bleu*. I would like some *brioche avec sel.*' He asks for a few other things, and he especially wants *champagne très sec*. And the man behind the counter says, 'When did you go to A&M?'

"The guy breaks into tears and says, 'How did you know?'

" 'Well, son,' he says, 'this is a hardware store.' "

That brought the house down in San Antonio. But besides being a good joke teller, Michener showed me that he has a sense of humor about himself. He mentioned that he regretted not having written a body of short stories. He once tried to write what is known as "the well-crafted English novel" and came up with *The Bridges at Toko-Ri*. And he thought he could have done more of those, but his mind just doesn't work that way.

"If I write a story next year about a man like you who's in radio and who has this great success and so on," he said, "the first thing I'd want to know is, What was his father like? Or what influence did his mother have? Or what town did he grow up in, and why was that town better than any other town? And pretty soon I've got eight hundred pages."

For all that I admire writers, though, I have to admit that they can be a little quirky, and I've got the stories to prove it. Take Gore Vidal and William F. Buckley, Jr., who give new meaning to the phrase "not talking to each other." They haven't been in the same room since they had that fight in 1968, after which lawsuits were filed and dropped. The two men hate each other so bitterly that they not only won't talk to each other, they won't talk *about* each other. And yet they're two highly educated men of letters. Through some unintentionally sadistic quirk of programming, both authors were scheduled to be on my radio program on the same night to plug their most recent books.

Vidal was on first, and he kept saying to me at the breaks, "Is he here? Where's he going to be when he comes?"

"He's going to be in the green room," I told him.

"How do I get out of here when we're done?" he asked.

"Don't worry," I said, "I'll walk you to the elevator." My producer, Chris Castleberry, had the task of getting Gore safely out through the elevator and ground floor maze. Meanwhile, Pat Piper also came to work that night, and he was bringing Buckley up personally from street level. I said to Vidal, "Wait a second, because I've got to wrap up here, and then I'll see you out and say good night."

Then I turned back to the microphone and said, "Thank you

very much for coming, Gore Vidal. We're going to pause
now—" And he was out of there like a shot, as if something
crazy was about to happen to him. A few minutes later, Buckley
came in from the other end of the studios. He sat down in that
cool way he has, very relaxed and poised. I said into the microphone, "Welcome back to hour number two. Our guest in hour
number one was Gore Vidal. . . ." Buckley's elegantly com-
posed face, the face that braved a thousand *Firing Lines*, con-
torted into a vivid grimace, as if he'd just sniffed ammonia. He
made a kind of snorting sound that I hoped his microphone
wasn't picking up and rolled his eyes. Suddenly it was Fear and
Loathing in Mutual Studios.

James Dickey is another writer I've enjoyed talking to. A poet
and novelist, Dickey is urbane, witty, and highly intellectual.
I don't read much poetry, and until a couple of years ago Dickey
had written only one novel, so my knowledge of his work was
fairly limited. When *Deliverance* was published in 1970, I
thought it was a great book. But he prefers to write poetry, and
so, despite the fact that *Deliverance* was a best-seller and the
movie version was a huge hit, he didn't write a second novel
for seventeen years. We had a great time when he came on my
show to plug that book, called *Alnilam*, but then the book just
died. Someone later asked me, "What happened with *Alnilam?*"

I think I can explain that right away: it had the world's worst
title. Imagine someone going into a bookstore and saying, "I'm
here to buy *Abuhlalhbilahb*." Or the talk show host: "My guest
tonight is James Dickey, author of— What's that again, Jim?
Ahbilahb. Did I get that right?"

How could an editor say to the marketing staff, "This is our
big hit of the year, *Alldiloll*. You'll have no problem finding the
right market for this book, folks, because that name tells us
right off the bat what it's about. What a headline-making title!"

I'm no expert, but offhand I would say the best book title I've
ever seen was *Your Erroneous Zones* by Wayne Dyer. Rollo
May's *Love and Will* was a close second. But *Alnilam?* I once
asked James Michener about the titles of his books, which have
to be among the least inspired of all time. He said he wasn't
much good at choosing titles, so he conferred with his editors,

who submit several possible titles for each book, and then together they choose the best one. That just makes me wonder what the alternative choices were for, say, *Alaska*. Do you think it came down to *Alaska* and *That Big, Ice-Cold State Up North?* Michener, at least, was honest about it. He said to me, "I like really wonderful titles. I think *Gone With the Wind* is a brilliant title. And *A Streetcar Named Desire* is great. But unfortunately, they've been used already."

Victor Borge used to tell a story about his uncle who invented a soft drink called 1-Up. It didn't do too well, so then he tried calling it 2-Up, but that didn't make it, either. Then he tried 3-Up, 4-Up, 5-Up, 6-Up, and then he gave up and killed himself. That story gave me the idea for a detective series called *Alaska Four-9*. It just missed.

One person who hasn't had that problem is Tom Clancy. Clancy is one of the great success stories of popular fiction, an insurance agent who also happened to be a military buff. Now he's a multimillionaire. Clancy spends a lot of his time reading about and studying military and naval technology. When he wrote *The Hunt for Red October*, he took a submarine inside out although he'd never been on one; it all came from reading and studying. I never saw fans for a thriller author like Tom Clancy's fans. Every light on the switchboard is lit up whenever he's on my show, and a lot of the callers just want to talk about the technology in his books.

One night I asked him why he was so fascinated with technical gadgetry. "The real inside truth about Tom Clancy," he said, "is that I never stopped being a little boy. I think of this complicated technological machinery as new toys, and I'm still fascinated with the way machines and gadgets work."

One thing most people don't know about Clancy is that, for all his intimate knowledge of planes and satellites, he's afraid of flying. He's much better about it now, he says, but if he has a choice, he'll take a train whenever he can—a car, an ocean liner, anything.

Another person who's afraid of air travel is the southern humorist Lewis Grizzard, who told me the story, which he swears is true, of how he formulated one of his rules about flying. The rule is, Never fly on any plane where the mechanic is named Bubba. He was on a plane once when he saw two mechanics walking on with their names stitched onto their uniforms. One was named Charles, and the other was Bubba. Bubba was adjusting some piece of equipment under a panel up near the front of the cabin, and Charles was watching. Charles said, "Okay, Bubba?" And Bubba said, "Ah, I think so. Yeah, I think it's okay now."

Then they closed the door. As Grizzard put it, "Bubba is sending me up to thirty thousand feet."

He said his fear of flying has gotten so pronounced that he likes to call the airline, find out the name of the pilot who's flying the plane he'll be on tomorrow, and go visit the guy. You know, see how he's doing, if he's having a good dinner, how he's getting along with the wife, and whether he's thinking about tomorrow's flight at all. When Grizzard toured to promote his book about fear of flying, he traveled by bus just to make his point. It was a nice bus, the kind of bus that Willie Nelson tours in, but still a bus. It may have been the only bus tour in the history of book promotion.

Garrison Keillor is another regional humorist, but with a very different style from Grizzard's. He is also one of the few authors who is as effective on the air as he is on the printed page. I knew that Keillor was going to go back on the radio just by his tone of voice when I interviewed him on TV. When he was on *Larry King Live*, at the first break he said, "Don't you wish you were on radio?"

"No," I said, "I like it here too."

And he said, "Really?"

"Don't you?" I asked.

"No."

Keillor is more comfortable on the radio or working at *The New Yorker*. My immediate impression of him is that he's very shy. The first time he did my television show, he was in the New York studio and I was in Washington, and when we broke for a commercial I didn't speak to him. I usually speak to guests during the breaks, unless I want to save something for the interview. But I never talk during the break if the guest is in a remote studio because that just feels strange to me. Apparently,

Keillor felt that because I didn't talk to him, it meant I didn't like him. He told his people that if I didn't like him—not his work, mind you, but *him*—then it would be uncomfortable for both him and me to do another interview. His people told my producer this and suggested I write him a letter letting him know that I did like him. My letter did the trick.

Garrison Keillor may be shy, but he loves to read his own work. I gave him a few poems to read, and then I read some of his poems, and he got a thrill out of that. I think he's a great broadcaster because he's a great storyteller. His voice is a picture. He is not an ad-lib performer, but he's so good that he sounds ad-lib, like Jean Shepherd. But unlike Shepherd, you know right off the bat with Keillor that everything is make-believe. And that's all right, because Jean Shepherd broke my heart years ago.

Jean Shepherd was one of my idols. Besides dozens of marvelous stories in books and magazines and on radio, he wrote a wonderful television show about Christmas and a kid who wants a Red Ryder rifle. I had always assumed that those tales he told about his childhood were based on real events, real characters. But when Shepherd was on my show, he told me that all those fabulous Jean Shepherd stories were invented. None of those people were real. When he told me that Itchie and Funky didn't exist, he broke my heart. His father wasn't the way he described him at all. That was created out of whole cloth. Shepherd said he's just a writer of fiction. I said, "You're destroying me."

"No, I write fiction," he said. He was very honest. "That was fiction."

"The stories in *Playboy?*"

"Fiction."

That broke my heart. In fact, he doesn't even like radio anymore. When I tried to get him to talk about it, all he said was, "Aw, radio. I'm a screenwriter."

Allen Ginsberg has never had the commercial success of the best-selling authors, but his position as a major figure in twentieth-century literature is likely to endure much longer. Maybe one of the reasons is that over all the years, Ginsberg has never compromised his work for commercial gain. When he came on my television show in Miami in the 1960s, he was the first person ever to appear there not wearing a jacket and tie. Back then we taped during the week and ran the show on the weekends, and it was a pretty prestigious show in that market. People got dressed up to come on television in Miami, but Ginsberg came on wearing patches. I don't know how else to describe it—he appeared to be in tatters. So I thought it was funny when, twenty years later, he came on my radio show in Washington, for which people routinely show up wearing jeans and a sport shirt, and he was wearing a coat and tie. I mentioned this on the air and asked him what had happened. "I ran into a really good Salvation Army," he said. "So I got this Pierre Cardin blue blazer for two bucks." Ginsberg's clothes may have changed a little, but not his attitude.

Allen Ginsberg published his great poem "Howl" in 1956. It overcame censorship trials to become one of the most widely read poems of the century. It has been translated into more than twenty-two languages, from Macedonian to Chinese. Ginsberg was crowned Prague May King in 1965 and was expelled by Czech police at around the same time he was placed on the FBI's "dangerous security" list. In recent years, he's traveled to and taught in the People's Republic of China, the Soviet Union, Scandinavia, and Eastern Europe. He's a member of the American Institute of Arts and Letters and cofounder of something called the Jack Kerouac School of Disembodied Poetics at the Naropa Institute, the first accredited Buddhist college in the Western world. That's a pretty interesting string of credits for someone who is not only a leading American poet but also a kind of emotional figurehead for the countercultural movement of past decades. I began by asking him why he chose poetry as his form of communication.

"Well, for one thing, it chose me," he said. "My father was a poet. So it's like a family business."

I recalled that I had once interviewed Ginsberg and his father together, and his father was wonderful. I asked Allen what he meant by "it chose me."

"I was born to it," he said. "Also, when I was young I had a kind of visionary experience related to William Blake which altered my life, I must say. It just was a different kind of awareness than I had experienced before. It turned me around, a little bit like the classical religious experiences you read about in William James. It was related to some poems by William Blake, and it altered my view of the universe. I just looked out the window and realized the universe was much older and much vaster than I'd thought before, when I was in high school."

"Being intelligent, though, you also knew that poets generally starve," I said.

"I had provided against that by getting seaman's papers," he said. "And so I had a job in the merchant marine, where you could save money. You know, in those days, back in 1945 or '46, you could ship out for a couple of months and come back with a couple of thousand dollars."

Ginsberg told me that he writes a lot of "dream poems," which is to say that he has a dream, wakes up, and writes the poem based on things that happened to him or were told to him in the dream. He told me an amazing story about a dream poem involving the great American poet and author of *Paterson*, William Carlos Williams—a man Ginsberg said is generally regarded as having changed the face of poetry in America. Williams was an interesting character in his own right, a doctor who practiced obstetrics and pediatrics among mostly poor families in the small industrial town of Rutherford, New Jersey, and wrote a large body of poetry in his spare moments.

"I met my poetry teacher, William Carlos Williams, in a dream," Ginsberg said. "And he started dictating instructions to me on how to be an older poet. So I woke up and wrote down the lines as I remembered them, and then I doctored it a little to add to it and finish it. The title is 'Written in My Dream by William Carlos Williams.' "

I asked Allen to elaborate on how he felt Williams changed poetry in America. "He invented a new way of writing down American verse line," Ginsberg said. "He listened to the American language as he talked it himself and others talked it, and he began measuring those rhythms and using them rather than using an old measure from England. I think Williams's attempt to find some kind of variable measure for American talk, American speech, to invent a new verse line, is the great breakthrough of the century, and I think it's work that has to continue. Not going back to sonnets and regular old English meter, nineteenth-century forms, but advancing forward to listen to our own talk and use the rhythms of our own talk."

"What makes a good poem?" I asked.

"I think you have to have a basic sense of rhythm," he said, "a certain kind of 'heart sacredness.' There would be some awareness of the fact that you're vulnerable and everybody has a soft spot. Even lizards love their children."

"Every word has some meaning?" I asked. "There are no throwaway words in poems?"

"No. I would say: maximum information, minimum number of syllables."

Later in the program, a caller wanted Ginsberg to talk about his meeting with Bobby Kennedy in the White House many years ago, a brief account of which the caller had read in Arthur Schlesinger's book on Bobby Kennedy. "I got back from Czechoslovakia," Allen recalled, "where I'd been kicked out after being elected King of the May, and I found out that the narcotics bureau was trying to set me up for a bust because I'd asked for a change in the law and for decriminalization of marijuana. So I went to Robert Kennedy's office to complain and ask him if I could get protection from illegal activities by the narcs. We got into a long conversation, and he wanted to know what I thought about the Black Power people relating to the hippies. Was there any kind of political liaison there? Then the conversation came around to Eastern religion, and I asked if he'd ever heard the Hare Krishna song. He said no. So I was singing 'Hare Krishna, Hare Krishna, Krishna Krishna, Hare Hare' to him and one of his administrative assistants, when Arthur Schlesinger stopped to listen. Schlesinger asked, 'What's that?' And I said, 'Oh, that cleans out the mind.'

"And Schlesinger said, 'The White House will need a lot of that.'"

One caller accused Ginsberg of having revealed Jack Kerouac's homosexuality during a symposium in the early 1970s. In response, Ginsberg said that he had simply admitted to having slept with Kerouac a couple of times. Furthermore, he didn't think that Kerouac was a homosexual, although he himself was and had been quite open about it since the age of eighteen. In fact, Kerouac was the first person he had told about it. This exchange started a flurry of calls about whether Ginsberg was saying that Kerouac was bisexual or homosexual or what. Ginsberg responded that he felt Kerouac was straight but that, as Kinsey had reported, the majority of American men have at one time or another had one or two experiences with the same sex, and Kerouac's happened to be with him.

I was pretty comfortable discussing homosexuality with Allen Ginsberg that night, but it wasn't always so easy for me. Years ago, I shared many of the prejudices that are still prevalent today but used to be more commonplace then. I owe my liberation from whatever stereotypes I've managed to escape to a remarkable man named Sergeant Leonard Matlovich. Sadly, like every other AIDS patient I've had on, about eight in all, he is now dead. Unlike them, or most other AIDS victims for that matter, Leonard Matlovich is buried in Arlington National Cemetery.

When I first met Leonard, he opened my eyes to the plight of the homosexual. He had won the Bronze Star and the Purple Heart in the Vietnam War, served three terms of duty, and was later on the cover of *Time*. He was a twenty-year veteran of the service and an outstanding military officer. One day he went to his commanding officer in the air force and said, "I wish to announce that I'm a homosexual." He was testing them. The air force flunked the test; they immediately discharged him. They had no evidence that he ever committed a homosexual act on the base with another officer on air force time, but they dismissed him just for *being* homosexual.

He sued them, and the air force would not cooperate during the trial. Judge Gerhardt Gesell was threatening them with contempt of court for dragging their heels on everything, and they finally settled out of court with Matlovich for $160,000. In the settlement, the air force removed his dishonorable discharge and honorably discharged him, so he received pension benefits and the right to be buried at Arlington Cemetery. He wrote a book about the experience in the early seventies and came on my show in Miami to promote it. I liked him right off, and I think he was extremely kind and tolerant toward me because practically the first thing I asked him was, "Why are you a homosexual?"

It was a dumb question, but like a lot of dumb questions it led to a great answer. Matlovich could have told me what a jerk I was, but all he said in reply was, "Why are you a heterosexual?" That stopped me dead in my tracks. Then he went on: "I want to ask you something. Do you know why you're attracted to girls? Don't tell me it's natural. I know you're going to say it's just natural, but can you tell me *why?* Why if you see a pretty girl do you get turned on?"

"I don't know," I said. "I always have."

"I'll tell you the truth," he said. "A pretty boy turns me on, and I don't know why either. So you don't know and I don't know. What do we care? I can't make you a homosexual. Do you think I could influence you, could write a book to tell you to be homosexual? Could you convince me to be turned on by women? You can't teach this stuff. My brother's a year older than me, married with three kids. We're very close. He's a macho kind of guy, and I've always admired him. I'm close to my father and close to my mother. When I was a kid, I liked dolls and I don't know why. My brother liked footballs and I never liked them. By the way, none of this affected my fighting in the air force. I grew up in the military. My father spent thirty-two years in the air force, and now I miss it. When I put on that uniform, I was a good fighting man. I earned my Bronze Star. But I knew it would be wrong to come on with anyone on the base, just as I knew it would be wrong for heterosexual males to come on with females on the base."

Sergeant Matlovich taught me something that day, and I've never gone back to the old prejudices since. From that day forward, I stopped saying "fag." Years later, Leonard came on my CNN show to talk about AIDS. He had been celibate for years. When the AIDS crisis came, he decided that if he was going to speak out on it, he would remain celibate. What he didn't know was that he already had AIDS. One day he walked into his doctor's office with what he thought was a common cold and was diagnosed with AIDS. He died like he lived, a courageous guy. But he said some things that day on television that probably shocked a few people in the audience, and not the way you might think. I asked him if he was bitter about anything—the wrangle with the air force, getting AIDS, any of it.

"I only have one regret in life," he said. "I'm a conservative Republican. I want the front yard, the backyard, the picket fence, the dog, the cat, taxes, and a lover. My only regret is that I've never been in a loving relationship."

When I asked him if he was opposed to AIDS testing, he surprised me again. He said he thought there *should* be testing—that everyone in the country should be tested every six months. "We're not opposed to testing," he said. "We're opposed to the Reagan administration's type of testing. When you leave so many holes in the system through selective testing—only new immigrants, prisoners, prospective marriage partners—it's useless."

He said that if every uninfected person in the country practiced safe sex or abstinence, no matter how reckless the people carrying the virus might be, it would mean the end of AIDS. Leonard also said, "If every homosexual in America just said 'I am a homosexual,' you'd have no problems from that day on. The world would be shocked at who is gay, but it would take the pressure off a lot of people. It's the best thing that ever happened to me. I should have said it in my second year in the service."

Matlovich was an inspirational character in many ways, not only because he went against type and expectation and forced you to think but because in the face of everything he was up against he maintained an optimistic nature. "In the long term," he said about AIDS, "all this is a blessing. Maybe that's just the way I deal with having a fatal disease, but in the long term, so much good is going to come out of this. The medical research will help with cancer and with all viruses, and it has renewed interest among physicians in public health as a field, as a valuable service to mankind."

When I asked him if he was afraid the AIDS crisis would lead to more antagonism against gays, he said, "This is one of the hidden blessings I was talking about." He had seen a woman on TV. She was from the mountains of West Virginia, and her son was dying from AIDS. "She said, 'I didn't know that my son was a homosexual, and now my son's dying of AIDS. But I love my son.' That woman is going to go back to the mountains of West Virginia, and when someone says 'queer' or 'faggot,' she's going to say, 'Don't you use that language around me. My son died of AIDS and I love my son.' Many of us in the movement have always said that if tomorrow morning every lesbian and every gay woke up and found that they were green or blue, it would change discrimination overnight. Because we are mothers, fathers, brothers, aunts, and uncles. Well, the AIDS virus has become that color. It may almost take something this insidious to bring people around, to shake them up and make them get over their hatred and their bigotry."

9

Radio Days

Talking with writers is one reason that, as much as I enjoy the money and the recognition that have come from my years on television, I still get my biggest charge from the kind of work I do on radio. It's not so much a question of roots, since I did a lot of TV in Miami when I was starting out as a broadcaster. It's the freedom, the time, and the communication with the listeners. I feel a special connection with the radio audience that's hard to explain. They stay tuned in, they don't click the dial, and I find that they share my native curiosity about a wide and unpredictable array of people and things. Maybe *unpredictable* is the key word, because before I begin an interview I often have no idea of the wealth of new information I'm about to stumble across. I can't think of a better example of the kind of interview that makes my job so much fun and that comes as a complete surprise than the one I did with the postmaster general of the United States, Anthony Frank.

Frank was appointed to that post in March of 1988, and I had him on my radio program a little over a year later. Until the 1970s, postmasters general were presidential appointments, but they are now appointed by the board of governors, which was created in 1971 to depoliticize the Postal Service. You now know as much as I did about the job of Postmaster General and the workings of the Postal Service before I met Frank. But by

the time he left the studio an hour later, I was brimming
with the sort of incidental but fascinating information that I
would love to know even if I weren't a professional interviewer.

Anthony Frank looks like any affable businessman in a dark
suit, probably because prior to becoming postmaster general he
was chairman of First Nationwide Bank of San Francisco, a
thirty-five-billion-dollar savings bank. And he runs the Postal
Service much like a rather large private business, although it's
also quasi-governmental. According to Frank, it does about
forty billion dollars a year, making it roughly the fifth biggest
business in the United States. "But we also do a lot of public
service," Frank said. "We do things that lose a lot of money,
like rural delivery, forwarding mail, all the rest of it. So it's an
interesting combination of business and public service."

By law, the Postal Service has to break dead even, and over
the last eleven years, cumulatively, they have, almost to the
decimal point. I asked Frank if there weren't a lot of surprises
in his work.

"Oh, a lot of surprises," he said. "One is the scope of the
thing. We have eight hundred thousand employees—more than
the U.S. Army—which makes us the biggest company in the
United States in terms of people. But we're big in every respect.
The Post Office buys more rubber bands than anybody else, uses
more vehicles than anybody except Hertz and Avis, and handles
five hundred million pieces of mail every day, six days a week.
But I was also surprised at the constraints that we operate under, such as very strong unions and no control over our own
pricing. Imagine that! A forty-billion dollar company and you
can't even do your own pricing. And even though we are de-
politicized, we get fourteen thousand communications a year
from the Congress. My associates or I testify about forty times
a year before the Congress. We handle forty percent of the
world's mail, so to whom would you compare us?"

Then I asked a question I've always wanted to know the answer to. Like millions of Americans, when I go to the post office
to buy stamps, I wonder why it is that the new issue has a
picture of Olympic athletes or little kittens or the state of North
Dakota. Why not Adlai Stevenson or Count Basie or thoroughbred racehorses? How *does* a stamp get to be a stamp?

"Well, let me put it this way," Frank said. "We issue twenty-five commemoratives a year, and I get twenty-five thousand suggestions. That gives you a little idea."

A commemorative stamp salutes a person or place, so those are in addition to birds, plants, and other things, like LOVE stamps. The Citizens Stamp Advisory Committee of about fourteen members makes all the decisions. On it are people such as Digger Phelps of Notre Dame, who is a big stamp collector, and James Michener, and they have to abide by certain rules. "Number one, you have to be dead ten years to be on a stamp," Frank said. "If we didn't have that, I don't know where we'd be. That is a real life-saving rule. Also, you have to meet the test of time, whatever that may mean. We are always working two or three years ahead to keep up with important dates and anniversaries. Obviously, we're looking ahead to the five-hundredth anniversary of Christopher Columbus in 1992. We're looking ahead to the fiftieth anniversaries of all the World War II battles, in ninety-one, ninety-two, ninety-three, and so on. We meet every other month. I generally don't meet with the committee, but I have the final say. I'm the one who has to sign off on the artwork and the concept."

So now you know who has the ultimate control over who gets to be on a stamp. In fact, though, if everyone on the advisory committee agrees on someone, Frank is going to go with it. "We don't knight people in this country," he said. "Issuing a stamp is as close to a pantheon as we get."

I was surprised to hear that the artist who creates the stamp, which can be a very painstaking job, is paid only $3,000. That doesn't seem like very much, especially when you consider that the Postal Service may print more than 160 million copies of that piece of art.

The conversation inevitably came around to the burning question of this or any other decade: Would there ever be a commemorative stamp of Elvis? Apparently, Postmaster Frank had been wrestling with that question, too. But for him it was no joke, since his office has been besieged with requests to put Presley's image on a twenty-five-cent stamp. "He clearly made a great contribution," Frank said. "He clearly has a great following. But as the congressman from Memphis wrote me the other day. 'There's nothing wrong with Presley's death. He only died from an overdose of twelve prescription drugs.' I have to sit down and think about that sentence for a little while."

Asked if the subject of a stamp must have an exemplary character, Frank acknowledged that they put W. C. Fields on a stamp some years ago, even though "he's been known to have a red nose." And then there were stamps honoring Ernest Hemingway and the Barrymores. So by the same token, Elvis and, for that matter, Judy Garland should get a shot. "Elvis didn't die in a very fine fashion," Frank said, "but that might not be a bad lesson to the youth of America. If he hadn't abused his body, he'd still be entertaining people."

I also got to ask him about a sore point, not only for me but for quite a number of people in the entertainment business, which is why Jack Benny hasn't been honored with a commemorative stamp. As I told Frank, I've been on a commission to get Jack Benny a stamp for years. We've presented our request a number of times over the past few years without getting a response. Johnny Carson is also on the commission, and Frank Sinatra's the chairman. Surprisingly, he said he'd never seen anything on it. We've had different postmasters general during that time—four over the last five or six years—so maybe it got lost in the shuffle. It's even less surprising when you look at who has and hasn't been honored with a commemorative stamp.

For instance, baseball may be the national pastime, but the first stamp honoring a baseball player, Jackie Robinson, wasn't issued until 1982. Since then, there have been only three more: Roberto Clemente, Babe Ruth, and Lou Gehrig, whose stamp had just been issued when Frank came on my show. But as he pointed out when I started naming possible future candidates: "How about Cy Young, who won five hundred and eleven games? Good Lord, we revere three-hundred-game winners, what about him?"

I have to like a postmaster general who knows his baseball stats. But then, that's why I love my job so much. Look at all the things I learned in an hour. I also found out the simple reason the Postal Service pushes stamp collecting. "You're selling a little colored piece of paper for twenty-five cents," Frank said. "That's what we bankers call 'permanent float.' You're lending me twenty-five cents in perpetuity."

It's like buying a traveler's check. A former executive of American Express told me that traveler's checks were their biggest profit makers, for the same reason. He thought those ads in which Karl Malden advised people to leave some traveler's checks in their wallets when they came back from a trip were brilliant. "They're always safe," he said, "and they're earning us six and a half percent every day you don't use them." I never thought about that as applied to stamp collecting. Lou Gehrig is going to make a lot of money for the Postal Service.

I was honestly thrilled to be sitting with the guy who has the power to make a stamp. But I was more thrilled to learn all those new things about stamps, and the best part is that I didn't even have to go looking for it. It came to me. That's further proof that I have one of the best jobs around.

Here's another example. One of the most surprising evenings I've spent on the radio was with the German-born actor Eric Braeden. Braeden is a soap opera star from *The Young and the Restless* who had played a role on *Rat Patrol* many years before, but other than that I knew very little about him. I expected very little from the interview. I was under the impression that Braeden was there to plug a new movie or TV special of some kind, but it turned out he was coming on to celebrate the fortieth anniversary of the German Federal Republic. I ended up wishing that he had been there longer, because he opened my eyes to a lot of the nuances of racism that I hadn't really considered before.

Braeden is in his mid-fifties and no longer has the German accent that he had when he played the character of Captain Hauptman Hans Dietrich in *Rat Patrol*. At that time Braeden was working under his given name, Hans Gudegast. *Rat Patrol* was originally telecast from 1966 to 1968, and Braeden's character was the commanding officer of a German armored unit in North Africa, part of Rommel's elite Afrika Korps. It was a role of the stereotypical German Nazi, which he now says he would never play again but which he was grateful for at the time. Braeden changed his name in 1970 to take a leading role in a Hollywood film called *Colossus: The Forbin Project*, whose producers felt they could not star someone with as German a name as Hans Gudegast. He took voice lessons to get rid of his accent and subsequently became involved in German-American awareness.

Braeden is now one of forty members of the German-American Advisory Board, along with the likes of House Speaker Tom Foley, Chief Justice William Rehnquist, Senator Bill Bradley, Warren Burger, Alexander Haig, Steffi Graf, and *Washington Post* publisher Katharine Graham. Eric Braeden came to the United States at the age of eighteen. He said he left Germany partly because of the war and partly because "America always provided for all of us a kind of dreamland. As a teenager I read a lot of stories about the American West, about cowboys and Indians. I remember growing up as a boy in Germany, being fascinated by American GIs, American films, American athletes."

I asked him if he didn't feel any rancor toward Americans as the victors in World War II. "I honestly don't think there was any rancor or hostility toward the Americans," he said. "In fact, it was the other way around. I think there was a sense of liberation. One thing that is forgotten in discussions of Germany in that period is that many of us felt liberated by the Americans. It was not only those who were imprisoned or in concentration camps who felt liberated."

Then I asked Braeden the obvious question: Is much of the anti-German feeling in America still based on hatred of Hitler? Braeden felt, justifiably perhaps, that this image was formed by Hollywood more than anything else. His point was that it is unfair to identify German-Americans with those twelve years of Hitler's reign. "There is more to me as a German," he said, "there is more to our history, than that damned twelve-year period which was so totally formed by that Austrian private."

Braeden underlines the need to remember what happened during that time. "It must be shown, it must be reiterated," he said, "and it is being done in Germany, as well it must be. No question about that. What I personally think is wrong is that we don't draw the *right* lessons from that period. We get caricatured images. We don't deal with the average person who was basically apolitical, who simply said 'Germany first,' as

many Americans say 'America first,' without critically thinking
about what was being said. By the time they became critical,
it was too late; the man was in power. No one at that time
knew in Germany, or in the world for that matter, what that
man would eventually lead to. It is that twenty-twenty hindsight that we indulge in so freely now that allows one to be
morally righteous. What we must try to do, and what films are
not doing, is to recapture what perhaps it was like when that
man started."

I brought the conversation around to the subject of the Jews
in Germany and the irony that, before Hitler, Germany was
one of the best places for a Jew to live. "What a lot of people
forget," Eric said, "is that the Jew was more successfully assim-
ilated into German society than any other society of the world.
That's a historic fact, and therein lies the unforgivable tragedy
of what happened. Because therein lies the reason that many
Jews, right up until the end, did not believe what was going to
happen to them. They *couldn't* believe it."

Next to the United States, West Germany is Israel's staunchest
ally today and is the only nation in the world that has continued
to pay reparations to its war victims forty years after the war.
Braeden said he used to play soccer for a Jewish team in Los
Angeles called the Maccabees. "I was one of two Germans on
the team," he said. "The others were Israelis and Ethiopians
and what have you, and we had a marvelous time with the
Israelis. They told us that when they grew up in the kibbutzim
in Israel, a lot of young Germans of my generation spent time
there. In 1967, when war broke out with Egypt, there was one
kibbutz where the Germans volunteered to take up arms against
the Egyptians."

Braeden acknowledged that Germans and Jews have to start
talking about the deep feelings between them. "There has to be
a dialogue about each other's perceptions," he said. "When I
meet a Jewish person, he often doesn't know I'm German. But
when I tell him where I'm from, I see a certain thing go through
his eyes, and I understand it now. If I were Jewish, I would
have the same feelings."

Some of those feelings came screaming to the surface when
we took calls in the second half of the show. The first caller

attacked Braeden for trying to "minimize" what happened during the twelve years of Hitler's power—which I didn't think he'd done at all. Another caller said he thought it was "disgraceful" that I was agreeing with my guest. In the caller's words, "Mr. Braeden is trying to perpetuate the myth that Hitler duped the German people and that before they knew it he was in power."

"Are you saying," I asked, "that German people are different from other people?"

"Absolutely."

"And Germans today are also different?" I asked.

"Yes," the caller said, "because they're still built from the same background that made them aggressive and warlike, whether it was the Franco-Prussian War or World War I or II."

"You think that's inborn?" I asked.

"That's correct," he said.

"In other words, a German baby is warlike, and an American baby is not?"

"An American baby may or may not be. But with a German baby, the chances are very good that he is going to follow his Prussian forebears."

That's the same insidious brand of idiocy practiced by the people who publicly destroyed Cat Stevens records because he supported the Ayatollah's threats against Salman Rushdie. Racism and intolerance aren't supportable just because the focus of hatred happens to be a people who themselves once supported those same evils. It would be hard to find a people on the face of the earth who haven't at some time been intolerant or been the oppressor, including Americans, Jews, and Africans. More than anything else, I have always been infuriated by anybody who hates a group as a group and hates individuals for no other reason than that they are members of that group. If you wanted to apply that principle to America, then all white Americans would have to be considered hateful because some previous generations of whites slaughtered Indians and practiced slavery. We should be paying reparations to both blacks and Native Americans, according to that way of thinking. Some black and Indian activists do advocate just that, but I don't hear many white Americans agreeing with them.

A woman caller went on at great length—much too great—about how all the German rocket scientists brought into this country after the war by Allen Dulles, brother of John Foster Dulles, were a real danger. "They have infected this country like a cancer cell," she said, "and we are going to be turned into another Germany if they can do it. They wish to destroy America, but slowly."

About then, I hit the button on her. Our final call summarized the full scale of the dilemma Braeden was trying to address. It was from a Jewish man in Chicago who began by wishing Braeden well but who went on to say that he thought history would ultimately work against Eric's argument. "I know that you can't characterize a whole people," he said, "but I'm afraid that while there are many good Germans, anti-Semitism has been so deeply inculcated in such a major part of the German population that generations hence—"

At this point Eric cut in to reiterate his point that anti-Semitism was far more rampant in other European countries than it was in Germany. The caller accepted that but insisted that anti-Semitism had been rampant in modern-day Austria even before Kurt Waldheim. We were running out of time, and Eric said he understood the caller's concern. "But it is people like you and me who have to talk," he said. "I have to tell you that I feel enormous pain about this period. Don't you think that my generation and I felt such shame and such guilt and such conflict over this issue when we found out what had happened? I found out in 1961 when I saw my first film about concentration camps. What do you think it did to Germans of my generation? It horrified us. How many conflicts do you think there are now in German families between fathers and sons—sons who demand an answer to that question, which often can't be answered succinctly by the older generation? It's a very, very painful thing for you *and* for me. You have to stop assuming that it isn't painful for me. It is damn painful for me."

Another interview that proved to be unexpectedly lively—though in hindsight, I should have expected it—was with William Bennett, the former secretary of education, who came on shortly after he had been appointed the new national drug czar by George Bush in 1989. He was a hot item in the news then,

but Bill Bennett and I go back a long way, well before he ever
became involved with the drug problem.

I first met Bennett when he was head of the National Endowment for the Humanities. That's a quasi-governmental organization funded by colleges and universities to promote the
teaching and love of the humanities. As I perceived it then, his
image was completely different from what it is today. I suppose
he was conservative, but that wasn't immediately apparent because Bill spent most of the time talking about Shakespeare and
the importance of teaching the classics in the schools and of
getting away from our emphasis on materialism. After he was
made secretary of education, I saw him a lot at the Palm, and
I had dinner with him a couple of times. We would talk about
education and smoke ourselves into oblivion. He smoked as
much as I did in those days. In fact, I had great sympathy for
Bill when he later took the job as drug czar because one of the
first things he had to do was quit smoking, and I knew how
difficult that can be.

Only when Bennett was named secretary of education by
Ronald Reagan did I realize he was a Republican. And at Education he completely surprised me—I thought he would be
dynamic and rooted in the arts, but he became a kind of hard-
line guy. Some of Bennett's positions on school issues seemed
antiquated to me. He wanted to bring back school prayer; he
wasn't so sure about sex education; and he admired Joe Clark.
His positions sounded completely contradictory to someone who
had been the head of the National Endowment for the Humanities. I could be wrong, but I can't picture a principal like Joe
Clark being funded by the Endowment. Yet although Bennett's
politics disappointed me, as a man he never has. I've always
liked him.

Bennett's appearance made a very compelling hour, even
though his people had been reluctant at first to let him go on
and field live phone calls. I didn't agree with a lot of what he
said about drugs, though, and in the heat of doing this show,
he made two statements that I left unchallenged.

The first was when he said, "The marijuana that we're talking about today is twenty to thirty times more powerful than
the marijuana of the late sixties. In potency it would probably

knock you out. If you were a casual marijuana smoker of the sixties, it would probably knock you out if you took it today." That's the kind of statement that appears to be virtually impossible to verify, but in fact the Drug Enforcement Administration's own most recent figures show that the THC content of marijuana has increased from about two percent to a maximum of eighteen percent, which would mean that in the most extreme cases some marijuana is about nine times stronger than it used to be. The irony is that this increase was largely caused by the government's crackdown on marijuana importation, which forced local growers to take up the slack by growing smaller quantities of more potent pot. As one economist at the Rand Corporation wryly put it, "This is the rare instance in which trade protectionism really worked."

The second statement came toward the end of the show when in response to a question about the link between drugs and poverty, Bennett said, "Drugs absolutely are the biggest cause of poverty today." That statement is an insult to most of the people who suffer the effects of poverty, and shows the worst of the old mentality, which holds that poverty is the result of weak will and degenerate living rather than the other way around. Much as I like Bill Bennett, that kind of rhetoric is beneath him.

Still, neither of those statements was the one that made the wire services after the show. Bill's response to a call-in question ended up as the lead item on the CBS news later that night and eventually appeared on the "Perspectives" page in *Newsweek*, where the week's most striking or ludicrous quotes appear along with political cartoons. The caller asked why we didn't get tough with the pushers as they do in Arabia, where they "behead the damned drug dealers." To my astonishment, Bennett said that the caller had an interesting point. "What the caller suggests is morally plausible," he said. "Legally, it's difficult, but—"

"Behead?" I asked.

"Yeah," Bennett responded. "Morally, I don't have any problem with it." And as if for good measure, he added, "I used to teach ethics." Maybe that was why his people had been a little hesitant about letting Bill take calls on the air.

When I run into fans who are regular viewers or listeners,

they sometimes ask me what's going on in my mind during these interviews and what we talk about during the breaks. I think they want to know if my mind ever wanders. In this particular instance, I have to admit that a strange reminiscence came to mind while Bennett was talking about the appalling depredations of drug use. It was a funny thing that had happened to me many years ago, and I realized not only that I wouldn't be able to talk about it on the air but also that it wasn't something I would want to mention to Bennett during the break. But I don't mind telling it now.

One night quite a few years ago in Miami, I was working pretty late. I had taped my TV show, written a column, and then done my radio show from nine to midnight. During the eleven o'clock news, my engineer told me that he'd just had a call from the all-night guy, who couldn't come in. We were strapped. I would now have to work till five A.M. and I was already whacked out. I'd put in a full day of work beginning at eight A.M. and didn't know where I would get the energy to sound upbeat for five more hours. I called my doctor, who lived three miles from the station and asked him, "Is there anything you can give me?"

"Well," he said, "I do have something. It's an amphetamine that's given to diet patients in Italy. It'll definitely keep you up for the night."

I asked him to bring it over. He drove to the station and gave me a little orange pill. I was reluctant to take the pill if I didn't have to, but by the time we were into the midnight news I was ready to go to sleep. I took the pill and washed it down with a cup of coffee. A few minutes later, the announcer said, "And now, sitting in for your all-night host, here's Larry King."

So far, all I'd been feeling was tired. I said, "Good evening, folks, nice to be here again." And suddenly I was going, "Hi! Sure! Welcome to the show! Wow! Let's get to the calls! We're going to have calls all night! Calls! Calls! Calls! Get 'em in!"

I was flying. The clock didn't mean anything anymore. I was so eager to talk to every caller who came on the line that I was finishing their sentences for them.

"Larry," one guy began, "I want to talk about the Dade County—"

"Commission!" I cut in. "That's what you want to talk about, and so do I! C'mon, let's talk about the Dade County Commission."

"Larry, I've got a question about President—"

"Carter! That's who you want to talk about, Jimmy Carter!"

I'd never taken anything like that pill in my life. I thought, Where has this been? Now it's five o'clock. My shift is finally over, and I am wide awake. I'm driving around Miami. I've got the car top down, the windows are open, I pull into Royal Castle—and I realize I am totally not hungry. I can't eat anything. So I go home, I'm reading the paper, trying to decide whether to have some coffee. I'm walking around the house in circles, smoking a thousand cigarettes, and about eleven A.M. I cave in. Within minutes I fell asleep. After that experience I decided I'd never use that stuff again.

As many surprises as I get by questioning people like Frank, Braeden, and Bennett, sometimes that's nothing compared with the answers my listeners get when they call in with questions. In fact, sometimes callers elicit a story or piece of information from a guest that I never would have thought of asking about. That's one of the reasons we take calls in the first place. I keep saying that it's ridiculous to get paid good money to do what I do, since I get such a kick out of it that I'd probably do it for free. But what makes it even more absurd is that often my listeners do the work for me.

I've interviewed Harry Belafonte plenty of times over the years, but one of the best stories I ever got out of him came from a question I never thought of asking. Harry was talking about his album *Paradise in Gazankulu* and about conditions in South Africa in general, and the talk had been mostly about race relations and geopolitics. Then we went to the phones. Someone called in from Detroit and all he said was, "Harry Belafonte, I like your music and I thank you for it. And I wanted to know how you got started."

Harry's answer was so eloquent and detailed that I just sat there listening. "At the end of the Second World War," he began, "I was working as a janitor's assistant in a Harlem apartment building. And one night I was given two theater tickets

because I'd repaired the venetian blinds for a young woman in
the building by the name of Clarice Taylor. She is the lady who
played the good witch in the Broadway version of *The Wiz*,
and she now plays Bill Cosby's mother on his TV series. The
tickets were to a play she was in at the American Negro Theater. It was the first time I'd seen theater, and when the lights
went down and the curtains opened and these people walked
on and began to talk to the human need, my heart danced for
joy. I didn't know quite why. My soul opened up, and I understood that for the first time in my life I had witnessed something
that I wanted to be a part of. There seemed to be a great sense
of purpose to what they were doing up there.

"When I joined that theater soon afterward, I joined it as a
technician because I thought I could use my skills as a venetian
blind repairman and as a stoker of the furnace in the building,
which was part of my job at the time. And also unloading garbage. But as I watched the process of theater and as I got to
know more about the performing arts, I found in myself a kin-
ship for it. A play written by the Irish playright Sean O'Casey
about Dublin slum life, called *Juno and the Paycock*, was un-
dertaken as an exercise by this black theater in Harlem, and we
had to put it on. And because we couldn't find an actor to play
the role of Johnny Boyle, the young male lead, I was required
to play the part."

Here I came out of my trance long enough to ask Harry
whether he didn't know Sidney Poitier around then. Belafonte
wasn't working as a singer yet, and I knew from talking to him
many times that he and Poitier had been friends since their
earliest days in Harlem. But I don't think I'd ever asked him
how they met.

"As a matter of fact," Harry said, "the day I walked into that
theater to register to become a part of it was the very same day
that Sidney Poitier walked in. And from that day until now, he
and I have been very close. I've got to tell you a story, very
swiftly. I was in a play called *Days of Our Youth*, and Sidney
Poitier was my understudy. I was paying a guy two dollars a
night to haul the garbage for me because I couldn't afford to
lose my janitor's gig. On this particular night, the guy took ill.
I had to go back to hauling the garbage, and Sidney Poitier

took over my part in the play. A man by the name of Light was putting on a black version of *Lysistrata* on Broadway, and he came from downtown looking for black actors, saw Sidney Poitier that night, and hired him for the male lead. The play was terrible, but it ran two nights. And on the second night, scouts from Twentieth Century-Fox out in Hollywood came to New York to look for a young black actor to play opposite Richard Widmark, then one of their biggest stars, in a film called *No Way Out.* That ended up being Sidney Poitier's screen debut. So I always tell Sidney his career is based on garbage."

I listen and I learn. That's the joy of it and, really, that's the only way to do a talk show like mine. I never pretend to be what I'm not. I was once on a radio show in New York when the host asked me, "What if you were walking down the hall in NBC and somebody handed you a note, sat you down, and said, 'Tom Brokaw's sick, you're on'? And the camera went on, and all you've got is this piece of paper and a camera. What would you do?"

And I know that I would say, as I told him then: "Folks, I'm Larry King. I was just walking down the hall. Someone handed me this piece of paper that said 'Tom Brokaw's sick.' And now I'm on. If we find out what's wrong, I'll let you know. I don't have an earpiece yet, so no director can talk to me. What I'm going to do for the next half hour is something I've never done before. I'm going to try to anchor the news. Now, probably during this half hour I'll turn to a wrong camera because I don't know my camera angles yet. And I may go to the wrong reporter. Please bear with me. Here's the news."

Now, what can happen to me? From then on, nothing bad can happen. If I look at the wrong camera, it doesn't matter. Who's going to tune out that channel? In fact, people start calling their friends to tune in. "Watch this guy, he's never anchored the news. He's going to try to anchor a half hour of this without an earpiece." I could even say, "Fuck it!" in the middle of that, and no one's going to say, "That schmuck." They're going to say, "Christ, he was walking down the hall, they told him to take over. How is he supposed to know what to do?"

But nine out of ten guys would say, "Good evening, I'm Phil

Randolph, sitting in for Tom Brokaw with the news"—and
screw themselves up trying to be what they're not. I would
never try to be what I'm not. The audience would know that
I've never anchored the news. And in that situation, I would
be doing it for myself. It may seem like a gutsy move, but it
ain't gutsy. It's a wonderful way to bring the audience into your
predicament. You can't lose. And people are with you more
than you think.

Nixon never learned that; most people never learn that. The
audience, the public, is always sympathetic to a need. As Edward Bennett Williams said, "The way to win a trial is simple.
Put the jury in the client's shoes. Once you've done that, you
can't lose. Once they're in his shoes, nothing matters, not murder or mayhem. If you can get them to think, 'Faced with this
situation, might I have done that?' then it doesn't matter if you
hacksawed your mother to death."

By using that one basic principle, I've gotten people to open
up to me who otherwise might look at me as if I were a Mar-
tian, and vice versa. People have asked me how I can interview
someone like Gene Simmons of Kiss, for example. I've never
heard a Kiss record or gone to a Kiss show. I don't really know
who Gene Simmons is. I started in the business in 1957, and I
never left Sinatra, Basie, and Ella. Presley was all right. I
thought the Beatles were crazy, and then Arthur Fiedler convinced me they were good. Maybe if I listened to Kiss records
or read a lot of press on them, I might think they were boring
or not for me. The same goes for any of the rock singers I've
interviewed, from Grace Slick and Joe Cocker to Huey Lewis,
Kenny Rankin, and David Crosby. Aside from an occasional hit
song, I don't know their work at all. But I can be fascinated
just by meeting a fairly ordinary-looking person and wondering
what makes him or her able to sell millions of records.

So I never pretend. I wouldn't say, "Your latest album is the
best." If they mention a song and I don't know it, I say I don't
know it. But I always let them know in a humorous way that I
feel like I'm ancient. So I may ask Gene Simmons or Grace Slick
to explain their music to me. If I do it right, I can make that
twenty-two-year-old who knows every Kiss song ever recorded
be interested in the answer, even though the question is asked

by someone who doesn't know who Kiss is. But you have to ask it in a genuinely curious way. For example, I love to ask, "How would you explain what you do to someone who didn't know your music?"

Even the fanatic has to be interested in that explanation. If Presley were alive, the Presley fan would be interested in hearing Elvis explain how he sings to someone who has never heard him. "If someone had never heard you, what would he be listening for? And how do you do it?" With rock groups, I also like to ask them who they look back to musically, and I get a frame of reference from that.

Pat Piper, my radio producer, loves to book those people for me. He does know their music, and he knows my audience knows them. And more often than not I end up getting a kick out of them, too. Joe Cocker was half zonked the night he was on, but I liked him. Although I don't have much affinity for rock 'n' roll, Cocker's "You Are So Beautiful" is one of the greatest songs I've ever heard. And even though he was a little drunk, he was fun because it was the kind of drunk I could play to. He wasn't going to say "fuck" or pass out at the microphone. He was not obnoxious, just loose. We were in New Orleans for a convention of the National Association of Broadcasters, so he kind of fit the mood of the place.

But I did have a bit of a problem getting him to focus on the questions. I asked him, "How did you get that tune, 'You Are So Beautiful'?" It took us ten minutes to get the answer because each time he started, he'd go off on a boozy tangent and I'd have to bring him back. First he said, "I thought you were going to say, 'How did you get in the building?' That wasn't easy either." And he told a story about the bar downstairs in the hotel. When I brought him back, he mentioned it was a Billy Preston song and then went off on a long, involved story about what had happened to his luggage earlier in the day. Finally he said he thought it was a hymn until Jim Price, the trumpeter, played the melody for him, and by then I was glad to get off that topic. Next I asked him about his drug problems, because Mercury Morris was going to be on the show later talking about *his*. I figured Joe would probably give me the same answer that everyone else gives these days—either that he was set up or that he's since learned how unimportant drugs are compared with music and personal freedom, or something like that. But not Joe. "I travel around the world, so I can live without it," he began. "But if I get a taste wherever I go of something I like, I think that's cool."

"Does it affect performance?" I asked.

"Uhh, yes," he said. "It brightens your ears sometimes to have a smoke of ganja or something."

"I mean, does it affect it adversely?"

"Haven't you ever had a taste yourself, Larry?"

God, was I sorry I'd asked.

I don't know why rock stars feel comfortable with me, but they seem to. For example, I think my biggest fans in San Francisco are Huey Lewis and the News. I've never heard a Huey Lewis album, and they're aware that I wouldn't know their stuff. Still, they were very nice to me. I certainly think that the other rock people I've interviewed know that I don't know their music and it doesn't bother them, probably because I'm never hostile or condescending the way some older interviewers are. In fact, I've really had a ball with some of them, like the time I had on Grace Slick and Paul Kantner of Jefferson Starship. We got off to a great start when I asked them how they'd come up with their original name, Jefferson Airplane.

"It was the name of a friend's dog," Paul said.

"This is totally new to me," Grace said.

"The whole name of the dog was Blind Lemon Jefferson Airplane," Paul said.

"No," said Grace, "it was the old blues singer, you told me."

"Well, the dog was named after the old blues singer," Paul said.

"I'm totally destroyed," I said. "One of the hippest names in the history of show business was taken from a dog?"

Then we talked about the various name changes and reincarnations of the band. Paul and Grace were not in any band at the time, but they were thinking of playing together again. When Paul said they didn't have a new name to go with the group yet, I said, "How about Spot?"

This made everyone crazy. "I like it," said Grace. "We'd probably get into a legal hassle if we tried to use Jefferson Airplane again, so maybe Spot would work."

"We could say we named it after Larry King's dog," said Paul. "Spot—Live in Nicaragua."

One by-product of taking this direct approach is that people who have a tendency to put you on if they don't trust you act a little differently if they feel you're being genuine with them. So even though some rock 'n' roll star *knows* that I've never heard one of his records, he's less likely to be sarcastic with me because I've admitted my ignorance up front. Of course, it helps if they happen to listen to my show while they're up late traveling across the country or trying to get to sleep in some hotel room. Gene Simmons told me that he listens to my show a lot on the road. Then he told me about the time he wanted to rename his band, which in the beginning was called Wicked Lester. The guys were driving down Kissena Boulevard in Queens trying to come up with a catchier name when he had the idea that they should call the group Fuck. They quickly realized that this might limit their airplay potential, so they settled on Kiss.

Simmons is also one of the few rock 'n' rollers who has admitted to me that what they do is really very simple and doesn't take much talent. Some guys say that to put you on, but he really meant it. "Let's not be pretentious about it," he said, when I asked him if, despite all the fun, Kiss didn't have to be pretty talented musically to make it for seventeen years. "The truth is, this is rock 'n' roll. I certainly don't place myself on the same level as a Shostakovich or anybody who's a musical virtuoso. This is ear candy. It's not meant to last more than a couple of years. This is here-and-now music, and you don't have to be a virtuoso to play it. It's not like jazz."

I'm glad that selling seventy million albums hasn't loosened his grip on reality. And I loved Gene's response when I asked him whether you don't become Establishment after seventeen years on the charts. "To a certain extent," he said, "if you're around long enough, you *absolutely* become Establishment. The hardest thing to do, if you're in a band like Kiss, is to keep your snout close to the ground to make sure the dirt actually gets in there. You can't be squeaky clean because then you become the enemy. On the day Mom and Dad like the same music their kids do, it's over. There *is* no more rock 'n' roll."

And make no mistake, Simmons meant it when he said he

wasn't squeaky clean. One caller brought up the subject of tel-
evangelists, and a little later the topic of women came up—as
it usually does with Simmons. He made no bones about the fact
that he lives for groupies. So, tying those two strands together
on the spot, Gene said, "You know, there *is* one thing I have in
common with TV evangelists. We both like to make our follow-
ers yell '*Oh, my God! Oh, my God!*'"

Simmons had lots more to say about women on the road. He
talked about the band's "after-school activities" in the "chicken
coup," a particular room of the hotel where they're staying.
One such night in Indianapolis, he said, he entered a room filled
with "an excess of local talent" (don't ask me to explain these
terms, folks, just use your imagination) and did what the band
always does at such moments—they just "hold their breath and
dive in."

Simmons likes managing and producing as much as playing
and recording. "I just hope that nobody ever suspects for a second that I'm getting away with murder," he said, "that I'm
having the time of my life and getting paid for it. It's amazing."

Is it even as much fun as being onstage? "I love all of it," he
said. "The best part of being onstage, incidentally, is doing the
shows and then running back to the hotel and doing as many
encores as you can."

Not long ago a friend of mine asked me how I could go from
doing back-to-back shows with headline-making revelations
about the PTL to an interview with Zsa Zsa Gabor. How could
I interview Frank Sinatra one night and Donald Regan the next,
and then follow them up with a show about pit bulls? How do
I get up for a couple of soap stars?

The answer lies in what Bill Hartack used to say: "There's a
race after the Kentucky Derby. And if you're in it when the
gate opens, you ride to win." So when the camera lights go on
for that third show of the week, and it's not Don Regan or
Frank Sinatra, I'm not going to throw it away. Besides, viewers
may be tuning in who never saw me before those big shows, so
I'd better be pretty good with the pit bulls if I want to keep my
new audience. The overall answer is that while it's different, it
isn't that different.

A second answer, though, is that no matter how exciting a one-night show may be, it's all the little nights that make my career and that make my job as interesting as it is. Those are the nights when I go on and don't expect anything special to happen and then an Anthony Frank or an Eric Braeden starts to talk and surprises me.

And then every once in a while an interview comes along that is so outstanding, that makes such an emotional connection with me, that I realize all over again why I do this job every day. Two that stand out in my memory were with the great folksinger Peter Seeger and Steven McDonald, the New York City cop who was wounded in action and left paralyzed.

McDonald came on my show ostensibly to talk about his experiences and his book, *The Steven McDonald Story*, but the interview turned into much more than that. It was the only time I can ever recall crying on the air. As a young police officer patrolling Central Park in 1986, Steven McDonald had come upon some teenagers who fit the description of suspected bicycle thieves. Caught off guard when one of them pulled a gun and fired, he was paralyzed from the neck down by a bullet to the spine. McDonald comes from a family of cops, so he knew what he was up against. I asked him what it was like to get shot, and he said the oddest thing was not feeling any pain, because of the damage to his spinal cord. He heard the gun go off, saw the puff of smoke, and the next thing he remembered was waking up in the hospital with his brother saying, "Don't die, Steve!"

His wife, Patti Ann, was two months pregnant at the time he was shot, and since their son was born he hasn't been able to hold him in his arms. Everywhere he goes he has a twenty-four-hour police guard. He still thinks he will make it back and will one day walk again. He still thinks of himself as a cop. When I asked if he would let his son be a cop, he said yes. "How do you feel about capital punishment?" I asked.

"I'm opposed to it," he said. "It doesn't accomplish anything."

He feels sympathy for the young black kid who shot him, although his wife doesn't. He would like to meet the kid one day, even though the kid's mother attacked the police for approaching her son in the park. She asked if they would have

approached a group of white kids playing in the park. Mc-
Donald's answer was no, and he wouldn't have approached
these kids if they hadn't fit the description. And the mother
said, "Forget the description. These were just fifteen-year-old
kids." She overlooked the fact that her fifteen-year-old son had
a gun. In any event, the kid will get out in a few years, since
the officer he shot didn't die and since the kid was a minor at
the time. McDonald wants to visit him and tell him he understands that those kids had different breaks than he had. "And
while it's never an excuse to shoot anyone, let alone a police
officer," Steven said, "I know that as a white kid growing up I
had opportunities he didn't have."

I've never talked to someone like that. With all the racism
rampant in our society, here's a guy confined to a wheelchair,
possibly for the rest of his life, showing that kind of compassion.
But McDonald is a wonder. He doesn't feel sorry for himself, and he has a great sense of humor. So when people ask me
who is the best interview I ever did, I could say Frank Sinatra,
or Mario Cuomo, or Bette Davis, but I could also say Steven
McDonald. He has all the qualities I want in a guest: passion,
knowledge, an ability to communicate. And there was something else about Steven McDonald. All the pain and suffering
he has been through have left him filled with understanding
and compassion that somehow encompass both police officers
and criminals, those who love the law and those who call cops
"pigs." We've often been told that compassion comes out of
suffering, but the reality is that those who have been hurt by
life are more likely to respond with anger, bitterness, and a
desire to hurt others in return. So I'm not surprised that when
I was listening to Steven talk, it got to me emotionally in a way
that my superstar guests usually don't.

Anyone who was old enough to be listening to the radio during
the summer of 1950 will probably remember the Weavers' version of "Goodnight Irene," which was No. 1 on the *Billboard*
charts for a total of thirteen weeks—longer than any No. 1 single in history, including Elvis and Beatles hits. What you might
not remember was that "Goodnight Irene" was not even the A
side of the single released by Decca. The A side was actually

the Weavers' rendition of an Israeli folk song, "Tzena, Tzena, Tzena."

I didn't know that either until Peter Seeger came on my radio show in 1986 at the age of sixty-seven. Many people associate Pete with radical politics, maybe because for many years he was a victim of the McCarthy witch-hunts. It's true he was black-listed in the '50s, kept off TV, and dropped by his record label along with the other members of the Weavers. But to me Pete Seeger has always been the quintessential American patriot, a kind of benevolent father figure for a lot of people who grew up in the '50s, '60s, and '70s.

Pete was deeply involved in the organized labor movement in this country in the '30s and '40s, the civil rights movement of the '50s and '60s, and then the antiwar movement of the '60s and '70s. More recently, he has been involved in environmental and antinuclear causes, too. In other words, each "radical" cause he has been associated with has eventually become main-stream. But what a lot of people don't know about Pete Seeger is that he also went to Harvard and can trace his family roots back to the *Mayflower*. There is no doubt in my mind that Seeger is one of the last living American heroes, and yet every time I referred to him on the air as "the great Pete Seeger," he winced. I finally asked him why he seemed to hate being com-plimented, and I loved his answer.

"I know that I'm only one link in a long chain," he said. "And the greatest musicians I've ever known have often been quite unknown people. Like, for example, Pete Steele of Hamilton, Ohio. He was a carpenter most of his life. He was absolutely the greatest banjo picker I ever heard. But he was a homebody and didn't like to travel, plus he had a big family. I don't really feel happy about the overemphasis on individuals which mod-ern life has given us. The media makes some people seem awful important and makes a lot of people feel like they're unimpor-tant. Once upon a time, everybody was working together and one person might be good at this, another good at that. But technology has overemphasized our differences, and I think we need to get a little more equalized. Things kind of get thrown out of balance. Now, however, I have to confess that I fall into the habit of so many older people who look around and say, 'I

don't like the direction the world is going.' I have to guard
against that."

"You never cared about your name in lights," I said.

"Oh, I guess it's kind of funny," he said. "I have to laugh."
Pete also said that he doesn't think of himself so much as a
singer anymore, but more of a song leader. He likes to get people to sing along with him and sing all kinds of different har-
monies, as he demonstrated on the show.

"I may be unduly discouraged," he said, "but I rather suspect
that in this age when there is so much music coming out of
loudspeakers, people probably don't sit around the kitchen and
sing as much as they used to."

"Did you consider yourself a protester?"

"In the early days, I guess I did. At this age of life, I now
feel probably a lot of songs are protest that people don't think
are protest. After all, a guy singing about unrequited love is
protesting unrequisition. A lot of people in church sing Protestant hymns. As a matter of fact, I remember vesper services at
my school where we sang, 'In spite of dungeon, fire, and sword,'
harking back to the Reformation. I also think that some of the
best protest songs have been humorous songs. There's a famous
Irish song called 'Lily Bolero' from the seventeenth century.
They say King James lost the throne because of it."

"So we've always had it," I said.

"I suspect we have," Pete said. "I once heard an Arab proverb
that went, 'When the king puts the poet on his payroll, he cuts
off the tongue of the poet.' "

We talked about a lot of things, including Pete's interest in
Indian rights. True to form, Pete wouldn't let his forebears off
the hook.

"We did a pretty good job on the American Indian," I said.

"I have to confess that my own ancestors were some of the
first ones to do it," he said. "They landed at Plymouth Rock
and fell on their knees, and then they fell on the Indians."

"You traced it back to the Rock?"

"That's right. William Bradford. He was the man who owned
the library."

"You're eligible for the Daughters of the American Revolu-
tion."

"Or the Mayflower Society. As a man said, though, 'Those of us who come from common ancestors, let us remember that some of them were very common.' "

"Or as FDR said, 'My fellow immigrants.' "

One of Pete's greatest contributions is his work as a chronicler and conservator of folk songs, not only from America but from all over the world. We talked about folk songs that night, and one of the most interesting stories he told had to do with the song "Wimoweh," also a hit for the Weavers.

"You should know that this song is an ancient song from South Africa," he said. "I met the head of the recording company from Johannesburg way back thirty years ago or more. I said, 'Do the Africans ever try to put political words in their songs?' He says, 'Oh, they try it all the time, but we weed it out.'

"Guess what? I asked him what this song meant. He said, 'Oh, it simply means: The lion is sleeping, the lion, the lion, the lion.' Later I found out that the last king down there, who was killed before the Europeans took over, was known as Chaka the Lion. And the legend said, 'Chaka is not really dead. The lion is only sleeping and will someday wake up.' "

I asked Pete how it was that he and the Weavers had come to be blacklisted.

"They accused us of being Communists," Pete said, "and we were unwilling to deny it. We just said, We are singing some songs, and if you like them, you like them, and if you don't, you don't. But how we vote shouldn't have anything to do with it. And that wasn't enough in those days."

Pete refused praise for standing up to the House Un-American Activities Committee during the 1950s. "Oh, you give me too much credit," he said. "You know what? Some people had a real tough time in the fifties, but my kids never went hungry. And I feel grateful not only to the First Amendment to the U.S. Constitution, which is a wonderful little phrase, but to the general spirit of American people in all sorts of places who stuck up for me. It's true that on occasion I had things thrown at me. But I also had lots of good people who supported me."

Toward the end of the show, a caller asked Pete if he considered himself religious.

"I used to think I wasn't," Pete said. "Then I decided that I really get the most religious feelings when I'm outdoors with the blue sky over my head. And I realized that these words mean different things to different people. I suppose some people might think I'm irreligious because I don't go to church regularly. But in a sense I feel it whenever I'm outdoors."

Maybe the most poignant moment of the night came afterward. My producer, Pat Piper, said that Pete told him that his hearing was going and that it was very distressing sometimes. He would sing or play with people and find it difficult to hear them. It wasn't something I was aware of while I was conducting the interview, and Pete would be the last one to make a big deal of it. But after Pat told me about it, I was more aware than ever that even this fixture of twentieth-century America is mortal. I hope Pete Seeger lives forever, but short of that, I wish he would get the kind of national acclaim he deserves, the kind that's usually reserved for astronauts, war heroes, and all-star athletes. I think he's earned it. Maybe the postmaster general would even consider him for a stamp.

10

Talk Show Hell

Fairness dictates that I give a little time to some of my silliest, most infuriating, and most disappointing guests—the kind of people who make the talk show circuit not because of any particular talent they possess but simply because of their celebrity.

Sukhreet Gabel is the perfect example of Andy Warhol's line about everyone being famous for fifteen minutes. If you remember, Bess Myerson's boyfriend was getting a divorce, and the judge in the case was later brought to trial herself for favoritism because her daughter, Sukhreet, had been given a job by Myerson. Sukhreet was the key witness against her mother, which many people considered strange, especially since Sukhreet proclaimed undying love for her. When I interviewed Sukhreet, she sincerely wanted to please me and to show how bright and serious she was, and yet she had nothing to say. Less than nothing. She wasn't content just to discuss the case that had made her ever-so-briefly famous. Sukhreet wanted to talk about Sukhreet. She said that she was going to be a singer and that she was already making the rounds of the clubs. But so far I haven't heard anything about a singing career, and neither has anyone else I know. Her mother's trial was the highlight of her life. Part of me wanted to do a jokey kind of interview and kid around about her obsession with celebrity, but I held back because I had a sense that there was something almost tragic about her. She was dressed to kill and had had hair and cosmetic make-overs in the previous few days. She appeared to be what Sukhreet Gabel probably dreamed of all her life. She had always watched television and now she was on it. The sad part was that the circumstances that had gotten her there—testifying against her own mother—didn't seem to matter a bit to her.

While I'm speaking of silly guests, I would be remiss not to mention Zsa Zsa Gabor. I've probably had her on more times than reason would allow, but my producers keep booking her—they say people love her and she gets good ratings. If I never had her on again, I wouldn't miss her. At least Zsa Zsa has some acting credits, but she got more attention for her trial on charges of assaulting that Beverly Hills policeman than for any of her recent performances.

Wendy O. Williams of the Plasmatics appears to have only two notable assets besides her outrageous stage behavior—and they were both falling out of her costume the last time she was on. People were actually calling in to complain that she was revealing too much, and they didn't mean about the music industry. I know Wendy has made a name for herself by buzz-sawing guitars and blowing up TV sets and cars onstage, but can anybody give me the title of one of her songs? Oh, of course, "Butcher Baby." How could I forget? I'd have to say Wendy has very good PR.

Nonetheless, I try to treat all these people the same way I treat all my other guests. I'm as courteous to Sukhreet or Wendy as I would be to George Bush—and for some viewers, there *is* no difference there. I try to ask serious questions. If the subject needs kidding, I kid them. I give them a frame of reference as an invited guest and let the audience make up their own minds. Those kinds of guests don't infuriate me, though. I may wonder how they got on the show, and I may feel sad about them at times, but they don't send me off my nut. William Rusher of the *National Review* infuriates me. He's okay off the air, but the minute he gets on the air he begins to grate on me. He's beyond conservative; he's a rigid ideologue. To him, conservatives never do wrong, liberals never do right. That drives me up a wall. So I've told my producers, "I like William Rusher as a guy. I would have dinner with William Rusher. But please, don't book him on the show. The man gives me headaches."

Anita Bryant is another example, although she has all but faded from the public eye. I knew her in Florida for years, where she lived near me and married a friend of mine. She was a sweet girl, a former Miss Oklahoma who had a nice voice. I always liked her as a person until she went way out. From time to time, she still calls to ask me to attend a rally in favor of changing the Constitution to allow prayer in the schools and things like that, so I don't have much to say to her anymore.

I didn't usually take public stands on the issues in Miami, except on civil rights, because I was an interviewer. But I really got caught up when she came out attacking gays in the late seventies. I said on the air that she was wrong to attack them, so she got mad at me, or maybe just hurt. She thought that because we were friendly I shouldn't have gone against her, but the truth is that, although I liked her and still do, I despised what she was trying to do.

But Anita called me one night back then, crying, "Larry, I can't believe it," she said. "I think you're attacking me personally."

I said, "If you take it that way, Anita, you're wrong. I'm never attacking you personally. I think your stand is whacked." I know she's been through some tough times recently. Her daughter had a divorce, the orange juice people dropped her, and she had some surgery. But she has an answer for all that, too. "The power of the devil, Larry. It's very strong," she told me not long ago when she came on my show to plug her new album. "That's what ruined my career. It was the stand I took. When the devil wants to get you, he is one tough guy."

To her way of thinking, the devil is responsible for everything. The devil made Jimmy Swaggart go to New Orleans. She actually said that. "Do you think God would have let Jimmy go to New Orleans? And when the devil gets a hold of you, he can ruin you. They got Anita Bryant's whole career."

She came pretty close to saying there was a gay conspiracy against her and implied that gays were somehow in league with the devil. In show business, where homosexuals have key posts in the advertising and recording industries, she was saying that if you take a stand against gays, you don't get records made. "But I knew that going in, Larry," she said. "They're a strong enemy. The devil's still a strong opponent of the Lord."

But my all-time major headache is Lisa Sliwa, a part-time model who is also the wife of Curtis Sliwa, the head of the Guardian Angels. When Lisa is wearing her Guardian Angels beret, she is a hanging judge. She has no sense of the Constitution. She wants castration for rapists. I said to her once, "That sounds like cruel and unusual punishment to me. What if we later find out that the guy didn't do it?"

"Well," she said without blinking, "that's the breaks."

I asked her if she realized that our whole law is based on the presumption of innocence, that it's okay for the guilty to go free as long as we don't punish the innocent. "You're kidding," she said. "You think we could live as a society if that's okay?"

"Lisa, that's in the Constitution," I said. "You must have the evidence. You must dot the *i* and cross the *t*. You have to have the search warrant before you break down the door."

"Why bother?" she said.

I found myself screaming, "That's what Hitler said!"

"You're comparing me to Hitler?" she said. "These are creeps, Larry. You cut their penises off."

Jean-Paul Sartre wrote, "Hell is other people." For me, I'd say that hell would be having Lisa Sliwa, Anita Bryant, and William Rusher as my only guests for the rest of time, on a show where they can give their opinions and I can't interrupt them. That is worse punishment than eternal hellfire.

Another guest who had an attitude was Dr. Bernie Siegel, the retired surgeon and former Yale Medical School professor and best-selling author of *Love, Medicine, and Miracles*. He was on my TV show to promote his new book *Peace, Love, and Healing*, and the first part of the interview went fine. Siegel takes an interesting stance, somewhere between traditional AMA medicine and the holistic approach of the New Age healers. He believes that a positive mental attitude is a better cure for illness than most medicine. He also believes in using love, the doctor's concern for the patient, to augment traditional medical cures. A few years ago, he risked his reputation by calling on all cancer patients to help heal themselves. He concerns himself with a lot of the extraneous factors that don't have to do directly with medicine as the AMA understands it, but his is a valid thesis, not unlike that of Norman Cousins. "Feelings are chemical," he told me. "What we feel is translated into something chemical that affects your body. Peace of mind, love, and hope are physiological."

Siegel went on to list the names of some people who had actually healed themselves of AIDS through nonmedical practices, although this was news to me. Then we went to the phones. The first caller was a man from San Francisco. He came on the line and said, "Dr. Siegel, I've got friends who are dead or dying from AIDS over the past ten years, and I think you're just another huckster who's looking to sell books, a snake oil salesman who gives people false hopes."

"Let me ask you a question," Dr. Siegel responded. "What is false hope?"

"False hope is snake oil. 'Here's the answer, buy my book and I'll save you.' "

The guy was obviously hurting, and he came off as both hostile and broken-hearted. There were a lot of ways Siegel could have responded to that combination, but he responded by getting pissed off, making a face, taking an attitude. His attitude was, "Hey, you're disputing me? You dare to attack my thesis?" What he actually said was, "I gave you specific names. If you think that they would be better off dead, then call them up and tell them to die because somebody gave them false hope. You wanna lie down and die because somebody said you have cancer or AIDS, go ahead."

The caller tried to ask another question and Bernie cut him off. "You wanna listen, please?!" He crucified this caller, and I was sitting there thinking, This is my love doctor? This is the man who believes in healing through a positive frame of mind, and he can't even accept criticism from one caller?

Thinking about it later, I realized that maybe Siegel's anger came from the frustration of trying to get people in the medical profession to accept his thesis. But this caller was not a professional; he was someone who had lost a lot of dear friends to a seemingly incurable disease, and I don't think anger or one-upmanship was an appropriate response. Siegel demolished the caller, and from that moment on I had trouble liking him; I felt that his true colors had shown through. I think a really caring doctor would have said, I understand how you feel, and gone on from there. Instead, he took it personally and reacted defensively and arrogantly. He may have been right technically, but he won the argument and lost a potential believer.

Speaking of defensiveness, there's nothing I like better than sinking my teeth into political debates, except one: abortion. I've found that moderating any debate on abortion is a no-win situation. I've done quite a few abortion debates over the years, on both radio and TV, and I've never enjoyed a single one. By now, people know how I feel about abortion—that women have the right to a choice. But as much as I bend over backward to be fair to both sides, I don't think I've ever learned anything in an abortion debate. And I don't think I've ever had anybody say to me during an abortion debate, "Oh, that's interesting," or "That's an angle I never thought of before." Neither side ever budges. In the fifteen years I've been moderating these debates, perhaps the first new slant I've ever heard was when Mario Cuomo said that it could be considered the essence of Catholicism, of Christianity, *not* to force a woman by legal means to follow a moral precept.

Another reason I don't like these debates is that the people involved hate each other more than political candidates do in a tough race. People in abortion debates won't look at each other, even if they're sitting inches apart behind the desk or on the dais. They despise each other, and it's very disheartening for me to be the moderator in that situation. And that's a shame, because there are some interesting facets to this issue that the debaters rarely bring up. If a pregnant woman commits a crime, for example, can you jail her? Since the fetus didn't commit a crime, why can you put the fetus in jail? If a fetus is already a person, doesn't it have rights? But a pregnant woman is never charged as two people. There is no separate legal individual until it's born. There's no social security number. There's no tax break to the parents until the child is born, even if it's a minute after midnight on New Year's Eve.

And I've never understood those pro-lifers who would allow abortion in the case of rape and incest. If they follow the natural law that forbids intervention to put an end to life, then

what difference does it make how the pregnancy was begun?
Politicians like Bush take that stand purely as a matter of ac-
commodation—they want to sound like kinder, gentler guys.
But the position makes no sense unless you are already pro-
choice.

Abortion is not the only topical argument that can get out of
hand, especially when I'm working with a split screen on TV
and I have somebody in the studio with me and maybe two
other people on remote. We'll be arguing some point, anything
from battered women to cryonics, when suddenly I'll hear the
producer in my earpiece saying to the remote guests, "Just jump
right in. Don't wait to be asked a question. Jump in there." I
understand that they want these people, who are sitting in a
remote studio somewhere with a camera pointed at them, to
feel they're a part of the show and to speak up. But it can make
for a hectic night, and it sometimes gives me the feeling that
I'm just another cut of raw meat being tossed to the TV lions,
along with the guest who has suffered a tragic loss or is revealing some embarrassing secret.

If there's anything worse than an infuriating guest, it's a boring
one. At least the infuriating guest can make for a lively show.
The boring guest makes me work twice as hard and still leaves
us with a lousy show. In that respect, my most disappointing
guest had to be Bunkie Knudsen, the so-called Whiz of GM.
When Knudsen was the head of Pontiac and Chevrolet in the
1950s and 60s, he was looked on as a god. His father, William
Knudsen, a Danish immigrant, had been a big wheel at GM
before him and is generally credited with having a large part
in the origin of the assembly line when he was with Ford. Bunkie Kundsen was probably the most respected name in auto-
motive circles after his father died in 1948. Sad to relate,
though, the Whiz of GM was all but inarticulate on the air.
He'd resigned from GM after being passed over for the presidency, had gone on to Ford, and he was then in charge of
Willys Jeep. And after that show, I knew why he had been
passed over. I was so disappointed, I was verging on rage. About
the only question I had left when I was finished with him was,
How the hell did he ever get to the top? I expected Bunkie

Knudsen to be tough, opinionated, savvy. But I kept asking myself, Why is he here?

He was there because he was a big name and he'd taken over the Willys Jeep company. The Willys PR department had gotten him booked on the show. So I began by asking him why he'd gone over to Willys Jeep.

"I always liked the Jeep," was Knudsen's entire answer.

"You wish General Motors had it?"

"Oh, I couldn't say that. I'm not sure about that, but I always liked it."

"What was your secret, Bunkie?" I asked. "What did General Motors have that the others didn't? What made them rise?"

"They had good cars, and, um, good sales."

By now I was convinced that I knew more about GM than he did. After all, I'd interviewed people who had designed cars for the big three automakers, and they had told me a lot about GM's remarkable success. "General Motors created internal competition, didn't they, Bunkie?" I said. "The Buick guy would want to outsell the Pontiac guy?"

"Yeah, that's true," he said. "That was done before I took over, though. Internal competition, that was a good idea."

Jonathan Yardley, the book review editor of the *Washington Post*, once told me that he knows by the first fifty pages if a book is any good or not. In other words, a poorly written, badly plotted, tedious book doesn't suddenly turn into a masterpiece on page 89. And you can usually tell if a movie's any good in the first twenty minutes or so, often less. For me, the first three minutes of an interview tell me everything I need to know about how it's going to be, and with Bunkie I knew he was major trouble after a minute and a half. I worked hard trying to drag anything at all of interest out of the man, but nothing I did seemed to work. And folks, there is no happy ending to this story. I went to the phones early that night, but nothing my callers asked could make the man any more animated or informative.

The only thing worse than a silly, argumentative, or boring guest is one who doesn't show up at all. Only two or three people have failed to show for one of my programs—that is, without formally canceling or calling in sick earlier in the day.

When we have even just a few hours to get a replacement or fill the time, it's not so bad. But waiting with an open microphone or cameras aimed at an empty seat gives me time to indulge in homicidal fantasies. One of the no-shows was Mike Tyson, who was supposed to be on my CNN show in 1989 and never appeared, never called. To this day, we don't know where he was for that hour. Instead we spent half an hour with Don King, his promoter, trying to explain why Mike wasn't there and where he might be, before we gave up waiting and went to a taped interview with Paul Harvey.

The only other person to do that to me was Mort Sahl, and he did it twice. Mort was booked on my radio program years ago and he didn't show. I did talk to him later, and he went through a long, convoluted explanation about why he couldn't get there. So we booked him again, and again he didn't show and didn't call. I have a theory about Mort Sahl. I've known him for a long time, going back to Miami. And for at least the last twelve years, every time I've run into him, he's told me that he's working on a screenplay with his friend Clint Eastwood. Yet in all these years, this film script has failed to materialize. So my theory is that Mort lives in some kind of dream world in which he imagines he is doing all sorts of things that he never actually does. So maybe on those nights when he was supposed to be on my show, he was home with Clint Eastwood, working on that screenplay instead.

And then there was one of my oddest moments on radio. It came about when I was supposed to interview Dick Howser, the former Yankee who was then the manager of the Kansas City Royals, at a dinner before the 1986 All-Star Game. Dick was suffering from cancer at the time, although we didn't know it. We were at the hotel that was serving as headquarters for the game, and we had been told on the phone that Dick would show up at a certain time. When he didn't, Chris Castleberry, one of my producers at Mutual Broadcasting, went out looking for him. He thought he had found him and brought him back to the show, but it turned out to be somebody who looked just like Dick Howser. In fact, when I first saw the guy, I thought it was Dick. We already had him on the air when I realized this was not Dick Howser.

Chris went back out to find the real Dick Howser, which he

never did, because Dick wasn't there. Apparently the cancer
was already affecting his memory, and he had forgotten about
the All-Star dinner. So I went ahead and interviewed the guy
Chris had brought back, who happened to be a manufacturer
of baseball jackets. He had a license with major league baseball
to manufacture all their hats and jerseys and satin jackets. I
was able to talk to him for half an hour about that, just winging
it. It wasn't a bad half hour, and the guy was very gracious.
He said that he got mistaken for Dick Howser all the time.

On many shows, that would have been a big deal, a very
embarrassing moment, and they would have tried to cover it
up somehow. I decided to go with it. The audience laughed and
had a good time because I admitted that we'd screwed up and
I made a joke about it. At the time we were angry at the PR
people, but as it turned out, of course, it was a tragic event.
Not long after that, Dick Howser died of cancer.

People sometimes ask me about my embarrassing moments
on the air, and, fortunately, there have been very few. I've had
many *potentially* embarrassing moments, however, of which the
Howser episode was only one. Others have stemmed from any
number of causes, such as our physical location.

Chris Castleberry has told me some hair-raising stories about
problems he's had with guests on my radio show, beginning
with getting them into the building. The building that houses
Mutual's studios is in the heart of Crystal City, Virginia. Crystal City has been built from the ground up in a matter of years,
and it resembles the futuristic city run by an electronic brain in
Jean-Luc Godard's *Alphaville*. It's all cubelike concrete high
rises, with a network of highways running through them. This
is the kind of place that, if you drove through it at night, you
wouldn't even think of getting out of your car. It's relatively
crime-free, but it's just ominous-looking. The building I'm in is
high-security because it also houses elements of the Navy Department. A complicated system of elevators and magnetic cards
makes it an exercise in technological overkill just to get up to
the studio.

Most guests are a little apprehensive coming there, not only
because of the building and the hassle of getting in but also
because of the time I do my show, from eleven P.M. to two A.M.

It's dark and deserted, and these people may have started their day in another city, doing the *Today* show or *Good Morning America* at six A.M. They're probably going to do another show tomorrow morning, and they tend to be a little disoriented. We lose guests all the time and may find them with only three or four minutes to go before air time. At that point they are usually frightened or upset or both. If they're any kind of celebrity, they're more likely pissed off. In either case, I just tell the audience that Chris is in an elevator somewhere looking for the guest and that when he gets here we'll put him on, and until that point we'll take calls.

So Chris has had to smooth some pretty ruffled feathers. When he found Ed McMahon, for example, Ed was in the underground parking garage of the building, which is a horrifying place to be even if you know the territory. By the time Chris got to him, the veins in his temples were popping out. He was with his wife, who was very quiet, and the first thing Ed said was, "You want me to do this show or not?" He was yelling. He was so furious, he wouldn't look at Chris. Of course, Chris knows that from the time he finds the guest, even in the underground garage, it's only a matter of a minute or two before he can have him in the studio with me. But the guest doesn't know that. That particular story had a happy ending, because once they got to the studio and I started talking to Ed, he relaxed right away. And after the show, Ed and his wife came over and told Chris that he reminded them of their son, who works with David Letterman, and that anytime he was out in California he should come and visit them. They were totally changed.

Some celebrity guests are concerned that we don't screen calls on the radio. Raquel Welch was booked to do my radio show right after my TV show, but after doing TV she decided she didn't want to do the radio show. My TV executive producer, Tammy Haddad, talked her into going ahead and doing it. She got to the studio and immediately announced she didn't want to do two hours. She said she'd do an hour, and we said fine, we can always go to the phone. Then she wouldn't give Chris the time of day, and there was nothing he could do to please her. She wanted fruit juice, and we had only Coke and Diet Coke, club soda, coffee, and that sort of thing. She asked one of her assistants if he had brought the fruit juice for her. He hadn't, and she started laying into the assistant.

I knew the situation from having been on TV with her, so I came in and gave her a big hug, and that seemed to loosen things up. She began to relax and she ended up staying the whole two hours. As I say, guests have always been very nice to me. I've never had any bad remarks come back to me through the producers. This is a little surprising considering that, particularly before my heart attack and surgery, I was often exhausted when I was doing the show. The show used to run from midnight to five A.M. and there were times when I would actually fall asleep in the middle of an interview. So Chris or Pat would hit the intercom button and say, "Larry, Larry, wake up" in my headphones. I had a knack for finding something to say when the guest or the caller finished speaking, even if I was half asleep. One time this happened with Alexander Haig after he was out of government, and fortunately he was very gracious about it. Chris told me that Haig came up to him after that show and said, "God, he works so hard. You'd better take care of this guy."

And then there was the time I wished I could have been anyone else but me. It happened about three or four years before my heart surgery, when I was doing the overnight radio show. I used to get pretty tired toward the end of those evenings, and one night during the three A.M. news I took a break for some coffee and a little nap. I went to sleep on the couch in the studio. When they played the theme for my show after the news, I would hear it coming over the monitors in the studio and it would wake me up. The theme runs just under half a minute, so the moment it came on, I got up. I put my glasses on, walked over to the microphone, and sat down. The rest of this story is based on what Chris has told me, since my memory of it is pretty hazy. He said he could see my chair start to tilt over very slowly. My headphone cord had wrapped around the chair, so it looked like a seat belt. I couldn't get out of the chair as it tipped over, but I didn't fall out either. I could see Chris fighting to hold back the laughter that he knew would tick me off. He was just watching, expecting me to extricate myself, but I couldn't. Finally, he came into the studio.

I didn't say a word to Chris and he didn't say a word to me. But he knew he had to get me up because the theme was winding to a close. The announcer was saying, "And now, here's Larry. . . ." And I was still on my butt. Chris had to pick up me and the chair together and wheel me back in front of the microphone. I was pretty embarrassed about the whole thing. At that point, Chris was laughing hysterically. I was getting pretty annoyed because it didn't seem funny to me, but I still didn't say anything.

Nothing like that has happened lately, but it's definitely true that my producers get to see me at my worst. And I have to thank them for being so patient and understanding at times like that. I just wish they wouldn't laugh so hard.

11

Flipping the Dial

One of the reasons I like my job is that I like broadcasting. I follow other talk shows, on radio and TV, and so I have some very distinct opinions about my colleagues, past and present. I mentioned some of them in *Tell It to the King*, but there's one I left out, I'm ashamed to say, and that's my all-time favorite, Paul Harvey. I don't agree with much of his politics, but I'd hire him in a minute. He's a classic radio personality. Harvey is not a newsman as I would define one—he does commercials, for one thing—but his delivery is impeccable, and his voice is spellbinding; he's a hundred percent better on radio than on television. I *cannot* turn him off. If I've got Paul Harvey on the radio, he stays on.

Paul has been one of my few idols over the years. I've expressed my admiration for him publicly, and he's been kind enough to respond. One of the nicest things he ever said to me, back in the early eighties, was, "Thanks for all you've done for radio. You've brought radio a lot of attention. The media doesn't like me, so I don't get a lot of press. But you've got so much press that you've reestablished the way people think about radio." Harvey is known for being extremely conservative, and they say he turned against the Vietnam War only when his son came of age. But I heard the show when he turned on the war, and he was eloquent.

Paul Harvey is also one of the best newswriters I've ever heard. He's never dull, which is one of the best things you can say about a newswriter. One line I heard him say when I was a kid still jumps out at me. An American plane had flown over Chinese territory and had been hit by enemy fire, but it managed to make its way back into friendly territory and landed safely. Harvey's whole comment on the event was: "American plane over Chinese waters—shot up, not down." That's writing.

Johnny Carson said once, "The only difference between talented broadcasters and ordinary ones is the ability to take risks." The good broadcasters are the ones who have learned how to separate themselves from the pack. It's not just having a special voice. They are *different*. And one of the things that makes them different is that they are themselves. I never met a great broadcaster who was not the same person off the air as he was on the air. Carson is one of the great television hosts, and part of the reason is that he's really Peck's bad boy. Johnny is also your absolutely favorite uncle. You'll forgive him anything. He's funny; he listens to you. He definitely hands you five bucks when he leaves the house. And he's aged well.

Johnny does some biting political comedy, although he doesn't get enough credit for it, but he is able to carry it off because of the Peck's bad boy image. Carson is not a great interviewer. His staff give him all his questions; they interview the guests all day for that show. But Johnny's a wonderful actor *off* what his guests say. He's never afraid to let his guest get a laugh. He knows that it's the guest's performance that matters. If people say that Don Rickles was funny on Johnny Carson last night, that's a plus, and Johnny understands that.

This reminds me of something Jackie Gleason once said. Gleason told me he would have really loved to play *The Odd Couple* onstage. I assumed he meant the Oscar Madison role, the slob. He said, "No. Felix."

"Why?" I asked him.

"I'd get more laughs as Felix," he said.

"But all the lines belong to Klugman," I said. "All the lines belong to Matthau."

"Yeah, but what do I *do* with the line? I want Oscar to get the laugh, then I want to be Felix off that laugh." That's the kind of sophisticated comic theorizing that Gleason was brilliant at.

Every so often I get a little taste of role reversal, when I go on talk shows and sit on the other side of the microphone for a change. It gives me a chance to check out the competition, but mainly I just try to have fun. When I'm on with someone like Arsenio Hall or Jay Leno or David Letterman, I can end up having a whole *lot* of fun. I was on David Letterman a couple of years ago, and I realized about ten seconds into the interview that Letterman's a hypochondriac. The audience knew that I picked up on it. We were talking about my book *"Mr. King, You're Having a Heart Attack,"* and I looked over to David as I was describing my heart attack and saw that his eyes were really intent. So I said to him, "Wait a minute, David, you want this heart attack. You wish this were *"Mr. Letterman, You're Having a Heart Attack,"* don't you? The ultimate hypochondriac thrill. And maybe there's cancer, too!"

Letterman was perfect. He didn't say, "Don't be silly." He said, "Jeez, now that you mention it. . . ." He began feeling his chest. "When I inhale here, I'm having a little pain."

The night before, Letterman had been on my radio show, and he was being his usual smart-ass self. I came back from a break after announcing our new stations: "WEXI in Memphis, WKCN in Charleston, South Carolina, and KAPE in Cape Girardo, Missouri."

"What I've wanted to know all these years," David cut in, "is how come every night, every week that you've been on the air for eleven years, you can add new stations?"

"Because," I said, "sometimes we lose stations. Like, we lost an old station in Memphis this week."

"Well, point that out," he said. "Because the way it sounds now is that you're on every station in every market in North America."

"You're right, I should be fair. We've lost a station in Memphis. We are now heard on WEXI."

"I used to say to myself, Man, Larry has got every station in the country."

"And Charleston, South Carolina, we lost a station there a while back," I said. David had me confessing all the stations we'd lost.

Later the same night, we had a wonderful little occurrence that captured the magic of the business we're in. We were taking calls for David. A guy called in from Fraser, Michigan, just outside of Detroit, and said, "Dave, you are number one on my list for comedy. God forbid if a bomb should drop on that studio right now, 'cause you're both my idols."

"What a thought!" I said.

"I listen to Larry every night," the caller said, "and I knew you'd be on tonight. I've been calling for two hours before the show, and I've been letting it ring. I'm working right now at a gas station. I'm an aspiring—that'll be one-forty—an aspiring broadcaster, and—"

"What's one-forty?" I asked.

"Someone's buyin' a pack of Lucky Strikes right now, and I'm the only guy here."

"Listen," said David, "let me buy the smokes for him. They're on me."

Then the caller said to the customer, "David Letterman says the smokes are on him. I'm talkin' to Larry King and David Letterman."

You could hear this all on the air. Then the customer said, "Yeah, sure."

The caller said to him, "No, turn on the radio." And he gave him the number on the dial. The guy in the car said, "Hey, I don't believe this! You're talking to David Letterman and Larry King."

Not to be outdone, I said, "Did he buy gas? I'll buy his gas."

Then you heard, "Five dollars on pump number two? All right, go ahead. I'll be out there in a minute."

It came to $6.40. The caller said, "Okay, I'll keep this receipt."

Four weeks later I had a speaking engagement in Detroit, and while I was there I did the television show *Kelly & Company*, which is an audience show like Donahue, only local. On the show I was talking about weird calls that I've gotten on radio over the years, and I mentioned the call from the gas station.

When the host went to the audience with the microphone to take questions, this guy pulled out a credit card receipt and said, "Remember me?"

The receipt was for $6.40 and was marked "No charge, courtesy of David Letterman." He had gotten into the studio audience to meet me and collect his money. I gave him $5, and I brought the receipt to New York, gave it to David, and David sent him $1.40. In fact, David signed the dollar bill.

After the radio show, David and I had talked about that caller. Letterman said, "There's one magical thing that radio has that television does not. As much as we try, by taking calls and sending cameras outside, television could never have created that moment."

Nonetheless, I've had some pretty funny moments on television with David. The next time I was on his show, nothing went the way it was planned. His staff had interviewed me for an hour beforehand and had come up with a whole string of stories I could tell, including the one about the night I was almost killed by the Israeli secret service. But David and I ended up having such a good time winging it that we never got to any of them. Instead, David started talking about my recent marriage and asking why, after previous marriages had failed, I would want to get married again rather than live together. I said the reason was that I wanted to have another child. "When you make that decision," David said, "then you can get married."

"I've made that decision," I said.

"So what are you telling us?" David asked. "Is there something we should know right now?"

"I'm going to start to try to have a child again in January," I said.

"Wait a minute," he said. "You're gonna *have* a child in January, or you're gonna start to *try*?"

"We would like to have a child around October," I said. "It's a good time to be born. You're a Libra, so you have certain breaks in life."

"So the project begins in January," David said, cracking up. "Is that what you're saying?"

"You're making it sound very formal, David. Are you putting this down? Wouldn't you like to be a father?"

"Sure I would."

"Okay, then wouldn't you like your kid to be born, say, in the fall?"

"I guess," David said sarcastically. "Why not?"

"You want a kid born in July?"

"It doesn't make much difference, does it?"

"Sure it does," I said. "You gotta walk with the kid, and it's hot out."

Later David asked if I'd like to take some calls, and I said sure. After the first two, I realized they were setups that were getting increasingly strange, like "What's the best way to get bloodstains out of drapes?" The third call was from a woman who asked, "Do you wear pants when you do your radio show?"

I cracked up, then I said, "Only when Letterman is on." I don't know what it meant, but it got a great reaction from the audience. It was one of those times when everything I did seemed to work. When I came off and went back into the green room, Tony LaRussa, the manager of the Oakland A's, was sitting there. He was scheduled to go on next and he looked a little concerned at having to follow that act. "For God's sake, Larry," he said. "It's like you just scored ten runs in the top of the first."

But as much fun as I have in a situation like that, there's no doubt in my mind that I live on the other side of the microphone, as the guy who asks the questions. The night of the San Francisco earthquake, my TV show at nine o'clock was pre-empted by live news coverage. By the time eleven o'clock rolled around, I was dying to go on the radio. My first guest was a seismologist, and my first question to her was, "What happened under the ground?"

"I've been on four networks today," she said, "and I've been interviewed twenty times, and no one's asked me that."

She went on to explain that a dozen tectonic plates rub against each other along underground fault lines and that when they hook onto each other, they build up tension until they finally snap apart. When you have a quake that registers over 6 on the Richter scale, it means that two of these plates that had locked together have broken apart. And she said the plate under the

Pacific Ocean is heading north toward Alaska, causing it to snag against the plate under the North American continent.

"What are the odds of it happening again in the same place?" I asked. She said it was unlikely because once the plates slide off each other they become stable, locked into place. But pressure can always build up along another part of the fault line. I knew they had had a quake that registered 5.1 a year ago that caused only minor damage. So I asked her why a 6.9 is that much different from a 5.1.

"Because it's not a proportionate scale," she said. A 6.9 is one hundred times stronger than a 5.1. A 7.5 is five hundred times stronger, and an 8 is immeasurably stronger than a 5. I don't remember the exact figures, but they were way out of proportion to the numbers on the scale. No one had asked her this, either. These are what I call "dumb questions."

Dumb questions are what we would ask in the street. Hey, what happened? I watched a lot of the TV coverage and the questions were mostly very good, intended to be helpful. But nobody asked the dumb questions. The basic things that I think everyone would like to know are the very things that the news reporters miss. They're afraid to look dumb. So as good as some of the network anchors are, they aren't going to ask, "What does an earthquake mean? Could it happen here in Washington? In New York? We know how to prepare for a hurricane, but is there any way to prepare for an earthquake?"

Dumb questions. They're dumb because the person asking the question is admitting he or she doesn't have the least idea what the answer is. If you're the anchor or the interviewer and you don't know exactly how the Richter scale works, why not just ask? If you already know, then you should either explain it yourself or get the expert you're interviewing to explain. "I understand it's an unequal scale, but most people don't know that. Could you explain it for the layperson?" But the fact is, most reporters didn't know that and didn't want to admit that they didn't know. Either that, or it didn't occur to them to ask the difference between a 5.1 and a 6.9, which is *really* dumb.

Political commentary shows are a specialized variety of talk show, but they're no less interesting to me than the general interview kind. There are plenty of good ones on the networks, but I'd like to say a few words about some of the right-wingers I share my CNN airtime with. It's not that I want to plug CNN, but just to point out that all those people who have been moaning and complaining about the so-called liberal bias in the media must not watch these guys. I give Ted Turner points for a lot of things—for example, he is probably among the most racially equitable employers in television—but I have to admit that I sometimes feel like the odd man out at CNN. With voices like Pat Buchanan and Robert Novak dominating the network's political opinions, it may be the most conservative major network in the country.

Robert Novak, who writes a syndicated column with Roland Evans and appears on CNN with him on the *Evans and Novak Report*, is a real character. He's a conservative with a sense of humor, and sometimes I suspect he's really a closet liberal who has a shtick going. I had him on my show with Mark Shields once and Novak said, "You know how bad Pat Buchanan's gotten? He made me a present of a new book called *Another Look at the Inquisition.*" Novak knows more about basketball than any person I have ever met. He's an extraordinary sports fan who scouts for the University of Maryland basketball team in his spare time and is very close to a lot of athletes on the team. That may surprise some people because Novak can be outspoken when it comes to racial matters, and basketball is the blackest professional sport in the country. But his politics seem so bizarre to me that I'm inclined to agree when people tell me he's an act. I don't know that for a fact, but I do know that the people who work with him, like his very liberal producer on *The Capital Gang*, Elizabeth Baker, adore him.

And I'd have to say that *Crossfire* was a lot more fun when Bob Novak was filling in for Pat Buchanan while Pat worked for the Reagan administration for a couple of years. That show was fairly unwatchable after Buchanan came back and was paired with Tom Braden. Braden was supposed to provide the "liberal" balance, but he is a former CIA operative, so just how liberal can he be? On too many shows they both seemed to be taking the same side, particularly on issues of morality. When you had Braden and Buchanan arguing about rock lyrics or pornography, there really was no argument at all. When Michael Kinsley, the brilliant columnist and former editor of the *New Republic* replaced Braden, the show became much more entertaining, not to mention balanced, and I love seeing Kinsley and Novak whenever Bob sits in.

Pat Buchanan is a nice enough guy, but something happens to him on the air. He tries too hard to defend people accused of extreme forms of racism or Nazism, and this leaves him in a preposterous stance. For instance, during the Salman Rushdie affair, he took the stand that it's improper for anyone to speak disparagingly about any religion. So you had the great American patriot Buchanan sticking up for the Ayatollah on principle. Could you even begin to calculate the ferocity of Pat's response had a liberal, for any reason at all, chosen to side with the Ayatollah on principle? But the key to this bizarre stand is that, although Pat's a Catholic by birth, he is really a fundamentalist at heart. He has generally sided with the fundamentalist Christians in this country and, whether he would admit it or not, I think he feels an affinity with Islamic fundamentalism too. It's basically the same stand, after all: fundamentalists hold that their belief is the only acceptable one and that anyone who thinks otherwise is an infidel. Pat believes that wholeheartedly. Lately he's been writing columns questioning America's support for democracy around the world and speaking admirably of Pinochet, South Africa, and Marcos. Can the deep end be far away?

Besides, I feel that the conservative movement, whatever it says, has festered a lot of racial hatred in this country and still does. Buchanan and Reagan both opposed the Civil Rights Act of 1964. They both opposed Medicare and social security. Nowadays they may say that they want employment based on merit only, not on artificial quotas that aim to correct past injustices. But they never spoke out for hiring on merit in 1945 and 1948 and 1951. Quotas didn't bother them then. When quotas were keeping blacks and Jews out of law schools and medical schools, we didn't hear from the Reagans and the Buchanans. In short, I think they're blowing it out their, uh, ears.

Talk shows continue to be popular with radio and television stations because they're cheap, they make a lot of money, and

they have high audience loyalty. Even if you give Oprah thirty
million dollars a year, it's still the cheapest show to produce.
Howard Stringer, head of CBS, told me, "I could put *Larry
King Live* on every night on CBS, from ten to eleven, and we'd
make more money than I now make in that time slot. It costs
me three million to buy a new episode of *Dallas*. I'm fighting
for numbers, and I get paid by the sponsors according to those
numbers. But you have to prorate things. For instance, let's say
I had to pay you two million a year, and I get a four share—
meaning four percent of all TV sets in America are tuned in.
And say I pay a hundred million a year for *Dallas*, and I get a
twenty-four share. I don't make fifty times the amount of money
in commercials. So I can have a better net at the end of the
year running *Larry King Live*. However, my affiliates would go
crazy because they would have a weak lead-in to their eleven
o'clock news, because you wouldn't match *Dallas*'s audience."

But cable has changed the whole game. "The same pie of TV
viewers is being divided into ever more pieces," Stringer said.
"Larry King gets four percent, New York Mets baseball gets two
percent, HBO with a movie might get three percent, a Show-
time comedy special might get another two or three, and so on.
What was once our thirty percent is now sixteen percent. We
can't charge as much for ads. So in a sense, you do better for
Turner than *Dallas* does for me."

But a network can't afford to keep getting a 4 share every
night, even though they might make more money. It's embarrassing to finish third, and so much of the business is ego. If you
go under a 10 in prime time, you blow your brains out. Later
at night it's a different story. Pat Sajak did around a 2, but
that's not bad because the audience dwindles as the night goes
on. In fact, radio holds people better than television. Television
drops every fifteen minutes. The first fifteen minutes of Carson
have a third more audience than half an hour later. Viewers
keep dropping off and off until you get down to, say, Bob Costas's *Later*, which gets a 1.5—but that's tremendous at one-
thirty A.M.

It sounds like they make a lot of money on news too, because
whatever they pay Dan Rather doesn't compare with what
Larry Hagman costs on *Dallas*. What I make in a year, Bill
Cosby makes in three segments. Cosby or *Dallas* could put Dan

Rather away, but Rather makes more money for CBS than
Cosby makes for NBC. Talk shows also hold their popularity
longer than series and sitcoms. They have a high loyalty quo-
tient, higher than soaps, once they get established. But you have
to be good, you have to have some charisma, and you have to
be timed right.

To me, the biggest phenomenon in talk shows in the last decade is Arsenio Hall. Although his show is almost more of a
variety show than a talk show, Arsenio still has the youngest
talk show audience in history. He's getting people who never
watched talk shows before, like urban blacks and the eighteen
to thirty-four age group. That means he has expanded the audience for talk shows, and he's giving new people a taste for
something they might not ordinarily watch. Eventually, some
of those people will tune in my show, or Bob Costas, and not
feel that it's something only older folks watch.

And then there's tabloid TV. In recent years, I've turned down
a couple of the tabloid-style TV shows. I decided against appearing as a regular on *Entertainment Tonight*, on which I was
asked to do my column. Hosting *Crime Watch*, a nightly show
about crime, didn't appeal to me either. All I would have to do
is wraparounds; it would take twenty minutes a day: "Good
evening, tonight's main story is in Phoenix. Let's go to Phoenix." But it would have hurt my image. Although I don't consider myself a reporter, Russell Baker says I am. "In the highest
sense, you're a journalist," he told me one night. "Your interviews are journalism."

"But I don't have the same kinds of rules," I said, and I don't.
I'm not evaluating or reporting on my guests, so if the occasion
arises to socialize with them, I don't have a conflict. Someone
for whom those rules have become hopelessly entangled is Geraldo Rivera. I like Geraldo as a person, and I've appeared on
his show. My only objection about Geraldo is that he says he's
doing journalism. I wish he would come out and say, "Our
show is a tabloid television show that looks for the kinkier,
weirder side of things." He made a name for himself by breaking that story about the Willowbrook scandal in New York some
years ago, but he has really changed since those days. David

Brinkley told me off the air that Geraldo is the last person he would ever call a journalist and that when Rivera was with ABC no one who was in the newsroom understood why he was there. What he did was not journalism. It was personal, and it was different. They just weren't quite sure what it was. But Brinkley said, "I never thought of Geraldo Rivera as a reporter."

On the other side of the ledger, Geraldo used to be my principal guest host, and he did a splendid job. The crew said that no one who ever sat in for me was nicer, more courteous, or more professional than he was. I have no doubt about that. Sylvia Chase tells me that if you ever need a stand-up guy in your life, Geraldo is it. When Sylvia had her problems with 20/20 because they wouldn't run her story on Jack Kennedy and Marilyn Monroe, Geraldo was the first to stand up for her, and he was fired for it. And I told David Brinkley that.

Rona Barrett also did a good job when she sat in for me on Larry King Live. She worked hard and was very nice to me, but she's had a rough time of it in this business. Rona used to be a major force in Hollywood and the gossip industry, and now she's reduced to being a guest host. That's the nature of the business, and certainly falling from popularity is no reliable indication of a decline in talent. But doing the Tom Snyder show was a mistake for Rona. Interviewing rock groups didn't suit her, and Snyder clearly didn't like her. They didn't get along, and that hurt both of them. Then Entertainment Tonight came along and entertainment information—the infamous "infotainment" craze—began to be covered by many more people. Rona was no longer special. Rona should have found a niche there, yet somehow she was overlooked.

As for gossip, I'm uncomfortable discussing a guest's personal life unless he or she has written a book about it or has become famous because of it, like Donna Rice or Jessica Hahn. But I don't take the approach of trying to find out who some politician slept with; I'm more interested in what it tells us about changing mores in America. Part of the reason is that I'm not curious myself about who my guests are sleeping with or have slept with. Some producers are a little bugged by that. "He had an affair ten years ago with rock singer Haley Wacko," they'll tell me. "Ask him about that." I don't care. If he once had a romance with someone who has since become famous, I might ask, "Is it interesting to see someone you knew early on suddenly making it big? How do you feel about it?"

If Geraldo sometimes seems to go beyond the limits of good taste, there is one talk show host who is beyond any concept of taste at all. If you've ever seen the *Joe Franklin Show*, you know what I mean. Joe Franklin has been on the air for forty years now. It must be the longest-running show in the history of television, although I don't know one television pundit who can render a believable explanation for this rather dumbfounding fact. Joe is a very nice guy who, to my mind, has no discernible talent. But who can argue with history, even TV history? When you go on the *Joe Franklin Show*, you may end up sitting next to a guy who presses records in his basement, someone who publishes giveaway TV listings, or a dancer who's not quite a professional yet—maybe she's dancing for the Kiwanis Thursday night. And yet the first time I went on, I was with Steve Lawrence and Eydie Gorme. We took over the show and had fun. The second time I went on—and I really ought to have my head examined for going on Joe Franklin a second time—I went on alone, and Joe wanted to do a gag. He didn't know what gag, but he thought it would be fun to open the show with something wacky. I was going to be his first guest, and he was feeling kind of collegial—you know, nobody here but us talk show hosts. "Let's do something different, Larry," he said to me.

"Okay," I said. "How about when the announcer at the opening of the show says, 'Now, here's Joe Franklin,' the camera comes on me. I'll be sitting behind your desk. And I'll say, 'Good evening, I'm Joe Franklin. My guest tonight is Larry King.' You'll be sitting in the chair, and you'll be Larry King. The first two or three questions, you answer as Larry King."

Joe was ecstatic. "Great idea! Wonderful, Larry! What a good gimmick."

So I sit in Joe's chair and the show opens, the theme music plays, and the camera comes on me. I say, "Good evening, I'm Joe—" and Joe leaps over in front of me, throws his arm around me, pushes his face into the camera, and says, "No, he's not really me! We're just kidding. *I'm* Joe Franklin! That's Larry King, that's not me. Good joke, Larry."

I like how Joe really went with the moment there. Then the guest who was following me had written a book on camp. I could see the book on Joe's desk and just from the cover I could tell it was about all sorts of things that are considered camp— clothes, movies, and so on. Joe introduced him by saying, "My next guest, Larry, has written a marvelous book on camp. Let me ask you first, Larry, before the guest comes on, have you ever been to camp? Did you go to camp as a kid?"

"I went once, Joe," I said, "but I don't think that's what the book is about."

"No, Larry?"

"No, I think it's about 'campy' things."

"Oh, *that* kind of camp," Joe said. "Oh, could be. We'll see when he comes on with this wonderful book."

The last guy on the show had windup toys sitting on the table. I don't remember if he designed them, sold them, collected them, or had regressed to childhood and just liked to play with them. But by that point I was so bored that I had begun regressing myself, and all I could think of to do was to wind up the toys and have them all going at once by the time the show was going off the air. And if you ever see me on the *Joe Franklin Show* a third time, you'll know that I've regressed so far that there's no hope left.

I don't want to sound like I'm griping, though, because I've been very lucky with my own career. This was made clear to me when I was in New York Hospital for my heart bypass surgery and Phil Donahue showed up unannounced. Phil sat around for two hours, and later we took a walk through the hospital, causing more than a few patients to do double takes. All the while, Donahue was telling me how fortunate I was to have the kind of show I do and how smart I was to stay with CNN. Considering what I'd been going through, it was a great kindness for him to show up like that.

I don't know if he was trying to make me feel a little better or just unburdening himself, but this is what he said: "Let's say, for argument's sake, that I make two million dollars a year and you make one million. All that really means is that if we're both into boats, I can buy a bigger boat than you. And if we're into mansions, I can buy a house twice the size of yours. Other than that, all it means is that I'm going to leave more to my heirs than you are. But our lifestyle is going to be exactly the same. You can live in an East Side apartment. You can have a limo meet you. But look at what you get for your million, as opposed to what I get for my two million. You get to do Congressman Gephardt on Tuesday night at nine o'clock, and I get to do priests who wear dresses."

Well, Phil gets to do a little better than that, too, but he's right about one thing: I wouldn't trade my life for anyone's.

12

Where There's Smoke . . .

I've written elsewhere about my heart attack and bypass surgery, so I'll spare you the details here. Let me just say that as a result of all the time I've spent in hospitals in the last couple of years, I can sympathize enormously with people who go into the hospital under ordinary circumstances. As a celebrity, I went in under the best possible conditions. I never checked in. It was, "Right up to your room, Mr. King." Forms? "You can sign them later." They couldn't have been nicer, and *even then*, it was the most difficult situation I've ever experienced.

That's because in a hospital you have no control. I got a further insight into the patient's perspective when I appeared as the commencement speaker at Columbia College of Physicians and Surgeons in New York City. That was one of the biggest thrills of my life because I was thinking of my mother and how she would have felt if she were still alive. I never went to college, yet there I was wearing the Columbia gown and surrounded by doctors. As we were sitting there before we went on, the dean told me that the worst experience of his life was being a patient in the hospital. I asked him why, and he said, "Because the doctor knows most of all how little control the patient has. When you're in the hospital, your total being is determined by other people. 'Roll him over, sit him up, take him back, sit him down.' And the doctor panics the most in those circumstances because he knows what's coming and how helpless he'll be."

Because of this, doctors don't follow rules well when they become patients. Dr. Bernie Siegel, the author of *Love, Medicine, and Miracles*, told me that every doctor should be a patient in a hospital for a week. That would change their perspective about what the patient experiences. Siegel is bold enough to suggest that this ought to be a part of medical school training, and I think he's absolutely right.

Maybe the best thing to come out of my heart surgery, besides the fact that it probably extended my life by a few years, is that I finally discovered the benefits of physical exercise. Afterward, I went down to my agent Bob Woolf's house in Florida to recuperate for a couple of weeks, and there I started walking every morning. It was late December, just the right weather in Florida, and I got to like it. Not only did I look forward to the walk every day, but I could enjoy it too because, thanks to the bypass, I had no shortness of breath. I experienced a great feeling of rebirth.

When I got back to Washington, I began walking every day. I'd walk the halls of my building when the weather was bad. I learned how to walk a twelve-minute mile, doing a quick pace up and down the hall. Later I graduated to the Trotter 540, an electronic treadmill which I now use almost every morning.

The funny part of my new fitness obsession is that I was always the kind of guy who laughed at people who did things like this. In fact, if my mother or friends could see me now, they would be hysterical. I'll make any excuse to walk. If I'm in New York, say, at the Plaza, and I have an appointment at 35th and Lex, I'll leave fifteen minutes early and walk briskly. The fact that I'm often recognized in New York makes it more interesting because people want to stop me on the street. I try not to be rude, but I have to keep moving. I smile and tell them I'm exercising. It doesn't look like exercise, just sort of a fast walk, and I'm in business clothes, so this tests their credulity. But trust me, folks. I'm really working out when I buzz past you on the street and don't stop to chat.

About six months following the surgery, I went to Lacosta with Wayne Isim, my surgeon, and spent a week reinforcing my new living habits. That isn't standard treatment, but he recommended Lacosta highly and he happened to be going himself. I was having dinner there one evening when the woman next to me said, "I don't know how to say this to you, but you saved my father's life."

I asked her how. "Indirectly," she said. "My father had a heart attack while skiing, and they brought him down to a remote hospital outside of Boulder. That hospital had t-PA because they had seen you talking about it on the *Today* show." It was still experimental, but any hospital could order it. "That drug saved his life," she said. "If you hadn't publicized it, the head of that hospital said, they never would have tried it out."

I spent most of my time at Lacosta with Wayne—breakfast, lunch, dinner, treadmill, sitting by the pool. For me to get a chance to talk to a heart surgeon for a week was a dream situation, and some of the stories he told me were wild. For instance, he once did a bypass on the great violinist Isaac Stern. Isim did not cut out the large artery that goes up and around the neck and shoulder and that is used in all heart bypass operations, because he thought it would have affected Stern's playing. When you use that artery to replace certain valves, it reduces the mobility in the shoulder. I still can't move my shoulder way back, for example, but I don't have to play the violin. Not that Isaac asked him not to use it; Isim decided on his own. He used extra veins instead because he couldn't imagine Isaac Stern without total mobility in the arms and shoulders. But when he told Stern what he'd done, Isaac said, "But, Doctor, is this something you *should* have used?" Stern was concerned that maybe the surgery wouldn't hold up under stress.

The heart surgeon rarely gets friendly with the patient because, unlike the cardiologist, he sees you once before and usually once after the operation, and that's it. He usually has a very small part in your life. After all, surgeons perform about sixteen operations on sixteen different heart patients a week. But one time, years ago, Wayne had to perform a bypass on a guy who was in the mob. That patient he remembers vividly. First he had a visit from the mob guy's friends, who informed him that they'd have their own protection outside the door. "And Doc," they said to Wayne, "he's out of here in nine days."

Wayne said, "He's out of here when I say he's out of here."

"No, he's out in nine days, Doc."

You may ask why a top surgeon like Wayne would operate on someone from the mob, but that guy's just a patient like anyone else. And besides, how could he refuse?

The Mafia guy wasn't the least bit concerned when the operation was explained to him. "Do what the fuck you have to do, Doc," was all he said. The man was scheduled for surgery in the morning, and one of the guy's friends said, "When does he go?"

"I don't know," Wayne said. "They schedule according to urgency and how much time we're going to allot to each case."

And the guy says, "Fuck all that, Doc. He goes first."

Wayne said, "No," and this time they had to listen. Then they wanted to be in the operating room. They didn't trust the aides, because they thought there could be a hit on. But Wayne wouldn't let them in the operating room, either. The one thing you can never have as a heart surgeon is pressure. There's enough pressure as it is having the guy's heart in your hands, in addition to the everyday pressures of the surgeon's personal life. Pressure is a given, but he is used to putting it aside. He doesn't need to add more. This Mafia guy said to him, "Anything happens to this guy, Doc, you're history."

Wayne said to me, "There was a permanency to that threat. I have to admit that I gave that case a little extra attention that day. One of the assistants mentioned to me that I was doing things I didn't usually do, like asking, 'Is the double clamp doubled?' The assistant said, 'You never asked that in ten years. We always double clamp the double clamp. Why are you suddenly asking?' The day that guy got out of the hospital was the happiest day of my life."

Wayne told me he has a running argument with a brain surgeon at New York Hospital who says to him, "You guys, you heart surgeons, you're the darlings of the hospital. Everybody loves you." This was after a full-page picture of Wayne ran in a big article in the *New York Times Magazine* about New York Hospital. The brain surgeon said, "The Department of Neurology here is just as good as the Department of Cardiology. We have never had any problems in the brain section. But I'm no hero because I'm the brain. You're the heart. The heart is just a fucking organ. You are a terrifically skilled plumber. I'm the brain. I decide everything. I go in and control memory, speech, thought, life. I tell the heart to pump. I'm the master of all I survey."

And Wayne said to him, "Yeah, we should have called the song 'I Left My Brain in San Francisco.' "

One of the other side effects of my heart attack is that I stopped smoking. It's been—let me see now—two years, seven months, and eleven days as I write this since I gave up cigarettes, and I have to say I don't miss smoking at all. The smell of smoke drives me a little wacky, but I would never ask anyone to put a cigarette out. I smoked too long, and know too well what that addiction is like, to ask that of anyone. If you've been a smoker, you should understand best of all how cruel it is to tell someone not to smoke. But Bob Uecker told me something that didn't really surprise me. He was a heavy smoker who'd stopped smoking five years ago, and he said he thought he'd have a cigarette one day, just to see what it would be like. Just one cigarette. He took two drags and said, "How did I ever smoke this shit? In fact, it tastes *worse* than shit."

My daughter smokes, and that's bad enough for me. Still, I don't find that lecturing someone about smoking helps any. I learned this when I was at Donna Mills's house once with William Devane, the actor. Devane is a serious smoker, but he didn't have a cigarette the whole time I was there—until the conversation came around to smoking. We started to talk about what a problem smoking is, how bad it is for you, and how good it was that I'd stopped. All of a sudden Devane lit up a cigarette. What you have to remember is that as soon as you start talking about smoking, a smoker wants to smoke. If you're an antismoker and you're around a smoker, don't talk about smoking. Don't make a speech, because the very word *smoke* is an encouragement. Devane smoked more during that conversation than at any time that day.

Seeing someone light up doesn't make me want to smoke, though. And the reason it's hard for me to tell someone not to smoke is that I know all those good feelings you get from lighting up. They're great feelings. The feel of a cigarette in the mouth is erotic. Cigarettes give you something to do with your hands. Health aside, it's a great habit. I said to C. Everett Koop, "You know, if they came out with a healthy cigarette, I'd be the first one on line."

And Koop said, "I'd be second."

It's probably been said before but it's worth repeating that Koop was the closest the Reagan administration ever came to a genuine national hero. He is not just against smoking; he *loathes* the tobacco industry. The last time he was on my show, after leaving office, I asked him why he was so vehemently against the industry. "Because of the sleaze," he said without hesitating.

"The sleaze?" I asked.

"The sleaze," he said. "Because they continue to say that no one has conclusively linked cigarette smoking to lung cancer and that no one has conclusively linked smoking to heart disease, when more than fifty-five thousand scientific papers have been published supporting my position that they *are* linked. And because they say, 'We're not trying to entice young people to start smoking. We only want them to switch brands.' That's garbage."

Outside of adultery, smoking may be the one subject that more people lie about to their spouses than any other. When Jack Lemmon was on my TV show, I spent some time talking with him prior to the broadcast. About fifteen minutes before we went on, Jack said, "Want to walk me into the bathroom?" I thought it a rather strange request, but I've long ago learned to humor movie stars. I walked him into the bathroom, and as soon as we were inside, he lit up a cigarette.

"Christ," he said, "I can only get eight or nine of these a day. The wife would kill me if she saw me lighting up, because I gave it up years ago."

Then he told me how he went back. He was shooting a movie when the director said, "I think it would be a good idea if your character smoked."

Lemmon said, "But I've quit for years."

The director said, "Then don't inhale."

That's like giving an alcoholic actor real whiskey in his glass and then telling him not to swallow it. So that sent Lemmon

back to smoking, playing a part in *Dad*. Certain parts call for
a character to smoke. For instance, in *Agnes of God*, the psychiatrist has to be a chain smoker. There's even some funny
dialogue about what kinds of cigarettes the various saints would
have smoked. In the film version, Jane Fonda was a terrible
smoker because you could see that she didn't ever inhale. She
just held the smoke in her mouth and blew it out again, which
looks ridiculous to a real smoker. Elizabeth Ashley, who's a
heavy smoker, was much more convincing in the Broadway version.

Then there was the time Michael Dukakis was on my TV
show. It's three weeks before the election, and we're taping on
a Saturday afternoon. Kitty arrives first, fifteen minutes before
Michael's due. Kitty is chain smoking. Meanwhile, her Secret
Service men are all pacing around with their walkie-talkies,
signaling each other. Finally one of them announces, "The governor is in the elevator." Kitty gets in two more deep drags,
then stubs the cigarette out. The ashtray with the lipstick-
marked butts gets dumped in a wastebasket and wiped out with
Kleenex. Then out comes the Binaca. She sprays her mouth.
And in walks the governor.

Michael goes on first and then we put them on together. During the whole time they're on, I know she's dying to light up.
After we finish, he has to leave the studio before her. The minute the elevator door closes, out comes the cigarette. It was
almost slapstick, and I couldn't help smiling. But Kitty was dead
serious. What I don't understand in all this is, What's he going
to do to her? What's Jack Lemmon's wife going to do to him,
besides register disapproval? That told me that as old as we get,
or as famous as we get, we're still little boys or girls afraid of
our parents' disapproval. I felt sorry for Kitty because I like
her. She's got a great sense of humor. I saw her after the election in a unisex beauty parlor on Rodeo Drive. I was having my
hair trimmed, and she came in and sat in the next chair. She
turned to me very casually and said, "We can't go on meeting
like this."

A short time after that, Kitty announced her drinking problem and went to dry out, and I presume that she has dealt with
her smoking habit too. The Columbia dean who sat next to me

when I gave the commencement address said that he once saw
Kitty speak at a conference on addiction. He thought she was
more honest about her own addiction and her own addictive
personality than anyone he had ever heard speak at a medical
convention. It makes me believe all the current studies that say
smoking is a more insidious addiction than drugs or alcohol.

Jackie Gleason smoked as he died. So did the great hockey announcer Dan Kelly, who died of lung cancer at fifty-two. His
son told me that on his deathbed Kelly said good-bye and died
with smoke coming out of his mouth. The day I had my heart
attack, four other men entered George Washington University
Hospital with heart attacks, all smokers like me. And three days
later, two of them were smoking again. I have a lot of trouble
understanding that because now it never enters my mind to
have a cigarette. When I get on an airplane, I don't even think
about it. But I'm very fortunate that I quit when I did, and not
just because of my heart.

For instance, I don't know what I would do if I were a smoker
now that they've passed the law banning smoking on all domestic flights. I recently gave a speech in Chicago. Would I
have gone to that speech if I were still a smoker? That's about
a three-hour flight. Could I go without a cigarette for that long
in the sky? When you're a serious smoker, the sky is the place
you most feel like smoking. Especially when the plane's bouncing, it's a comfort, a familiar friend. What if we got hung up
over Chicago for an extra hour, flying around in the clouds? I'll
tell you the honest truth: I would have lit up. The flight attendant would have come over and said, "Put that out immediately." Passengers might have yelled at me. But if I were still
an addict, I would have lit up. And if I were a smoker these
days, I would definitely not fly to California. There's no other
way to say it. If I were still smoking and someone wanted me
to come to California, they would have to charter a private
plane.

The smoking rules that used to be in effect on airlines were
interesting rules, though. Let's say you were on a smoking flight
a few years ago—a flight of more than two hours—and the
flight was booked solid. And let's say the last person who got

on got a seat in the smoking section but was a nonsmoker, and he or she said, "I don't wish anyone to smoke." That became a nonsmoking flight. The rule stated that people in the smoking section either had to be smokers or not be bothered by smoke. If anyone who was placed in the smoking section was bothered by smoke, all he or she had to do was tell the captain. The captain then declared, "This is a no-smoking flight because a nonsmoker is seated in the smoking section."

I know all this because that happened to me on a U.S. Air flight before I'd stopped smoking. We nearly beat the poor guy to death. The pilot announced it after we took off, and we knew who the nonsmoker was because he had boarded late and most of us already had our cigarettes out. The guy behind me wasn't a smoker, but he said, "It ain't me. Smoke don't bother me." I swear, grown men were punching him. One guy lit up and blew smoke in his face: "Fuck you." The nonsmoker called the stewardess and she made the guy put out the cigarette, and he was later arrested at the airport. But think of it. We're all dying to get lung cancer and heart disease and hitting this poor guy who wants to be healthy. That was right before my heart attack.

I would still be doing things like that if I smoked. On the flight to L.A., I would probably test the smoke alarm in the lavatory. I always smoked in movies. If the usher found me, what could she do? "Please put that out, sir." So you put it out, but you had your three drags. To the nonsmoking reader, this sounds bizarre. Jack Lemmon, millionaire movie star, is hiding in the bathroom. Kitty Dukakis is spraying Binaca in her mouth. Larry King is trying to sneak smokes in the lavatory on an airplane. But it's all true. Now I fly and never think of it. Like I said, I'm just lucky.

In fact, it was on a flight from Los Angeles to Washington that I ended up talking to James Garner about his smoking habit. Garner was heading for Richmond to film the final scenes of the TV movie *My Name Is Bill W.* Garner still smokes, but he's got it down now to five cigarettes a day. His wife doesn't know he does, and he chews gum and mints and sprays Binaca. I asked him how, even after open heart surgery, he could still smoke. He said he didn't think five a day would kill him, although some doctors might dispute that. He has the five cigarettes timed out across the day. "My next one is at quarter to ten," he told me. "It's only three hours away. I can't wait till quarter to ten."

Garner keeps the cigarettes in a little pack inside his leather jacket. It's funny to me now to see grown men with this habit. Johnny Carson and I spent some time together when we appeared on a broadcast of the Television Hall of Fame. Our dressing rooms were next to each other, so it was really a hoot. I was there to install David Susskind in the Hall of Fame, and Carson installed Jack Benny. Johnny and I talked about football and about smoking. He is still a smoker. He was amazed that I had been able to quit and asked me how I did it. He said to me, "I bet a lot of people tell you that you're an idol to them because you stopped smoking and then they stopped smoking."

"Yeah," I said, "it's kind of embarrassing."

"Well, you're an idol to me," he said. "Except I don't listen to idols. I still smoke. How the hell did you stop?"

"I had a heart attack," I said.

"Yeah," he said, "but how the hell did you stop?"

George C. Scott has heart trouble and nearly had to have heart surgery. When I was shooting my scene in *The Exorcist 1990* with him in Georgetown, he was puffing away between takes. He was telling me, "You look terrific, Larry. Heck, man, you look great. How do you do it?"

"The heart attack scared me," I said. "That may have helped me into exercising and eating right. But I'll tell you, George, I really think quitting smoking had a lot to do with it."

He just cursed. "Aw, fuck! It's the hardest fucking thing to do!"

I said, "But George, you've got a heart problem."

"What the hell?" he said. "I'm sixty-seven years old, Larry."

And he smokes nonfilters, too. Now I watch people smoking with a certain amazement. The author Peter Maas is a chain smoker. He recently sat on my radio show for two hours chain smoking Mores. His eyes were red, but I couldn't ask him to stop. And the great Bette Davis came on my show just a short time before she died. She was so sweet and looked so frail in her little white gloves. She said to me, "You and I have the same disease—the camera. We love it more than anything else.

Anyone who loves us should understand that. My four husbands would have been better off if they had all understood it." It was a great hour, but she never stopped smoking the whole time she was in the studio. She never asked, "Do you mind if I smoke?" One entire hour of smoke in my face. The next day she called me to say how much she had enjoyed the interview, and I wanted to say that I would have enjoyed it more if she hadn't smoked so damn much. After she died, I wished that I'd had the courage to say something to her about it. But Bette had been smoking all her life and never thought about stopping. She smoked in her films because everybody smoked then. It was considered racy and elegant, and a cigarette made a great prop on-screen.

Not long ago, at a party at Mark Russell's house, I spent the whole evening talking with Antonin Scalia, the newest Supreme Court justice. And the first thing we talked about was smoking, because Scalia still smokes. He sits on the bench all day, and on every break he goes and has two cigarettes. He can't stop, either. Herb Cohen stopped smoking the day I had my heart attack. He used to smoke cigars. He stopped smoking that day and hasn't had a cigar since, just from my having a heart attack.

And then there was the late Bart Giamatti. I'd known Bart for quite a few years, going back before he was named president of the National League. In fact, I had met him through Edward Bennett Williams when Bart was president of Yale and he used to come to Oriole games. He was also an insomniac and he liked to listen to my radio show at night. Shortly before he died, I defended him on the radio for his Pete Rose ruling. I thought Rose was clearly in the wrong, and I said he was making fools of us. Everyone knew he gambled, but Rose was still refusing to admit it, although he finally did sometime after Giamatti's death. On the radio that night I said that I thought Giamatti had handled the Rose matter fairly, with class and grace.

The day before his death Bart called to thank me for saying that on the air. He said you really need your friends at a time like that, and that's how you know who your friends are. He invited me to go to the World Series with him and congratulated me on my impending marriage. On a previous occasion

Giamatti had told me I was a hero to him because I'd stopped smoking, and if anyone could inspire him, I could. So during this conversation, I asked him how he was doing with his smoking. He said, "Not so good."

During our last interview I had asked him how much he smoked, and he'd said he wasn't sure. He thought maybe three packs a day. I'd suggested that he count his cigarettes for one day, and now he told me that he'd stopped counting after four packs. In the course of that two-hour program alone, he had smoked a pack and a half, so I knew how bad off he was.

"Am I still your role model?" I asked the last time he called.

"You're still my role model," Giamatti said, "but I'm not doing anything about it."

But he had agreed to appear on my television show, which would have been his first public appearance since the press conference announcing his decision in the Rose case.

The day after I spoke to him, I went to get my marriage license and stopped by the CNN office, which was nearby. When they told me that Bart Giamatti had had a heart attack, I was stunned. I could still hear his voice in my head from the phone conversation the day before. But I shouldn't have been so surprised, because he had all the signs. He was fifty-one and looked sixty-five. His father had died of heart failure. They found that Bart had had a silent heart attack once already, and he never went for checkups. Had Giamatti gone for a stress test years ago, his heart condition would have been picked up because he had major blockage. This was a guy who was president of Yale and commissioner of baseball and who nonetheless was addicted. That's what Koop called it afterward, the death of another addict. Bart had even said to me on the air, during that last interview, "Why do smart people do dumb things? We have never had an answer to that."

A little while after Giamatti's death, I heard from a friend I hadn't seen in quite a while. Hawley Rodgers is the headmaster at Oldfield School in Glencoe, Maryland, where my daughter went to high school. He is a Yale graduate, class of 1960, as was Bart Giamatti. Hawley sent me a copy of an article Bart had written for *Yale Alumni Magazine* in 1977 that dealt with the effects of becoming emotionally involved in a sports team.

Bart was a lifelong Red Sox fan, and that year Boston had lost the pennant to the Yankees in the rain on the last day of the season. The piece is called "The Green Fields of the Mind." It is lovingly and lyrically written, and if you can track it down from Yale, it's well worth the effort. It begins: "It breaks your heart. It is designed to break your heart. The game begins in the spring, when everything else begins again, and it blossoms in the summer, filling the afternoons and evenings, and then as soon as the chill rains come, it stops and leaves you to face the fall alone. You count on it, rely on it to buffer the passage of time, to keep the memory of sunshine and high skies alive, and then just when the days are all twilight, when you need it most, it stops."

Reading that again and thinking of Bart Giamatti makes me all the more furious at cigarettes, smokers, and the tobacco industry. And it makes me crazy to watch my daughter smoke now. Chaia stopped smoking after I had my heart attack. She was in the hospital with me, and she got sufficiently scared. So why is she smoking again?

The other day Chaia was at my apartment and she wanted to smoke. She had her cigarettes with her, but no lighter. We found an ashtray but I couldn't find matches anywhere. Finally I remembered an old lighter someone had given me as a memento. But imagine: Larry King had no matches in his house. Hard to believe, man. Hard to believe.

Awareness of smoking, its dangers, and its offensiveness happens to be at an all-time high. But over the years, I've discussed all sorts of maladies and health concerns with many famous people. One of the least talked about but probably most common ailments is depression. All sorts of people you might least expect are apparently vulnerable to this condition. Art Buchwald, for instance. Art has a way of making illness and operations seem routine. Just before I went for my heart surgery, he said, "Listen, unless you have seven bypasses, we don't want to hear about it, Larry. Seven, that's a good story. If you're a four or a five, I'll give you ninety seconds, that's it. The club is too big. No one cares. You know what we care more about, Larry? Measles." Buchwald happens to suffer from severe depressions, and

I've had discussions with him on the topic in which he was able to make me laugh at the whole thing.

Dick Cavett also has depressions, but he can't make it sound funny the way Buchwald can. Cavett takes lithium, as did the late Joshua Logan, who was the first prominent person to do so. Logan was the great director of *South Pacific* and *Pal Joey* and won many Tonys. Apparently you have to take lithium every day, and at a certain time, for it to be effective. Tony Orlando is another guest I've talked to about depression. He heard Joshua Logan recommend lithium on a television show and went to see a doctor about it. Tony was friendly with Freddie Prinze, who took his life because of chronic depression. Tony thinks lithium would have saved Freddie's life.

Cavett made some interesting comments about depression on my show when a caller asked if it was true that he had once checked into a funny farm for a week because of depression. "Do you mean," Dick answered, "what Jean Stafford used to call the 'hat factory'?" Cavett then acknowledged that there was a time during the run of his PBS talk show when things got pretty bad. "I was having maybe the third classic episode of clinical depression," he said, "during which I could do my show but found it almost impossible to do anything else."

He mentioned talking to Rod Steiger about depression, Steiger having gone through a year or more of a much deeper case. It was astonishing to find out that so many outwardly productive people were meanwhile battling this awful disease. "I could function at work," Cavett said of his depressions, "although I didn't think I was any good. I realize that just about every other year of my life I've had a period where I knew I was below normal level. I was having trouble listening to people. I was convinced that I had no talent and that at the end of the show they would come over to me and say, 'I'm sorry, but you didn't make any sense out there. We're going to have to bring someone else in for a while.'"

That sounds like my own worst nightmare.

All this talk about smoking and depression leads inevitably, I suppose, to the subject of death. The problem with death isn't only, as someone once put it, that it's the ultimate inconvenience. Foreknowledge of death affects you most of the time you're alive. For instance, I think organized religion, for all the good it has done some people, has caused more calamity than any other concept in the world. And it's all because of fear of death. Most religions are predicated on the question What happens after we die? Religion's best friend is death: if we lived forever, we wouldn't have religion. Of course, Shirley MacLaine is saying that we *do* live forever, more or less, and she still believes in spirituality. But although I don't agree with her any more than I do with Swaggart and Falwell, at least hers is a fairly harmless, nonintrusive version of spirituality, as opposed to the fundamentalists' and the mainstream churches' versions.

I have a theory, incidentally. If Christ knew that when he was crucified he was going to his Father and that it was wonderful where his Father is, in paradise, and that he'd come back one day to bring us with him to paradise, then what did he sacrifice? But if he didn't know, then I think he sacrificed a great deal, because he risked a great deal. It all comes down to a fear of death. The world would be a different place if we lived forever. Life would be infinitely more precious. If you died only by murder or accident, automakers would not build faulty cars. We would have the safest automobiles anyone could imagine. But people would not be contributing much to churches and synagogues.

I've been in the business so long and interviewed so many people in those thirty years that it's inevitable that quite a few of them have died. Bobby Darin was the first famous person I ever interviewed, even before Adlai Stevenson. One night Bobby had walked into Pumpernik's in Miami, where I started out in radio interviewing, so I called him up to the microphone and we had a great time together. I remember walking along Collins Avenue with him after the show, just talking casually, and the subject of death came up. He was mainly concerned with keeping his career going at a high pitch. "Mack the Knife" was out and was doing great on the national charts, but he knew he had a rheumatic heart. He kept saying, "I'm not going to make it to seventy years old. I want it all now." He got a lot of it, but he never made it to forty.

274   L A R R Y K I N G

More than anything, it's important to keep our sense of humor about the great equalizer. Malcolm Forbes once contacted me about a book he was doing called *They Went That-Away*. I gave him one story. It was about Buddy Rich. When Buddy was dying, the nurse leaned over and asked him, "Is anything making you uncomfortable?"

Buddy opened one eye and said, "Country music."

That is a true story told to me by Frank Sinatra, who heard it from the attending nurse.

I have another true story about death, which came to me from Milton Berle. It's about the great actor John Garfield. Berle said, "John balled anything that walked," and Berle apparently was in a position to know. He said he was in the next room when John Garfield died. They had two women up in their hotel suite in the afternoon, and they were each having sex in a different room of the suite. In the middle of making love, Garfield had a heart attack—he was thirty-nine—and he died. Berle heard the woman yell and he went running in to find her lying there with Garfield dead on top of her. Berle just said, "Holy shit!"

They extricated Garfield and the two women left. Berle somehow got him dressed, put him on the floor, called an ambulance, and told them he had just keeled over. The story was one of those perennial rumors I had heard many times, but now it turned out to be true. What a way to go.

Not long after Lucille Ball died, I had Bob Hope on my show. I could see how her death weighed on him—and also how he was trying to push the whole subject out of his mind. For instance, he would emphasize something that she did that he doesn't do. "Lucy shouldn't have smoked so much," he said. "I don't smoke. I'm fine."

I ask people who are Hope's age about death because I'm fifty-six myself now and I've had a couple of close calls. I want to know how they deal with death's inevitable approach. "What does it feel like," I'll say, "when you see people of your age group, friends and contemporaries, dying?" Milton Berle came on my radio show two weeks after his wife, Ruth, died. He had to get out of the house. Ruth was very funny and talented but always took a back seat to him. She had been in the hospital, and she happened to die the night Lucille Ball went in with a heart attack. In fact, the first thing Lucille Ball asked in the morning was, How is Ruth Berle? They didn't tell her, and soon Lucy was dead, too. But there was virtually no news of Ruth's death because the media were fixated on Lucy. When I heard that story, it reminded me of Aldous Huxley, a great writer who suffered the bad fortune to die on the same day that John Kennedy was assassinated. I didn't see anything about Huxley's death at the time, so for years I didn't even realize he was gone. The first thing I said when I learned Huxley was no longer alive was, "When the hell did he die?"

We make a big deal about people like Lucille Ball who died after long lives in which they've made great achievements and contributions. But I think we should pay a little more attention to some of the people who die before their time. When I interviewed Terry Bradshaw, the great Pittsburgh Steeler quarterback who led his team to four Super Bowl wins, he talked about the other great quarterbacks who played at his high school in Shreveport, Louisiana. One, I knew, was Joe Ferguson. "But the best of the three," he said, "was a guy named Ray Draper. He was about the best quarterback I ever saw. Then he went to Vietnam and was killed in action."

And who knows how many potentially great athletes have been lost to drugs? Len Bias, the Maryland basketball star who died after snorting coke, was only the most visible. Red Auerbach told me that Bias, who had signed with the Celtics shortly before he died, would have been a major superstar of the two-million-dollar variety. But Bill Bradley had a more chilling story. He said the best basketball player he ever saw was a kid in Harlem. Some of the NBA guys go up there on Sunday afternoons and play outdoors in the Harlem league, and Bradley said this kid would run you into the ground. But he was a coked-up kid. As Bill put it, "He'd play a tremendous game, and then he'd go sniff and sell." The kid finally just disappeared, and Bradley never saw him again.

It's easy to tell stories about the deaths of celebrities, but when somebody dear to you dies it's a little harder to find the words.

My father died when I was ten, and my mother died fifteen years ago, and until recently I'd been lucky to not lose anyone else close to me. I have tried to replace my father with various father figures over the years, beginning with Charlie Bookbinder, who actually got me started in the business of interviewing people. Charlie owned Pumpernik's restaurant in Miami, and it was his idea to set up a radio microphone there and have me interview whoever walked in. While I was living and working in Florida, Charlie looked after me and gave me all kinds of fatherly advice. Duke Zeibert took over that role somewhat when I moved to Washington, and to a lesser extent so did Edward Bennett Williams. But Ed was more like a strong uncle and a close friend rolled into one. So when he died, it came back to me all over again just how devastating a loss like that can be.

Simply put, Edward Bennett Williams was the greatest man I ever knew. I heard about his death at the Republican convention in New Orleans. I was at a party given by the *New Orleans Times-Picayune* when Art Buchwald came over to me and said, "Eddie's gone." I knew he had been sick with cancer for some time, but those words hit me like a truck. I went back to my hotel room that night and found messages from more than a dozen radio stations and publications asking for my comments. I spent most of the night on the phone talking with people about Edward Bennett Williams. George Will and I talked about getting a plane back to Washington, but it would have been very hard to go and come back and do our shows. So I missed that funeral, and I'm sorry I didn't get a chance to pay my respects.

I spoke to Mario Cuomo the next day, and Mario told me that he had spoken to Eddie the day he died. "I think I've lost this one," Williams told him. Ed had fought cancer for so many years and thought he had licked it several times, but he knew that the end was near. He had grown to hate doctors, especially those in Washington. I had said, "Well, where's the best medicine?"

He said, "The best medicine starts with National Airport."

When Eddie hugged me at his daughter's wedding the year before he died, he had the look of cancer for the first time, that terrible yellow color. All the years he'd been fighting it, he never looked like he had cancer. You knew it was there and you knew he'd had surgery, but he never looked bad. In fact, that was what used to drive him crazy. He'd say, "I have this disease and I don't feel any pain." And, of course, it never affected his work habits. He'd still be in the office every day at seven A.M. When I spoke to Eddie just before I left for the Republican convention, he said that he was feeling a little tired. I could feel how frail he was when he hugged me. Ed was a big bear of a man and very strong, and I was beginning to get the sense that he was finally going.

About a month before he died, we had taken a walk along Connecticut Avenue, talking about the unfairness of death and about how his religious belief was keeping him strong. "Larry, you don't want to know about this," he said. "This is a son of a bitch. I don't want to die."

"If you're a believer," I asked him, "why should you be afraid to die?"

"I'm not afraid of death," Eddie said. "It's just that I like this so much. Am I going to get to know who's the next president?"

Edward Bennett Williams gave the soundest practical advice of any man I know. I would certainly want him in a courtroom with me. I think about Eddie every day since he's gone and I can't think of anyone else that I could say that about, including my parents. I'm an agnostic. I don't believe that there's anything out there, but sometimes I think that Eddie's looking down or that Eddie's talking to me. I can still hear his voice.

Sammy Davis, Jr., wrote in his autobiography about the man who had been his conductor for most of his career and who died of a heart attack. Sammy said that at the funeral he thought about how the late Bobby Darin had always liked this guy, whose name was George, and that now Darin could have George as his conductor. Sammy went on to say that sometimes he felt he could sense George's presence in the room when he was recording. After all, George had been his conductor for thirty years. Before Eddie died, I would have dismissed all that as maudlin sentimentality. But now I understand what Sammy was talking about. I have to admit that sometimes I sense Eddie's presence, although I can't really explain it. I just have the feeling that I could call him up on the phone at any time and talk to him. There's no one who can take his place. I asked Larry Lucchino, who was Ed's law partner and who took over the Baltimore Orioles after he died, "Who's taking over the law firm now?"

Lucchino said, "Caesar has no heirs." He also said, "The trouble now is that I judge other people by his standards."

I've talked to Art Buchwald and Ben Bradlee and I know they feel the same way about Ed's death. "There are still some days," Buchwald told me, "when I'm going to lunch and I say, 'Where's Eddie? Where's Eddie to have a drink with?' "

Ed was always there for me. He wrote the letter to get my daughter into Oldfield School when we moved to Washington, because his daughter had gone there. He was with me the night Chaia graduated. He was a frequent adviser to Jesse Jackson, something not generally known. And his Catholicism, his faith in God, never wavered. He used to say, "How can you not believe? You mean this is an accident? Come on. Are you crazy? If I didn't believe, this would be intolerable." For all that, Ed Williams was a pessimist who used to say, "Pessimism is just intelligence."

When I returned to my show after my heart attack, Ed came to the TV studio with Angie to cheer me on. My guest was the head of the FDA, Frank Young, who was talking about the new AIDS drug, AZT. When Frank walked into the studio, he was shocked. "Larry, good to see you again," he said.

I said, "I'd like you to meet two of my friends, Edward Bennett Williams and Angie Dickinson."

I thought Frank would faint. "These people are just here to watch?" To him, Ed Williams was as big a figure as any movie star or national politician.

But best of all, Edward Bennett Williams had a wonderful sense of humor. After my heart attack, I went down to Florida and stayed near Eddie's compound on Key Biscayne, and then he flew me back in his private plane. We went out to Memorial Stadium where his Orioles were playing. Everyone was very concerned about me because I had just had a heart attack. They were saying, "Larry, how are ya? How ya feeling?"

Ed got really mad; I could tell he was ticked. "I've got fucking cancer," he said. "Heart attacks are a dime a dozen. I got the Big C, man."

That night, we went out to eat, and as we were getting ready to order we were still arguing the merits of cancer versus heart disease. "Well, I'll tell you one thing," Ed said, resting his case. "I can eat anything on this menu."

13

All the News That Fits ...

In line with my own advice about admitting things up front,
let me say right off that I had originally placed some of the
following stories in other chapters throughout the book. The
only reason they're here is that my publisher didn't want to
leave them where they were, which shows you how much clout
I have. The only thing we agreed on was that the stories were
good enough to stand on their own, so here they are.

In 1988, I emceed a show entitled "The First Annual Evening
of Jewish Humor" at Davis Hall in San Francisco. The program
was produced as a benefit for the Jewish Community Federa-
tion by Bob Harris, who runs a comedy club called the Other
Café. It was a great bill, with Henny Youngman, Steve Landesburg, Richard Lewis, Rita Rudner, Jerry Seinfeld, and local
San Francisco comic Bobby Slayton. Somehow Robin Williams
had heard that the event was taking place, and he showed up
backstage. I asked him if he would like to go on. He said, "But
I'm not Jewish, Larry."

I said, "Okay, if I can think of a way to work it out, will you
go on?"

He said, "Yeah." And just before the last comic finished his
routine, I had a brainstorm. The audience was getting ready to
leave, and I went out and said, "It's been a wonderful night.

But the title of tonight's program sort of offends me because we of the Jewish faith are known for our open-mindedness and tolerance, and everyone on the stage tonight has been Jewish. Probably almost everyone in the audience is Jewish. I was backstage while Mr. Landesburg was finishing up, and I thought, I'm going to open the stage door to the street, and the first person who comes along who's not Jewish, I'll invite him in and ask him to come up onstage, just to see what that would be like. And I found this young man straggling alongside the building, and he said he was not Jewish. So I made him the Shabbes goy."

I pleaded with them to treat him kindly since he was obviously out of his element but was game to try this out. I think they knew something was coming, because in explaining how disoriented he was, I told the audience that when I said to him, "Good evening," he said, "Good morning." And as I said that, Robin Williams came from the wings, did a double cartwheel onto the stage, and leaped into my arms. And Robin is not a light guy. Naturally the place went wild, and Robin was in peak form. He started by saying that he was picking up all the Jewish energy in the hall, that he could feel it coursing through his body, and then he kind of went into a trance. And in the trance, he channeled George Jessel. Robin did the best George Jessel imitation I've ever heard, but it was George Jessel speaking New Age Jewish wisdom from beyond the grave, as Jessel might have purveyed it. Robin somehow segued from that into the Israeli ambassador pitching for contributions. It was Israel's fortieth birthday, but it was also the height of the Intifada, and he managed to handle it all in a way that had this very pro-Israel audience laughing at itself. Moments like that make me realize exactly why Robin Williams is a national treasure.

Williams is a brilliant improvisational comedian; he does some of his best work off the top of his head. Don Rickles is the same way. I once went to dinner in Las Vegas with Rickles and brought Chaia, whom he hadn't seen since she was an infant. Rickles used to kid Chaia's mother, Alene, when she was younger than Chaia is now. He would walk onstage, look down, and say, "The wife, Larry?" Then he'd look at her and say, "Trixie, you don't have to work the bar anymore. Holy Christ, Trixie, you made it to the main room."

This time, before I came in the door, someone said to him, "Larry's here." Rickles started talking loud. "Hey, it's Larry King, he got big with a heart attack! He needed a heart attack to get big. He was doing okay, but Jesus Christ! You want press attention? Going to fall down at my show tonight? This would help me a lot, Larry, if you could have the second one tonight right in the middle."

We went to dinner at the Golden Nugget and he told a great story about Princess Margaret. It's a true story, and classic Rickles. This is some years ago. He's in England and he does a command performance. At the end of the performance, Princess Margaret would like to see him alone for a private conversation. Everyone's a little worried; they're nervous because he'd lambasted the queen in his performance. Margaret sits down and she says to him, "Donald, I understand you live near your mother."

Apparently they have a dossier on each performer, so they know all the particulars about his life. He says, "Yes, I do. I live near my mother."

"I understand your mother is seventy-three," she says. "Is that right?"

"Yes," he says.

"*My* mother is seventy-three," the Princess says.

"Amazing," Don says.

"And your mother has emphysema, does she not?"

"Yes."

"*My* mother has emphysema."

"Your mother smokes?" Don asked.

"My mother smokes. Isn't it amazing? Your mother's seventy-three, my mother's seventy-three. My mother lives near me and you live near your mother. My mother has emphysema and your mother has emphysema. My mother smokes and your mother smokes. How interesting that we, from different continents, have mothers who are so alike."

And Don says to her, "The one difference is—at your mother's house, there's a flag on top."

Rickles has a way with heads of state. One time he was at a state dinner at the White House along with Frank Sinatra. Don told it this way: "Sinatra's outside on the lawn going, 'I'm still big.' Then, as we're leaving, I grab the president and whisper into his ear. The Secret Service leans forward like, What are you going to say? And I say to Reagan, 'Y'ever in Vegas, you need anything, you call me.' "

Rickles also told me a funny story about being on an airplane with Bob Newhart, who's a very nervous flyer. Newhart and his wife travel all over the world together, but for Bob every flight is as if it's his last. Newhart and his wife are Catholic and they carry rosary beads. During the flight, he'll run the rosary beads through his hands. He looks straight ahead. He doesn't look out the window. Rickles, on the other hand, is very nonchalant about flying. He feels that if your number is up, your number is up, and there's no sense worrying about it. So one time they're all sitting together in first class, and the plane's coming in for a landing. Newhart's seated on the aisle. His wife's by the window. And Rickles is in the middle row reading a paper.

All of a sudden, Newhart's wife looks out the window and says, "We're too high up for a landing."

Newhart grabs the rosary beads and starts kissing them and rocking back and forth saying, "We're definitely too high." Rickles looks over at them and says, "How the fuck could we be too high? You think the pilot doesn't know what's going on? Do you know better than the pilot?"

Then, suddenly, the plane takes right off again and starts climbing. A few moments later the pilot comes over the intercom and says, "Sorry about that, folks. We were coming in a little too high, ran into some wind pressure, and we'll have to bank around and come in and try that again."

Newhart starts yelling, "This is it, it's all over!" And the wife is going, "I told you we were too high."

Tommy Lasorda, the Dodger manager, has often been accused of being more interested in celebrities than in baseball. That's not true, by a long shot, but Tommy fuels the accusation by using celebrity batboys during Dodger games, including the likes of Don Rickles. Once Lasorda even had Rickles take a pitcher out of a ballgame—not a spring training game, but a regular-season game. The pitcher on the mound happened to be Alejan-

dro Peña, who doesn't speak much English. Rickles was wearing
a uniform because he was the honorary batboy that day. This
is in the fifth inning at Dodger Stadium, the other team is getting to Peña pretty good, and Lasorda tells Don to go take Peña
out. Rickles says to Lasorda, "Hey, Tommy, it's a real game.
There are forty thousand people out there."

Lasorda yells, "Fuck it! Take him out."

Rickles goes out to the mound. Nobody in the stands knows
who he is. He's got a number on his back, but it's not even
listed in the program. And Peña says, "Who de fuck are you?"

Don says, "Look, don't embarrass me. Just please come out
of the game."

Peña says, "I no know you, man. You no on this fucking
team. I no fucking know you!"

Joe West is the umpire behind the plate, and after a minute
he comes walking to the mound. When he's not working baseball games, Joe's a country and western singer. He gets to the
mound to break it up and he sees Rickles. God's honest truth
he says, "Don, a week from Sunday we're going to be at the
Golden Nugget, four people. Would you write this down?"

Peña's fuming now. "What de fuck is going on?"

Rickles is taking a pad out of his pocket and writing. "That's
four for Joe West in Vegas. At the dinner show?"

"Yeah, the dinner."

Then West says to Peña, "He said to leave, you leave."

One year during spring training, Lasorda made Albert Brooks
a batboy, and Brooks almost killed Bill Madlock. Albert doesn't
know the first thing about baseball, but when you're honorary
batboy the umpire expects you to perform some actual batboy
chores four or five times during the game rather than just sit in
the dugout. Albert was told to get the bat away from the plate
when a player gets a hit. He was very conscientious and watched
what the other batboys were doing, picking up the bats and
tossing them toward the dugout after a hit. When Albert's turn
came to go to work, the batter hit a long sacrifice fly as Bill
Madlock was tagging up at third. Brooks went out to the plate,
picked up the discarded bat, and tossed it away. No one had
told him that there was a runner on third, though, and he ended
up smacking Madlock in the leg with the bat as he was coming

down the line. Madlock fell, got up and scored, and then had to be removed from the game.

We know a lot about major league ballplayers these days, but not so much about umpires. Not many people know, for instance, that major league umpires, unlike ballplayers, coaches, and managers, have to make their own travel arrangements. They get an American Express card that's billed to the league, and they get per diem expenses. But they make their own hotel deals. And umpires have a lot of deals with hotels. Since they get a certain number of free tickets to each game, they might, for instance, give the hotel manager tickets to the Orioles game and pay $60 for a room instead of $100. Their flights are all billed directly to the league, but they make their own reservations and have to find their own transportation to and from the airport. They get a three-week schedule in advance, and they can get to each city any way they want—bus, car, train, or plane—but they had better be there. Often one umpire from the crew of four is better at arranging travel, and he does all the booking.

This casts an interesting light on what it must have been like for the scab umpires who worked during and after the umpires' strike a few years ago. When it was all scabs during the strike, they worked together on travel. But a few of the scabs stayed on permanently after the strike was settled, and they were, as you might expect, ostracized by the other umps. If the crew had one former scab in it, the scab had to take care of himself. If the scab got on the flight with the others, that was his business. They had to use the same dressing rooms, so three guys would talk to each other but not to the fourth.

I learned a lot of this from Dave Pallone, who not only was a scab but also was the first umpire to come out and admit he was homosexual. I like Dave a lot, and he was very nice to me. He's a fan of mine. But when I was with him I could never get out of my mind the awareness that he took work away from guys who were picketing. I just don't like that.

Jerry Dale, a National League umpire, once gave me a very good analysis of why it's difficult to umpire. He said, "There is one attribute an umpire must have that is the complete opposite of what a player has. What a player is very good at, an umpire should never do, and that is to anticipate. The great player anticipates. The great umpire never anticipates. You don't put your right hand up until the player is tagged out. You have to remove anticipation totally. Here comes the player for the plate. Here comes the ball. You wait. The great player gets that jump, he anticipates that the ball will get past the right fielder, so he takes that extra base. The player cannot say to himself, 'I have no idea what's going to happen. There are runners on first and second. I have no idea what I'll do if the ball is hit to me.' The great umpire, in contrast, has total patience and no anticipation. If you anticipate and your hand goes up and the fielder drops the ball, you just made a wrong call in front of forty thousand people."

I'm a union man all the way. The great American labor leader Walter Reuther had a profound effect on me. He always believed that the unions prevented communism in America, that in the 1930s conditions were so bad that the country might very well have gone all out for communism if the unions hadn't been so successful in redressing many of the workers' grievances.

They can sometimes go a little far, though, as I found out when I was hired to play my small role in *Ghostbusters*. I was flown to New York to shoot my scene in that film and was told that a limo would pick me up at the airport. I got off the plane and started looking for a limo driver. What I saw was a burly guy about six-three, wearing a lumber jacket and carrying a little paper sign that read KING. As I followed him to a big stretch limo waiting by the curb, I realized that this guy, who looked like Rocky, was my driver. "You don't look like a limo driver," I said.

"I'm with the Teamsters," he said, "and we have a contract on any movie made in New York City. The contract requires that we do all the moving associated with the movie. We move the equipment, we move the people coming into town, and we drive the Ghostbusters vehicle, except for the times when it's being filmed. If it's not actually being shot but it has to be moved from Seventy-first Street to Seventieth Street, Aykroyd can't drive it. So I was assigned to pick you up today. The studio provides a stretch limo, but a Teamster has to drive it."

As we were driving along, I asked him, "What if I wanted to make a movie in the city and *not* use the Teamsters?"

He just turned around and laughed. The implication was clear: I'd have a hard time making a movie without my knee-caps.

I've mentioned that my friend Duke Zeibert was quite a heavy gambler in his day. "I used to go to Las Vegas with eighty dollars in my pocket," Duke would say, "and lose forty thousand, sixty thousand."

I asked him if he ever put a limit on himself and then told the house to forget it. A gambler would do that—tell the house, "Don't let me take out more than twenty thousand dollars in chips." But in Vegas, according to Duke, if you say, "I want forty thousand dollars' worth of credit and that's it," you don't get any more. They want to get paid.

"What was the biggest bet you ever laid?" I asked him.

"The biggest football bet I ever made was twenty thousand, when twenty thousand meant something," he said. "The busboys bet twelve thousand now. I'm talking about twenty thousand in 1958."

It was the NFL championship game between the Giants and the Colts. The Colts were four-point favorites, and their owner, Carroll Rosenblum, had bet on the game. He had bet his own team, but they had to win by more than three points to pay off. The game was tied and went into overtime. The Colts drove up to the Giants' one-yard line. Naturally, you'd expect any team in that situation to go for the field goal. Why risk a fumble, when three points will win? But Rosenblum needed to beat the point spread, so he sent word to have them run it in. Unitas gave the ball to Ameche, who ran it in for the six points, and they beat the spread. A strange story later surfaced about Rosenblum, who died while swimming in the ocean. He was a tremendous athlete and a very good swimmer, and the talk was that the mob had got to him for some reason or other. Maybe he beat the spread one time too many, who knows?

But Duke Zeibert didn't always come out a loser. In fact, he won one of the weirdest bets I ever heard of. As Duke tells the story, some bookies were running their bets out of a house when the police came and occupied the house next door and put a spike on the bookies' phone. The cops listened to the bookies' conversations for several weeks and eventually arrested them. They brought the case to court and Duke, who knew the bookies, got Edward Bennett Williams to act as their attorney. Williams told Duke he was pretty sure they would lose the case in court but would probably win on appeal. One of the bookies who had been indicted bet Duke that they wouldn't beat the case and gave him 10 to 1 odds. The bookie was betting against himself, or maybe he was just hedging his bets. In any case, Duke bet him a hundred bucks. He wanted to bet more at those odds, but the bookie wouldn't take more action than that. Sure enough, Bennett took the case, lost it in the lower court, and won the appeal. And Duke won his thousand dollars.

While we're on the subject of sports and gambling, here's a sports trivia question that you could win a lot of bets with. To my mind, it's the best trivia question ever asked, because no one ever gets it. The question is, What opposing pitcher has the best lifetime record against the New York Yankees, with a minimum of 15 wins? That means you can't give me a guy who's 4 and 0 against the Yankees.

The answer is Babe Ruth. Ruth was 17 and 3 against the Yankees when he was with the Boston Red Sox. But don't be crazy. Before you put a lot of money on the bet, ask if he's read this book first.

One of my favorite gambling jokes was told to me by Larry Merchant, a graduate of my alma mater, Lafayette High School, and now a sportswriter at ESPN. This bank president is looking over the accounts in his bank one day. He notices that one of his depositors makes deposits every Monday: $500, $1,000, $700, $1,500, $800. But only deposits. He has never made a withdrawal in eleven years.

So the bank president goes out to one of the tellers and says, "You know this fellow?"

Teller says, "Oh yeah, we know him. He's a nice guy, comes in on Mondays."

Bank president says, "You know this guy never makes a withdrawal?"

Teller says, "Yeah, always deposits, all in cash, every week."

President says, "Well, I'd like to meet him. This is one of the greatest bank accounts I've ever seen." He asks the teller to send the guy in to see him next Monday.

So next Monday they send the guy in to see the bank president. Guy knocks on his door and says, "You want to see me?"

Bank president says, "Yeah, please come in. I'm fascinated with your account. It's incredible. What do you do for a living?"

He says, "I'm a gambler. I bet on things."

President says, "Wait a minute. Gamblers mostly lose. But all you make is deposits, no withdrawals."

He says, "I don't lose. It varies what I win, but I never lose."

"That's amazing," says the bank president.

"I tell you what. I'll bet you five hundred dollars," he says to the bank president, "that you have three balls."

Bank president says, "What?"

He says, "I'll come back here at nine tomorrow morning with a witness. You take down your pants, I check you out. I bet you five hundred dollars you have three balls."

Bank president says, "You got a bet."

Next morning at nine, the guy arrives. He's got a friend with him. They close the door. The bank president drops his pants, and the friend faints. Bank president says, "What's that all about?"

He says, "I bet him a thousand bucks that tomorrow morning at nine A.M. I'd have a bank president by the balls."

Harry Morton was an emcee in a nightclub and a maître d' who managed comedians. He was also an inveterate practical joker, but one time, purely by accident, he had the tables turned on him. The chef in a nightclub in Brooklyn where Harry worked had the best-shined shoes Harry ever saw in his life. Harry was a bug on shined shoes. He used to say to this guy, "I never saw shoes shined like yours."

The chef said, "Well, I live in Harlem, and they got a shoe store there that's the best. That's where I get my shoes done."

"Listen," Harry said, "if I brought my shoes to you every week—I'll pay you extra—will you take them up to Harlem and have them shined?"

"Be happy to do it for you," said the chef. So for three years, every week, Harry would bring in five or six pairs of shoes. The chef would take them up to Harlem and have them shined.

Then the chef quits. Harry gets really depressed. He goes a week or two without having shined shoes. Finally he says, "Screw it, I'm driving up to Harlem." He gets the address of the shoe store from the chef and drives up to Harlem. He knows he can't do it every week, so he brings twenty pairs of shoes with him, his entire collection. He gets out of his car carrying twenty pairs of shoes and goes into the shoe store. Suddenly cops jump out behind him, in front of him, all over the place. They throw him up against the wall, take all the shoes, and start ripping them apart.

Turns out the shoe store is supposed to be a big drug supermarket, and the cops are investigating unlikely occurrences there. Here's a white guy in Harlem, carrying twenty pairs of shoes into a drug den. They say to Harry, "Who are you?"

He says, "Harry Morton."

"Show us your driver's license."

He does. "You live in Brooklyn?" they say. "What are you doing here?"

"I'm here to have my shoes shined." They take every shoe and rip it apart, looking for drugs. They're tearing the heels off, slicing up the insides. And he's saying to them, "You guys are in big trouble."

He never did get compensation from the City of New York. In a way, you can't blame those cops. Or maybe it was God's way of paying Harry back for all the practical jokes he'd pulled over the years.

Another Harry Morton story that I love shows how vicious his sense of humor could be. The TV show *Songs for Sale* was very popular from 1950 to 1952. *Songs for Sale* was a showcase for aspiring songwriters who had their songs performed by young singers including Tony Bennett, Rosemary Clooney, and Peggy Lee, backed up by Ray Bloch and his orchestra. It was originally hosted by Jan Murray and later by Steve Allen. Both Bennett and Rosie Clooney were virtual unknowns when they started on the show, and it boosted their careers. The songs were rated by a panel of judges (including, at different times, Mitch Miller and Barry Gray), and the winning song each week got published. In the last year it was on, you could also win money, maybe as much as a thousand dollars. It was a great idea.

Harry Morton was Jan Murray's manager during the time he was hosting *Songs for Sale*. Very late one night, Harry is driving on a rain-swept street in New York when a motorcycle cop pulls him over and walks over to Harry's car. Harry hates cops, for obvious reasons. He opens his window a little and hands the cop his driver's license. On his driver's license it says "TV producer." Every year he would change his occupation, and this year it said producer. So the motorcycle cop says, "What do you produce?"

Harry says, "I do *Songs for Sale*."

"I wrote a song," the cop says. "I want to get on that show. Can you get me on that show?"

Now any question of a ticket has been forgotten. It's three o'clock in the morning, but Harry says to the cop, "Follow me, we're going to Jan Murray's house."

And this motorcycle cop follows him through a driving rain-storm to Jan Murray's house. They get there and they knock on Murray's door. By now it's close to four in the morning. Harry says to the cop, "Look, Jan's a quick study. When he opens the door, just do your stuff."

Jan Murray opens the door. He's half blind, rubbing his eyes, and here's a motorcycle cop in full leathers, soaking wet, singing some ridiculous song at the top of his lungs in the pouring rain. And Harry's standing behind him, pointing at the cop and making the universal sign for "He's nuts." To this day, I don't know if Jan Murray ever forgave him.

We're all prone to a joke now and then. I recently had a chance to interview Jimmy Carter on my radio show when he was promoting the book he wrote about his experiences as an outdoorsman. I don't prepare questions before I do my interviews, just as I don't read authors' books before they come on. I usually have an idea about what area I'm going to explore, especially if my guest is in public life. But in Carter's case, I decided to depart from my usual procedure for once.

"It is a great pleasure to welcome to our microphones," I

began, "the former president of the United States Jimmy Carter, the author of *An Outdoor Journal: Adventures and Reflections.* And it's not generally known by our listeners, even though I grew up in New York City, that this is one of my areas of expertise. I've never let the president know it before, so I have a few questions in that area before we take calls from listeners."

"That'll be a shock," Carter said, under his breath.

"Concerning bone fishing," I asked, "and this has been driving me crazy, I have always used adjustable drag on my reel when going for bone fish. I used thirty yards of seven-weight line and two hundred yards of backing. What do you use?"

Carter laughed appreciatively. "That's a pretty good combination," he said. "Bone fish, pound for pound, are the most ferocious and best fighting fish on earth. I think you might need a *little* more backing, but thirty yards of fly line would be very good."

"Okay, let's go to bass," I said, warming to the topic. "Do you think that smallmouth really go for smaller worms than the largemouth?"

"I don't fish for smallmouth with worms anymore," Jimmy said. "I use a white mudlow minnow. So remember that the next time you go out."

"Well, in Brooklyn, we used worms," I said.

"That's pretty good," Carter said. "There's some good fishermen in Brooklyn."

"Do you think two-color worms are more effective for bass than single-color worms?"

"Yes," he said.

"Do you think I know what I'm talking about?"

"I really do," Carter said. "Plastic worms are great, and they're very expendable. You have to buy a whole bunch of them, but if I don't get any results with one-color worms, I switch to the two-color. Purple head, pink body, work fine."

Carter was being such a good sport that I finally broke down and confessed that I had been asking questions prepared by Pat Piper, who knows these things because he actually goes fishing. I don't know if Carter really thought Larry King from Brooklyn knew so much about fishing tackle, but I had a good time putting him on.

* * *

A lot of prominent people can take a joke. Albert Brooks once told me a story about Jonathan Winters that would have seemed unbelievable if I didn't know just how goofy Winters could be. He is one comedian who doesn't need an audience or a TV camera to make him do weird things. As you listen to Albert's excitement, I think you can get a picture of a budding comic genius undergoing the inspiration of a lifetime.

"Jonathan Winters is a wonderful man," Albert said. "Let me tell you a great story, because I know he'll never remember this. I used to live about two miles from the Beverly Hills Hotel when I grew up. And when I was in grammar school, it must have been in seventh grade, I was in the candy store of the Beverly Hills Hotel when Jonathan Winters walked in. He was my *idol*. There was nobody like him. He was all by himself that day and he was doing fifty minutes, like, for a Tootsie Pop. I mean, this guy was doing material for gum. I was a little kid, and he came up to me. He just started doing routines, and he was *on*, he was brilliant, he was funny. I said, 'Would you come home with me?'

"He said, 'Yeah, sure.'

"So he came home with me. I swear to God on my life. My mother was cooking in the kitchen. I walked in and I said, 'Look, Mom, Jonathan Winters!'

"Winters went wild: 'Oh my God, eggs! Oh my God, they look like the eyes of a monster!' He did forty-five minutes in my kitchen. What other comedian would have done that, gone home with me? Milton Berle drove me a mile and left me off in the middle of the street—he wouldn't come all the way home. I swear to God, it was the only time anything like that ever happened. I said, 'Would you come home and meet my mom?' And he came home with me."

Here's another story about a boy and his mom. Jackie Stallone is Sylvester Stallone's mother and a wild character in her own right. She promotes women's wrestling in California, and she reminds me a little of Zsa Zsa. When Jackie was on my TV show, a guy called in imitating her son. Apparently this guy was an aspiring comic and had a great Sylvester Stallone routine. Well, Mrs. Stallone bought it. She had a three-minute conversation with a total stranger she thought was her son. The guy called our office the next day and it all checked out. He even did the impression for us again on the phone. Jackie told me she doesn't like anyone her son dates. She thinks he's a great boy, and they're very close. But maybe she just doesn't spend much time on the phone with him.

I've already talked about how Frank Sinatra forgot he owned *The Manchurian Candidate*. But Frank isn't the only celebrity who can't remember everything he owns. Bill Hartack, the jockey, told me he was sitting in his house one morning when a letter arrived from a bank. "Dear Mr. Hartack," it read. "You have had $10,000 in this bank for three years and we have not had any activity on your account in that time. Please inform us of your wishes." It was the standard letter they send about inactive accounts. Hartack flipped. He had completely forgotten about the account. Bill had been riding high and he was rolling in dough, so maybe he'd deposited a check there for some reason and then forgot about it. But ten grand was ten grand. He ran out to his car, drove over to the bank and withdrew it immediately.

And then there was Irving Berlin. Throughout his nineties and until he died at the age of 101, he was completely reclusive. He went out maybe once a day in a wheelchair and didn't see any visitors. But he still had a secretary and his music publishing company. Rosemary Clooney told me she used to like to call up every Christmas just to say hello. She always left a message through the secretary. But one time she called and Berlin happened to answer the phone himself. She said, "Irving, it's Rosie Clooney."

"Rosie, how are you?" he said.

"I'm feeling wonderful," she said. Then she started to talk about what a good time they had making *White Christmas* with Danny Kaye and Bing Crosby.

"Yeah, what a wonderful time," he said. "Rosie, as long as I've got you on the phone, tell me something. Isn't taco a food?"

"Yeah, it's Mexican food, Irving. Why?"

"Well, I've got a royalty check for 'Puttin' on the Ritz' by something called Taco. Who the hell is Taco?"

"That's a rock group, I think," she said.

"You're kidding."

"Yeah, that was a big hit, Irving."

"I know, it's a sizable check. That song is fifty years old, Rosie. Hey, thanks for calling." And he hung up.

Speaking of putting people on, Henri Lewin is the funniest non-professional comedian I've ever heard, and a great put-on artist. Henri has gotten rich in the hotel business. In fact, his business card reads, "Henri J. Lewin, Millionaire." He's a sixty-seven-year-old German Jew who got out of a concentration camp during World War II at the age of fifteen and still has a thick accent.

Henri used to be chairman and chief executive officer of Aristocrat Hotels Incorporated, which owns and operates the Sands in Vegas, which they bought for $110 million. He uses a long cigarette holder and wears a monocle. When he's not wearing his monocle, he has a pair of half-glasses that sit down on the bridge of his nose.

Lewin grew up in prewar Potsdam, across the street from Albert Einstein and next door to Rommel's mother. "We used to think Einstein was crazy," Henri says, "because he talked to himself as he walked down the street. And even as a young man he wore his hair that crazy way." Henri's father was the mayor of Potsdam and owned two hotels there. Max Schmeling, the boxer who was world heavyweight champion in 1930–32, and Hanussen, the famous clairvoyant, lived in his house.

In 1937, Henri was put in a concentration camp in Spandau, just outside Berlin. He was there for thirteen days and was released because the commandant in charge of shipping people to Dachau was the son of the police chief of Potsdam and had grown up knowing Henri's father. This commandant recognized Henri and his brother and had them released, whereupon they promptly escaped to Shanghai. There Henri became president of the Foreign Hotel Employees Association of Shanghai. "It was the first time in the history of China that white people served the Chinese," Henri told me. "Under the English mandate, that was a no-no. But we were refugees with no money, no food, nothing. I went to the big hotels there, the Park and the Palace and so on, and told them I would bring waiters from

Germany, Switzerland, and all over Europe to wait on the Chinese patrons. I made a lot of money, and with the money I opened a nightclub, where I also performed."

But on December 7, 1941, the Japanese took over Shanghai, and Henri was once again imprisoned. Somehow he managed to slip out of his confinement at night, hook up with the underground, and wreak havoc on the railroads. He was down to about seventy-two pounds then, by his own reckoning, so no one suspected that he was capable of such shenanigans. After the war, Henri made his way to San Francisco and got a job at the Fairmont Hotel on Nob Hill. The rest, as they say, is hysteria. When I introduced Henri Lewin to my radio audience one night, he immediately began to crack them up with one-liners, which he writes himself. His first line was, "From all the introductions I ever had, this was the most recent one."

"That's true, when you think about it," I said.

"I actually canceled a dentist's appointment to be here," he said. "I think I made a mistake."

"Why do you wear so much finery, Henri?" I asked. "You wear spats, diamond collars in the shirt, rings, a forty-thousand-dollar Rolex watch, gold bracelets, handmade suits. Why do you dress like this?"

"I just came back from a pleasure trip, and I wanted to look good," he said. "I took my wife to the airport. By the way, I recently came back from Russia. I tried to make a deal there to build a hotel in partnership with the Hilton organization. And while I was there I saw something which is amazing. I saw for the first time a Russian car salesroom, where they sell cars like we do in America. I went in, there was a Russian fellow selling cars, and I heard this conversation with a customer. The salesman said, 'You know, these are really beautiful cars.' The other fellow says, 'Yeah. You make 'em in red?'

"Salesman said, 'Any color you want.'

" 'Do you have four-wheel brakes?'

" 'Four-wheel brakes.'

" 'Do you have automatic windows?'

" 'Absolutely.'

" 'Great. When can I get it?'

" 'In ten years, on July 10.'

" 'In ten years, July 10? Can you deliver it in the afternoon?'
" 'Why?'
" 'Because I've got my telephone in the morning.' "

I should say that one of Henri's favorite sayings is "If at first you don't succeed, skydiving is not for you." He also said, "I've traveled around the world and no one knows better than I that you can get as drunk on water as you can on land." Henri has his own philosophy of money. "Having money is a comfort," he says. "It's nice. But if you work for money, you will never make it. You must work because you like your work, because you find pleasure and satisfaction in it. I'm sometimes so busy I forget to collect. But then the next morning I wake up and talk to my rabbi, and he reminds me that's a sin."

Henri loves to kid other hotels when he stays there. My show was being broadcast from the Four Seasons Clift Hotel in San Francisco, and Henri couldn't resist taking a stab at the place, which is really one of the most elegant in the country.

"I was here this morning in this fine hotel," he said, "and I called the waitress up for room service, and I said, 'I'd like to have two eggs with the yolks broken, overcooked bacon, and burned toast.'

"And the girl said, 'Mr. Lewin, we can't do that.'

"I said, 'Yes, you can. You did it yesterday.' "

Henri also has some serious stories to tell. "When the war was over," he told me once, "Max Schmeling tried to get in touch with me, but I never returned his calls because I figured he was a Nazi. Then about ten years ago when I was running all the Hilton hotels, Schmeling called me in my office at the Las Vegas Hilton. He was in Hamburg, Germany, at the time, and he said, 'Henri, this is Max Schmeling. I want you to do me a favor.' "

Henri was caught off his guard, and he stayed on the line. Max had heard on the radio that Joe Louis, whom he had fought years ago, had died, and his body was being displayed at Caesar's Palace. Max was wiring a large sum of money to Henri and he wanted Henri to take it personally to Louis's widow. Henri agreed, and when he spoke to Mrs. Louis and gave her the envelope from Schmeling, she said, "Oh, Henri, you wouldn't believe it. Max is the dearest man. He helped us

through all the years. Whenever Joe was down or needed anything, Max Schmeling always supported us and gave us whatever we needed."

Lewin was dumbstruck. "I called Max in Germany," he said,
"and told him, 'You are a great guy, I want you to know. You
have my friendship forever, and I want you to come over and
be my guest here.'" They are friends to this day, and Schmeling
is a regular visitor at the Sands. But Henri is friends with a lot
of extraordinary people. His office is like a museum. He has the
shoes Elvis wore at his first performance in Las Vegas and
the jacket and belt from his last performance there. He has
the guitar Johnny Cash played in jail, an autographed copy of
Mao's *Little Red Book*, and a Haggadah signed by Moshe
Dayan.

Henri told me that he booked Elvis Presley into the Las Vegas Hilton five or six times and that the thing that most impressed him about Presley was his musicianship and his pipes.
"Presley was the greatest musician I ever met," Henri said,
"and I'll tell you how I detected that. He was an absolute
nothing during the day. He ate the wrong foods. He lay on the
couch, and made no sense of anything you discussed with him.
He was very polite and always called me Mr. Lewin, never
Henri. But if you wanted to have a conversation with him,
you had to talk about things he was interested in, like karate,
about which I don't give a damn. He had no scope. But the
minute that man went onstage, he could hear every note that
was being played by the last musician in the back row of the
band. And if their tempo or intonation was off the least little
bit during rehearsal, he made them stop until they got it right.
Sometimes he would stop them fifteen times on one song. He
was absolutely in command of everybody in the band. And
during the performance, he could change the tempo, slow it
down or speed it up, when he knew he had the audience going."

Henri also said that, in that big ballroom at the Hilton that
holds two thousand people, Presley could lay the microphone
down on the floor and sing "O Sole Mio" unamplified and you
could hear him in every corner of the room. "Julio Iglesias
can't do that," Henri said. "Frank Sinatra can't do that with-

out a microphone. But Presley could. It's not just luck that he became so famous. The man had tremendous pipes and an unbelievable ear. He was a musician. But that was all. The minute the show was over, the guy was nothing."

Henri once told me the difference between the three primary religions, as summed up in the following story. An announcement is made by the world's scientists that in fifteen days the world will be buried under ten feet of ice. We all have only fifteen days left. What would the Pope say? The Pope would say, "Lord, we hope we have lived a life of mercy. And we die in the knowledge of Jesus Christ's warm hands holding us, taking us to his bosom. We trust with forgiveness and understanding." The Protestant National Council of Churches would say, "Lord, may we live these final days in the Christian ethic whereby we have lived our lives. May we take care of our fellow man. May we do good deeds and be judged accordingly." And the head of the Rabbinical Council of America would stand up and say, "Well, we got fifteen days to learn to live under ten feet of ice."

Henri Lewin is also good friends with Bill Cosby and can attest to the fact that Cosby is one of those celebrities who is beloved by the little guys—the people on his staff, the aides, the assistant, the chauffeurs, the maids—because he treats them the same way he treats the big stars. For all the millions of dollars that he's made and all the success that he's had over the years, Bill Cosby is one of the most genuine people in show business and one of the least spoiled.

One night when Lewin was on my show between breaks, he told me a funny story about Bill Cosby. On a Friday afternoon in San Francisco, Cosby called Lewin's office and said, "I need to go to the airport and I'll be driving Bill Harrah's Rolls-Royce." Bill is the well-known casino owner. Cosby asked Lewin, "Could you get somebody to go with me and bring the Rolls back to the garage? Someone from Harrah's will pick it up on Monday."

Henri had his secretary get a driver from the convention services department. She told the young man, neatly dressed in a suit and tie, to bring the car keys to her office when he returned to the hotel. When the young man returned from his mission, this was his story. He said, "I met Mr. Cosby in the garage. There was a black man with him, who was also going to the airport. Mr. Cosby wanted to drive, so they sat in the front seat and I sat in back. And all the way to the airport people kept straining their necks to try to see who this VIP passenger was in the Silver Cloud Rolls-Royce with two black chauffeurs."

I have my own Bill Cosby story. I was having dinner with Cosby during the time of my contract dilemma, when we did a show in Atlantic City. I said, "Bill, I've got heart surgery coming. I've got Ted Turner offering me a new deal at more than twice the old salary. But I think I'm going to leave Ted because King World's package includes an offer of a million five, and CNN is talking a million two."

He just nodded and smiled. "I don't even know how to weigh offers like that," I said. "I mean, what's the difference between a million five and a million two?"

And Cosby said, "Three hundred thousand dollars."

Cos told me a great story about money at dinner. He still takes a lot of gaff for making all those commercials even though he's already rich beyond belief. "No one writes a check to me," he said, "whose company is making less than I am. The production company that does the *Cosby Show* makes more than me. NBC makes a lot more than me. Coca-Cola and Jell-O pudding and Kodak make plenty more than I make. All these people can afford it, and they all choose to pay me. Why would I turn that down? But I don't forget where I came from."

I asked him how he meant that, and then he told me a story about his wife. His wife's a sharp lady and she handles a lot of his business. One time they received a check for a syndicated package deal. It was hand-delivered to his house, and it was the largest check he'd ever seen in his life, which is saying something. The check was certified and made out in the amount of fourteen million dollars, payable to Bill Cosby. He showed it to his wife, who went numb. Cosby is obviously a very rich man, but fourteen million is fourteen million. "We're doing very well," he told me, "but I'm shaking. I've got antique cars. I've got a Rolls-Royce. But a check for fourteen million dollars is an unreal check. I call up my tax accountant. I say, 'Come over here right away. I want you to take this check and take out what's going to taxes. Give me back the check I keep.' The accountant picks up the check, goes away, comes back, and hands me the new check. It's now made out for $7,942,000. And my wife goes, 'Oh, jeez.' Kind of disappointed it's shrunk so much.

"I said to her, 'I'll tell you what you do. You get in your Rolls-Royce, and you go up to 137th Street and Lenox Avenue. You walk into a grocery store there. Just show them the check and tell them how disappointed you are. And then run your ass down through Manhattan while they chase you. And I will be one of the chasers.'"

Postscript
to the
Paperback Edition

Plenty has happened to me since the hardcover version of this book originally went to press, but one event stands out above all the others by far. Covering the war in the Persian Gulf was undoubtedly the most unusual piece of work I've ever done. For one thing, I did my television show seven nights a week for four weeks through the heart of the war. That's 28 straight nights of broadcasting. The previous summer I'd had a warm-up hosting the Goodwill Games in Seattle—17 consecutive nights, anchoring four hours each night. Two days before the Games ended, Iraq invaded Kuwait. This caused Jay Leno to remark: "Man, those Goodwill Games really helped, didn't they?" But nothing could have prepared me for the intensity of covering the war during those weeks of January and February.

From a professional point of view, we were exhilarated because in the early stages of our invasion of Iraq, CNN's ratings beat all three networks and their affiliates in homes wired for CNN, and *Larry King Live* was leading CNN. Not only were people watching me and CNN around the world, but I later heard from Dan Quayle that most nights in the White House, President Bush and John Sununu would stop to watch my show. On one level, of course, they wanted to get a feel for the political spin that the events of the war were generating in the media, and how the public was responding based on call-ins. But even more surprisingly, they wanted to be brought up to date on events in the Gulf. It may seem strange that with spy satellites and the whole intelligence-gathering network that the U.S. had over there, the White House would turn to television to find out what was happening. But television is so instantaneous that it was used by both sides in the war to get information. In that respect, TV has changed forever the way wars will be waged.

On a personal level, it was a new experience far beyond just working for 28 straight nights. I had never done anything where I discussed only one topic for that period of time, on TV as well as radio. Anybody who had a movie or a show opening, a book or anything else to promote was bumped from the show unless it had some bearing on the war. The only exception to that rule was Steve Martin. His latest movie, *L.A. Story,* had just opened, but he had gone to the Gulf to entertain the troops. We talked about his new film, but we also spent time talking about the troops.

An air of the surreal hung over the whole experience for me, though. For instance, one night early on we were talking about one of the first American prisoners of war taken in Iraq, Marine Maj. Joseph Small, and we put his picture on the screen. Three months later, I was talking to Maj. Small from the Bethesda Naval Hospital. It was as if the usual five-year span of a major war had been compressed into a few months' time.

During that interview, incidentally, I found out something I didn't know before. When a serviceman or woman was taken prisoner during the war, their branch of the service assigned an assistance officer to come and assist the POW's spouse and parents. And it so happened that the Marine assigned to the family of Maj. Small was named Capt. Larry King. As Jack Paar used to say, I kid you not.

That surreal feeling went further. Here we were at war with Iraq, and the Iraqi ambassador would be on my show, taking calls from a viewer in Toledo, Ohio, who might be asking the ambassador when he thought the war would be over, or what the Iraqi government planned to accomplish. One night I had on the Iraqi ambassador to the U.N., Abdul Amir al-Anbari, when a couple of callers used his first name—you know, "I have a question for Abdul." Al-Anbari went ballistic.

"Listen, listen, listen," he blurted. "Gentlemen, gentlemen, you don't call an ambassador by his first name!" I agreed, and suggested callers address him as 'Ambassador.' The next night, the Saudi Arabian ambassador to the U.S., Prince Bandar bin Sultan, was on and he said to me, "You can call me by my first name, or anything you like. I'm a regular guy, not like those Iraqis."

It was all so theatrical that after a while, the whole war began to seem like some kind of made-for-TV movie. I can't say that it was anybody's fault. Maybe it's the unavoidable result of broadcasting an event of deadly significance on the same medium that brings us soap operas, mini-series, and baseball games. How do you keep the medium itself from downsizing the significance of the event?

And the war did become a daily event. The nation's attention was riveted so fixedly on the Gulf conflict that certain figures became famous just by being associated with the war on a daily basis.

You expect General Norman Schwarzkopf to be a celebrity after leading the troops. That's only natural. But do you remember Pete Williams, the feisty, crewcut Pentagon spokesman? When he was on we got flooded with calls—not about what he was saying, but about *him*. Pete later told me he received a number of marriage proposals, both over the phone and by mail, from women who had watched him give the daily briefings. People became addicted to those briefings, too. When they were discontinued, many viewers called in, asking, "Where's my 10 A.M. briefing?"

General Tom Kelly, who did the media briefings in Washington, also became a celebrity. After a lifetime in the military during which he was not known outside of a small circle of colleagues, he became famous overnight. And there was a side of him that loved the sudden celebrity. If you remember, he liked to play to the audience at times. A reporter once asked him a question that seemed to go on forever, one long run-on sentence. Kelly started to answer it, then paused and said matter-of-factly, "Someday I'd like to see that sentence diagrammed." The press cracked up. Now he's retired from the service, writing a book, and out on the lecture circuit.

If you were in Washington during the war, you soon realized that the war was all anyone talked about. It was as if everything had come to a halt. Life seemed to be put on hold. And as much as I enjoyed the increased attention focused on my show and the heightened sense of urgency in what I was doing, I also felt ambivalent about the situation. On the one hand the war was an extraordinary event, and I was in favor of the decision to intervene in Kuwait. On the other hand, I wish the government had been more honest and admitted that we went in to protect our access to oil. If Peru had invaded Ecuador, for instance, we would never have gone in. What would have happened if white South African troops had invaded Mozambique, and we had gone to defend the black government of Mozambique? Would we have had the same support back home? Racism clearly played a role in all this, too.

On an even deeper level, I believe that, as a nation, we had a desperate need to feel good about ourselves. Witness the wave of self-congratulation at the end of the war: Let's have another parade. Let's have another welcome home ceremony. Let's wave the flag again. Unquestionably there was a great need for the celebration, as though we could make up for the muddled feelings about America's international role that had descended on the country during and after the war in Vietnam. But let's face it: in the case of Iraq, we were not playing a major league team. It was like the Dodgers beating Albuquerque, which was the comparison I made on my show. And one of my guests responded, "Yes, but if you're a Dodgers fan and the Dodgers had lost 13 in a row, you'd feel good if they beat Albuquerque."

On the plus side, at least the doomsayers turned out to be wrong, the ones who said that thousands of American soldiers would die. Yet we still don't know how many Iraqi soldiers died as a result of our bombing raids, a number which some estimates put at well over 100,000—and my guess is that the government does not want the public to know. Meanwhile, Saddam is still in power.

But the major hidden agenda of the war, to make Americans feel better about themselves and their place in the world, was certainly accomplished. One proof is that I have never seen the public so nearly unanimous in support of a government

action. The war didn't last long enough or generate enough
American casualties to lend much momentum to the antiwar
movement. One night on Mutual we did a call-in show that was
beamed into Saudi Arabia through Armed Forces Radio.
Listeners just called in to say hello to their loved ones overseas.
It was an emotional three hours during which we must have
taken 200 phone calls. I was crying during parts of the show.

The other major effect, which I've already alluded to, was the
extent to which the instantaneous nature of the television
coverage of the war played a part in the actual conduct of the
war. I was in Miami during the Vietnam war, and although I
interviewed people like Generals Maxwell Taylor and Lew
Wald, our broadcasts weren't being beamed over there. So even
though journalists had more access to that war, and the
reporting was less tightly managed by the Pentagon, the
American media had no worldwide impact equivalent to what
CNN had during this war.

Unquestionably, this war also changed the way war will be
covered in the future, both for better and for worse. The point
has been made that the Pentagon, trying to avoid the antiwar
sentiment that grew out of the open coverage of the Vietnamese
conflict, severely managed the media coverage of the Gulf War.
Our reporters were nonetheless able to go into the country
under attack and report from the inside. Of course, everything
they were able to see and to talk about in their reports was
managed by the Iraqi government. CNN's Peter Arnett was
criticized for reporting only what the Iraqis allowed him to
report. But as Ted Turner later pointed out to David Frost, when
viewed from a world perspective, the Iraqi censorship was no
worse than our own government's.

Arnett's interview with Saddam at the height of the war was
both astonishing and frustrating. Imagine Edward R. Murrow or
Walter Cronkite being invited to go to Berlin to interview Hitler
in 1944 or '45. Would they have turned down the offer? On the
other hand, interviewing Saddam is my idea of pure hell. He is
the ultimate interviewing nightmare: ask him a question and he
launches a filibuster. I think Arnett did as well as he could under
the circumstances. But I'm not a newsman, so if I'd had the same
opportunity I would have tried to personalize the interview,

which is what I do best. First I would have asked Saddam about the now-infamous conversation between him and Ambassador April Glaspie. What did she really say to you that day? How surprised were you at the world reaction?

Then I would have taken it further back, and asked him about his motivation in becoming a dictator. Who needs this? You're a prisoner of your own power, aren't you? What's it like to be surrounded by guards 24 hours a day? I would have tried to explore the man. Even that would have been difficult, of course, given the rambling way Saddam talks and the fact that you can't very well keep cutting him off.

I took a similar approach with Ollie North, by the way, when I later interviewed him about his book, *Under Fire*. "Do you," I asked him, "ever run into people who *don't* know you?"

"Yeah," he answered, "just the other day."

He told me he was sitting on a plane next to a guy who had no idea who he was. The guy looked at him and said, "so what do you do?"

North said, "I was a colonel in the Marine Corps. What do you do?"

The fellow said he was a computer salesman and asked Ollie's name. "I'm Ollie North. Nice to meet you."

"Frank Jenkins," the guy said. "Nice to meet you. What do you do now that you're out of the Marines?"

"Well, I'm in business for myself. I go around the country and give speeches."

"Hey, that's great. I really enjoy selling computers."

There was no recognition at all. Bright guy, sitting in First Class, but he just didn't register the name or the face. It may seem inconceivable to us that someone in mainstream America who travels on airplanes and deals in computers would not know who Ollie North is. We simply assume that celebrity is all-enveloping.

Incidentally, I'd put Ollie North in the same category as G. Gordon Liddy: someone I never expected to like. I found North personable and funny, easy to be around, even though politically speaking I couldn't be further from where he is. Even after Reagan shafted him, and although he must feel betrayed by Reagan, North still holds him blameless. Like a lot of other conservatives, I guess, Ollie just can't believe that Reagan was bad for this country.

The effect of the intensive CNN coverage of the war on my own private life was also extraordinary. I went to Amsterdam to interview Audrey Hepburn for a TNT special, and all over the airport people were coming up to me for autographs. Back here, I'd gotten used to a certain amount of recognition, and it had never really bothered me before. Now it's hard for me to walk down the street in Washington. When I went to OTB last time I was in New York, everyone started coming over to talk to me. I left after two races. I tried to do a fast walk through Central Park for exercise, but people kept stopping me. It's nice, it's flattering, and after a while it becomes a real intrusion.

I was walking down Madison Avenue with my friend Herbie Cohen recently and people kept coming over for autographs. Herbie reminded me of the time ten years before when we had been reminiscing about our childhood while we were walking along Madison Avenue. Back then, we just started skipping down the street the way we used to do when we were kids. He had a rubber ball with him and we started playing catch. I could never do that now, and it makes me sad. Anyone can spill tomato sauce on their shirt in a restaurant and not think much of it. If I do it and people see me, suddenly it's, Oh, there's Larry King the slob.

During the past year, my wife Julie and I, who had just gotten married when *Tell Me More* was written, separated and reunited. One of the highlights of that year was the week we spent in Montana with Ted Turner and Jane Fonda, who will probably be married by the time you read this. Ted has a 110,000 acre ranch called the Bar None near Bozeman, with 1,100 head of buffalo. We picnicked together, we went to Yellowstone, we went horseback riding. One night we were driving around with Ted and we got lost. Suddenly the car was surrounded by buffalo, but we didn't panic. You always feel safe with Ted Turner; you feel like you're with Captain Courageous. There are certain guys you'd feel okay walking down a dark alley with, and Ted is one of them. The Atlanta Braves were nine games out of first place at the time, and he was disappointed but philosophical about it all. It was right before the All-Star break, the Braves had just dropped three of four to Los Angeles, and I don't think he had any inkling that they were going to the World Series.

One afternoon he took us all up to the highest peak so we could look down at his spread. You could see Bozeman off to one side and Yellowstone off to the other. It was very majestic, but Ted has a way of being funny about it. I said, "God, all this acreage!"

"Yeah," he said, "but it's not a lot of money either. This whole thing only cost 22 million."

On second thought, that comes to only $200 an acre, so maybe he's right.

Between Ted and Jane, I was forced to be very healthy. It's hard not to be when you're around Jane Fonda. Every other morning we exercised, either walking or hiking, and had our health food drinks. Ted even helped me get off the sleeping pill Halcion by taking a slightly smaller dose every night—it took me about three weeks, but it worked. I learned how to fly cast and I didn't shave for a week, watched very little television, and slept nine hours a night. I had a good time in a way I never expected to have.

I'm more optimistic now than I've ever been. I've got new five-year contracts at CNN and Mutual, and a fifth book coming next fall on growing up in Brooklyn. I'm planning to buy a townhouse in D.C. after 10 years of living in Arlington. My old Brooklyn pal Herbie Cohen lives near me now at the Watergate, so at the age of 58 I feel like I'm on the corner again. In fact, when I call him on the phone and his wife Ellen answers, I say, "Can Herbie come out and play?"

I recently won the Graham MacNamee Award, which is given annually to a former sportscaster who has done well in another field. Ronald Reagan won it the previous year. I was a sportscaster early in my career in Miami and later did color for the Dolphins broadcasts. My first CNN television and Mutual radio shows are now in the Museum of Radio and Television (formerly the Museum of Broadcasting) in New York City, and I'm very proud of that.

      ❖   ❖   ❖

Based on 35 years of interviewing people, I believed Anita Hill. My gut feeling is that she was telling the truth. Clarence Thomas studiously avoided any reference to race throughout the hearings, except when he could use it to his advantage by disarming the senators and the television audience. When he talked about a "high-tech lynching," he only trivialized the tragedy of actual lynchings. That wasn't a lynching; people were killed at lynchings. Admittedly, I wasn't a Thomas supporter to begin with, but if I were a conservative I would have been disappointed by his testimony, too, because I think he copped out.

That said, I agree with critics who attacked the senators for being more interested in how they come off on national TV or in scoring points against the other side than in ferreting out the truth. Senators are lousy questioners. Some observers said they should have used experienced trial lawyers who didn't have a political stake in the hearings. But the problem there is that it wasn't a court of law. I think they would have been better off if they'd hired people like me and Mike Wallace and Ted Koppel to ask the questions.

If there was one thing I would have done that none of the senators did, it would have been to question Thomas on how he could possibly have avoided watching Hill's testimony on TV. Howell Heflin dropped the ball right there. He expressed some incredulity when Thomas said he hadn't watched her testify, but then he moved right along and nobody really came back to that. If somebody made those kinds of egregious accusations against you, I think you'd want to hear every word—if only to find flaws or inconsistencies in the testimony with which to refute it. That is, unless you already knew what she was going to say.

And I certainly would have asked him about the story in the *New York Times* quoting a fellow Yale Law School student to the effect that Thomas had an interest in pornographic films back then. If he refused to answer on the basis that his private life was none of our business, I would have asked if his grandfather wasn't part of his private life, too. And his childhood, and the nuns. He was the one who brought his private life into the hearings, so why stop with childhood?

By the way, my producers tried to get Anita Hill on my show, and I'm sure *Nightline* and all the rest were trying just as hard, but she turned us all down. She may well go on the lecture circuit at some point to talk about the issue of sexual harassment. But if she were simply interested in focusing attention on herself, as many Thomas supporters kept insisting, then she missed a golden opportunity to do so in a setting that would have been much more favorable to her than the Senate hearings.

I felt sad when we lost Gene Roddenberry, the creator of *Star Trek*. I had dinner with him once in L.A. and all he wanted to talk about was politics and morality. He was an unabashed liberal who wasn't ashamed to say that he put a lot of his own sense of political morality into the *Star Trek* scripts on TV, and later as producer and executive producer of the film sequels. If you go back and watch those shows now, you'll see that underneath all the adventure with strange alien beings, the themes usually revolve around deeper psychological and sociological questions. It may sound corny, but the *Enterprise* was really trying to spread love and understanding throughout the universe.

I still do plenty of flying, and I have to say that it hasn't gotten any easier, and the service hasn't gotten any better. My main gripe is that they still won't tell you what's actually happening. Not long ago I was flying to Pat Sajak's wedding on New Year's Eve. It was a little foggy, and we were just about to land at National Airport in D.C., when the plane suddenly began to climb back up at a fairly steep angle. The pilot didn't make any announcement; the flight attendants didn't say a word to us. I later learned that because of the fog we had nearly collided with another plane on the landing strip. We were finally diverted to the airport in Richmond, Virginia, and I never made it to the wedding. But the really weird part was that as we were climbing back up at this 45-degree angle, one of the passengers began to stand up, a little panicky. And a flight attendant barked at him, "Sit down, sir! We're landing!"

The venerable *New York Times Magazine* ran an article on me with a title that didn't make any sense to me: "The Maestro of

Chin Music." The writer told me *he* didn't know what it meant and he had to ask the editor. The editor told him "chin music" was an old vaudeville term for performers who just talk. To me, chin music always referred to a pitcher who brushes the hitter back off the plate with a pitch up and in—under the batter's chin. But this editor said that in the old days, what someone like Will Rogers did, because he didn't sing or dance or work with a partner, was chin music. Go figure. By the way, when the *Reader's Digest* reprinted the article, they called it "The King of Talk."

Part of why I like my work is that sometimes I get paid to do things just for fun. Like the time I got to play myself on an episode of *The Simpsons*. Homer is diagnosed as having only 24 hours to live, so he tries to settle his affairs with everyone, but they won't have anything to do with him. By then he has just a few hours left so he slumps into a chair, whereupon he finds a copy of a tape called "Larry King Reads the Bible." He listens to me reading the Bible, and he falls asleep. They told me to end it any way I like, so I say, "That's the end of the Bible. I think the San Antonio Spurs are going to win the NBA, and I'm goin' over to Duke Zeibert's for matzoh ball soup." The Spurs later played that part of the show during a home game to thunderous applause.

   Homer doesn't die, of course. It turns out the doctor misdiagnosed him. But my favorite line in that show had nothing to do with me. The doctor tells Homer he has 24 hours to live. Then he says, "Wait a minute. Make it 22 hours—I kept you waiting."

And then there was the time President Nakasone of Japan was being interviewed on C-SPAN. I don't recall what topic they were talking about—it may have been the loosening of restrictions on American imports coming into Japan. But he was saying that he would be presenting his case to the Japanese people on a TV show over there. Someone asked him if he was going to take phone calls. And the president of Japan said, "'Who do you think I am, Larry King?"

It was after the Gulf War had ended and just before Bush had that trouble with his heart. Dan Quayle was on the show, and I wore one of those bright floral print ties that were in fashion then. I liked the tie, but Quayle thought it was the ugliest tie he'd ever seen. He said, "That tie's so bad that if you give it to me, I'll wear it to the Oval Office tomorrow morning as a joke."

I gave him the tie and a few days later I received a photo of Quayle wearing the tie, George Bush cutting it in half with a pair of scissors, and James Baker watching the whole thing and laughing. Your tax dollars at work, folks.

LANDMARK BESTSELLERS FROM ST. MARTIN'S PAPERBACKS

THE SILENCE OF THE LAMBS
Thomas Harris
_____ 92458-5 $5.99 U.S./$6.99 Can.

SEPTEMBER
Rosamunde Pilcher
_____ 92480-1 $5.99 U.S./$6.99 Can.

BY WAY OF DECEPTION
Victor Ostrovsky and Claire Hoy
_____ 92614-6 $5.99 U.S.

LAZARUS
Morris West
_____ 92460-7 $5.95 U.S./$6.95 Can.

THE GULF
David Poyer
_____ 92577-8 $5.95 U.S./$6.95 Can.

MODERN WOMEN
Ruth Harris
_____ 92272-8 $5.95 U.S./$6.95 Can.

BESTSELLING BOOKS

FROM

ST. MARTIN'S PAPERBACKS

FLASHBACKS: On Returning to Vietnam
Morley Safer
_____ 92482-8 $5.95 U.S./$6.95 Can.

THE SILENCE OF THE LAMBS
Thomas Harris
_____ 92458-5 $5.99 U.S./$6.99 Can.

BORN RICH
Georgia Raye
_____ 92239-6 $4.95 U.S./$5.95 Can.

WEST END
Laura Van Wormer
_____ 92262-0 $5.95 U.S./$6.95 Can.

THE WESTIES
T. J. English
_____ 92429-1 $5.95 U.S./$6.95 Can.

HOW TO WIN AT NINTENDO GAMES #2
Jeff Rovin
_____ 92016-4 $3.95 U.S./$4.95 Can.